THE DOCUMENTARY FILM

06

THE DOCUMENTARY FILM MOVEMENT
An Anthology

Edited and introduced by
Ian Aitken

Edinburgh University Press

Published with financial assistance
from The John Grierson Archive,
University of Stirling.

Selection, arrangement and introductory materials
© Ian Aitken, 1998

Edinburgh University Press
22 George Square, Edinburgh

Typeset in Palatino Light
by Pioneer Associates, Perthshire, and
printed and bound in Great Britain by
The University Press, Cambridge

A CIP record for this book is available from the
British Library

ISBN 0 7486 0970 9 (hardback)
ISBN 0 7486 0948 2 (paperback)

CONTENTS

LIST OF ILLUSTRATIONS

—⊲⊳—

ACKNOWLEDGEMENTS

I would like to thank the executors of the John Grierson Archive for granting permission to reproduce the following papers by John Grierson in this book: 'English Cinema Production and the Naturalistic Tradition', extracts from 'The Character of an Ultimate Synthesis' and an untitled lecture on documentary, *'Drifters'*, 'First Principles of Documentary', 'Education and the New Order', 'The Documentary Idea', 'Art and Revolution' and *'I Remember, I Remember'*. I would also like to thank *Granta* for granting permission to reproduce 'Answers to a Cambridge Questionnaire', and Faber and Faber for allowing reproduction of Grierson's 'Preface' to Paul Rotha's *Documentary Film*.

Thanks are also due to Farrar, Straus and Giroux Inc. and Random House for granting permission to reproduce Paul Rotha's 'After-thought', from his *Documentary Diary*; the British Film Institute for granting permission to reproduce Paul Rotha's 'Films and the Labour Party'; *Sight and Sound* and Elizabeth Sussex for granting permission to reproduce 'Cavalcanti in England'; Carcanet Press for permission to reproduce Humphrey Jennings's *'Listen to Britain'*, 'The English' and 'Surrealism'; and A. P. Watt Ltd for permission to reproduce Jennings's 'Introduction' to his *Pandaemonium*. Wherever possible, attempts have been made to locate the rights holders of all the material contained in this book. This also applies to the eight photographs: sources are acknowledged for the three film stills in Chapter 1, but the portraits in each of the five subsequent chapters were obtained from the BFI and copyright could not be traced. The publishers will be happy to make amendments in future editions of this book.

I would also like to take this opportunity to thank the management committee of the Grierson Archive, both for affording me the opportunity to carry out further research in the Grierson Archive, and for generously contributing a sum of money towards the production costs of this book, which has enabled a larger number of papers by Grierson to be reproduced than would otherwise have been the case. I would also like to thank the Research Committee of the Faculty of Art, Media and Design, University of the West of England, for supporting me in this project. Thanks are also due to Jack C. Ellis for his correspondence, and to those who have contributed their opinions and advice to this project.

Chapter 1

INTRODUCTION

The documentary film movement has had a considerable impact on British film culture and, although the period of its greatest influence was the 1930s and 1940s, its legacy has continued to make itself felt in various ways up to the present day. The documentary movement has also been the subject of considerable critical debate, over both the role which it is perceived to have played in the 1930s and the influence which it is felt to have had on contemporary film and television. Indeed, few areas of British film history have been as controversial, or have received as much critical attention, as the documentary film movement.

A number of different, and competing, accounts of the movement already exist. According to one interpretation the movement's leader, John Grierson, elaborated an important theory concerning film's relationship to modernity and democracy. Grierson, a man impelled by profound conviction, formed a group of committed disciples in order to realise that theory. The film-makers of the documentary film movement then challenged the entrenched forces of reaction and monopoly within the film industry. A struggle ensued which was eventually lost, and the documentary movement faded from the scene, finally defeated by those whom Grierson once referred to as those 'cold English bastards'.[1]

However, this interpretation of the documentary movement is not the only one available. Another suggests that the movement and its leader played a pivotal role in stifling the growth of a critical British film culture, and in establishing a realist paradigm which critically marginalised the avant-garde. According to yet another interpretation, Grierson and his film-makers were a set of well-meaning but bungling amateurs, unable to adapt to quickly changing circumstances, and

responsible for undermining attempts by others to establish an effective system of public film-making in Britain.

This introduction will assess these interpretations of the documentary
movement. It will begin with a comprehensive overview of the movement between 1918 and 1972, and then examine the films produced by
the movement and the historical context from which those films
emerged. Grierson's ideology and theory of documentary film will then
be examined, and the critical literature which has appeared on the
movement from the 1930s onwards will be described and assessed.

JOHN GRIERSON AND THE DOCUMENTARY FILM
MOVEMENT 1898–1972

The founder of the documentary film movement, John Grierson, was
born near Stirling in central Scotland in 1898. On leaving school he
enrolled at Glasgow University, but, before he could commence his
studies, war broke out, and he enlisted in the naval minesweeping
service. He returned to Glasgow University after demobilisation in
1919, and eventually graduated with a Master's degree in philosophy
and literature before taking up a temporary appointment at Durham
University in 1923. Whilst at Durham he succeeded in obtaining a
scholarship to study immigration problems in the United States. He
arrived in America in October 1924 and remained there until his return
to England in January 1927.[2]

Although Grierson's research project was initially concerned with
the study of immigration, he quickly became more interested in issues
of mass communications and broadened his project to include these.[3]
One of the most significant influences on him at this stage was Walter
Lippmann, a writer on public relations and propaganda issues, who
argued that a contradiction existed between the egalitarian principles
underlying democratic theory and the hierarchical nature of modern
mass society.[4] Lippmann's ideas were influenced by a more general
context of conservative ideology, prevalent in America at the time,
which questioned the validity of universal franchise and emphasised
the necessity of rule by specialist elites. However, Grierson disagreed
with Lippmann's sceptical approach to democracy, and argued,
instead, that modern democratic structures could work if adequate
public information systems could be constructed. From that point on
the idea that public education, communicated through the medium of
film, could help to preserve the framework of democracy became the

foundation of Grierson's theory of documentary film.

As his period of tenure in America came to an end Grierson became aware that in Britain the Empire Marketing Board (EMB) had become one of the largest government publicity organisations of its kind. He contacted the EMB in 1927 seeking employment, and was eventually appointed there as Assistant Films Officer.[5] Between 1927 and 1929 he produced a plan for film production at the EMB, and the first film to emerge from this was *Drifters* (1929). The EMB Film Unit was established the following year, and Grierson hired his first two apprentice film-makers: Basil Wright and John Taylor. These were closely followed by J. D. Davidson, Arthur Elton, Edgar Anstey, Paul Rotha, Marion Grierson (John's younger sister), Margaret Taylor, Evelyn Spice, Margaret Taylor (John Taylor's sister), Stuart Legg and Harry Watt.

However, the expansion of film-making activities at the EMB was soon undermined by other events within the organisation. Grierson had initially been attracted to the EMB as a potential source of documentary film production because of its apparent size and importance. Unfortunately, the EMB proved to be an untenable and transient institution, and anything but a secure foundation for the documentary movement. Originally founded 1n 1924 as a response to calls for effective protection for British trade within the empire, the EMB largely failed to appease the proponents of protectionism, and the introduction of major tariff reform legislation in 1932 and 1933 rendered it irrelevant. It was eventually abolished in September 1933. However, just prior to this, Stephen Tallents, the Secretary of the EMB, and the man who had initially employed Grierson, managed to secure a new appointment at the General Post Office (GPO), a condition of which was that the EMB Film Unit should also be transferred there.[6]

Shortly after transfer the Film Unit moved to larger premises, and acquired sound-recording facilities. These developments enabled it to increase the overall standard of its output, and, in particular, to produce sound films for the first time. However, the overall quality of the facilities and resources at its disposal remained relatively low, and this continued to affect the quality of the films produced throughout the 1930s. Alongside this enhancement of the movement's resource base a number of new appointments were made, the most important of which was that of Alberto Cavalcanti, a Brazilian who had made avant-garde films in France during the 1920s, and had worked with directors such as Jean Renoir, René Clair and Jean Vigo.

In 1935 Stephen Tallents left the GPO in order to take up an appointment at the BBC. Around the same time Grierson and a number of the other film-makers also decided to leave in order to develop the documentary movement outside of the public sector. Edgar Anstey was the first to go, establishing the Shell Film Unit in 1934. He was followed by Donald Taylor, Paul Rotha and Stuart Legg, who set up the Strand Film Unit in 1935, and then by Basil Wright, who established the Realist Film Unit in 1937.[7] Grierson himself finally resigned in June 1937 in order to set up Film Centre, an organisation dedicated to the co-ordination of documentary film production. By 1937 the documentary film movement consisted of four production units (the GPO Film Unit, Shell, Strand and Realist), a journal, *World Film News*, which was launched in 1935, and Film Centre. Underlying this apparent expansion, however, was the fact that a significant division had emerged between those film-makers remaining inside, and those outside the GPO. Cavalcanti, Watt and Jennings remained at the GPO, giving the development of film-making there a particular inflection, whereas the films made outside developed in quite different directions.

In 1939, Grierson left Britain in order to take up a post as first Film Commissioner of the National Film Board of Canada, a post which he held until 1945. In 1940, with the outbreak of war, the GPO Film Unit was transferred to the Ministry of Information (MOI), and given the title of the Crown Film Unit. It remained at the MOI until the end of the war, when the Ministry was disbanded and replaced by the Central Office of Information (COI). The Crown Film Unit was then transferred to the COI. In February 1948 Grierson returned to Britain in order to take up an appointment as Controller, Film, at the COI. Between 1948 and 1950 the documentary movement found itself placed, in theory at least, in the best position it had ever enjoyed, with a good resource base, improved technical facilities and a large modern studio at its disposal. However, this promising situation soon deteriorated, and, in 1950, Grierson resigned from his post. In March 1951 he was placed in charge of Group 3, a production arm of the National Film Finance Corporation, and charged with overseeing the production of quality, socially purposive films. However, Group 3 ceased production in July 1955, with considerable financial losses, and Grierson left the organisation the same year.[8]

After 1955 the documentary movement continued to decline and disperse. Grierson's next major role was as a presenter on Scottish Television between 1957 and 1967, where he fronted the programme

This Wonderful World. After that he worked as an occasional freelance university lecturer at McGill University in Canada. Edgar Anstey set up British Transport Films in 1949, and ran it up to 1974, making over five hundred films for British Transport and other corporate sponsors. He was joined there by John Taylor and Stuart McCallister. Arthur Elton established the Shell Film Unit in 1936 and ran it until his death in 1973. Alberto Cavalcanti worked with Michael Balcon at Ealing Studios until 1946, directing the important *Went the Day Well* (1942), and producing some of the key films of the war period, including *The Foreman Went to France* (1941). After that he worked as a film director in Europe, Brazil and America, making his last film, *Herzl: The Story of Israel*, in 1967. Harry Watt directed films for Ealing Studios up till 1959, when he made his final film, *The Siege of Pinchgut*. Humphrey Jennings worked for the Crown Film Unit between 1939 and 1948. His last film was *Family Portrait* (1950), made for the Festival of Britain in 1950. He died the same year as the result of a climbing accident. Basil Wright produced and directed films for the Realist International film company between 1946 and 1953. He then worked as a freelance director, making his last film in 1960, and writing a book on the history of film, *The Long View*, in 1974.

The final major figure within the documentary film movement, Paul Rotha, worked as a freelance director and producer from the 1930s to the 1960s, making his last film, a Dutch feature called *De Overvall*, in 1962. After that he remained active as a writer, publishing, amongst other works, *Documentary Diary* in 1972, the year of Grierson's death. One of the most important of the young film-makers employed by Grierson, Rotha was semi-detached from the movement, coming and going over the period, and occasionally at odds with Grierson. In addition to his work with the documentary movement, Rotha also made a number of films for commercial documentary film companies, including *The Face of Britain* (1934), inspired by a reading of J. B. Priestley's *English Journey* (1934).

The lesser members of the movement took on a variety of roles after 1945. Donald Alexander stopped making films after 1948. Ralph Bond produced films up to 1948, and then became Vice-President of the Association of Cine-Technicians Union, a post which he held until 1974. Denis Forman worked for a short time with Grierson at the COI until 1948, after which he was appointed a Director of the British Film Institute (BFI). Like Harry Watt, he joined Granada Television, acting as

Managing Director there between 1964 and 1974. J. B. Holmes worked for the Crown Film Unit until 1948 and, between 1954 and 1961, was commissioned by Shell to produce films in Africa and Asia. He then worked as a freelance producer until his death in 1968.

Other minor figures included Stanley Hawes, who worked with Paul Rotha in the mid-thirties. He worked for the National Film Board (NFB) of Canada between 1940 and 1946, and became head of the Australian Film Board in the mid-1950s. He was active as a film producer and film policy advisor until the mid-1960s. Pat Jackson left the Crown Film Unit in 1944 and then worked as a freelance film director, making his final film in 1963. Ralph Keene founded the independent documentary production company Greenpark Productions in 1940, and remained there until 1947. Between 1951 and 1953 he advised and produced for the Government Film Unit in Ceylon, and worked at British Transport Films from 1955 until 1963. Jack Lee worked at the Crown Film Unit until 1946, after which he worked as a freelance director, directing, amongst other films, *A Town Like Alice* (1956) for Rank. He made his last film, *Circle of Deception*, in 1960. Stuart Legg worked for the NFB of Canada between 1938 and 1948, and, between 1950 and 1964, as a freelance producer.

A final group of minor figures included Len Lye, who made films for the GPO, Shell and Realist Film Units between 1939 and 1951; Norman McLaren, who worked with the GPO and Crown Film Units, and at the NFB of Canada; Evelyn Spice, who also worked at the GPO Film Unit before joining the NFB of Canada in 1939; Alexander Shaw, who worked at the GPO, Strand and Crown Film Units between 1933 and 1947, and at UNESCO until 1970; and, finally, John Taylor, one of Grierson's first recruits, who worked at the EMB, GPO, Strand, Realist and Crown Film Units between 1946 and 1948, then made occasional freelance documentary films until 1964.[9]

The film-makers within the documentary film movement came from predominantly middle-class and professional backgrounds. Most came from London and the home counties, and some from Scotland. Apart from Grierson, all the major individuals who contributed to the formation of the movement were born between 1902 and 1910. All were, therefore, in their mid-twenties or younger by the time of *Drifters*, and some were extremely young when first employed; Pat Jackson and John Taylor were only 15, and the documentary film movement was inaugurated in 1930 by Grierson, 32 years old, Wright, 23, and Taylor, 15.[10]

The personnel of the movement were almost all university educated, and there is a considerable Cambridge connection, with Alexander, Elton, Holmes, Jennings, Legg, Wright and Forman all educated there. Most also went to public school, and one route into the movement appears to have been through Marlborough College and then Cambridge. However, Grierson and Watt were educated at Glasgow and Edinburgh Universities respectively, and both went to grammar rather than public schools, whilst Cavalcanti was educated at a military high school in Brazil, and Rotha attended the Slade School of Fine Art.[11]

None of the above can be classed as having had academic careers of any distinction, and all left academia to become film-makers. This is particularly the case with the two Scots, Grierson and Watt. Watt failed to complete his studies at Edinburgh, whilst Grierson failed to complete the research fellowship which he was awarded in 1923. In papers written during the late twenties he indicated that he had little patience for 'the bespectacled professors', and little inclination to pursue an academic career, whilst Watt also adopted an anti-intellectual posture in his writings.[12] One area of differentiation which can be made within the movement, therefore, is based on a cultural contrast between a robust, even anti-intellectual approach taken by Grierson and Watt, and the Oxbridge and public school-educated culture which Wright, Jennings, Taylor and others emerged from. Another area of differentiation concerned homosexuality: whilst Wright, Cavalcanti and others were gay, Grierson consistently exhibited an overt hostility towards homosexuality.[13]

One significant factor connecting those mentioned above is that few were old enough to have been directly affected by two of the most important radicalising events of the first half of the Century: World War I and the General Strike of 1926. Their backgrounds also, to some extent, immunised them from a direct experience of social deprivation during the 1930s. Even Grierson, who grew up near a deprived area of Scotland, and who served during the war, was relatively distanced from both the social hardship around him in Scotland and the horrors of the Front Line.[14] Although he was 28 at the time of the General Strike, few references to this crucial event appear in his writings.

Two final points to be considered in relation to the personnel within the documentary movement relate to issues of gender and race.

Most of the members of the documentary movement were male. Evelyn Spice was the most significant female film-maker to emerge from the movement. Ruby Grierson, John Grierson's sister, died in 1940, and Marion Grierson, another sister, effectively left the movement in 1946.[15] Although the presence of these women reveals a willingness on Grierson's part to employ women as directors – a willingness which, to some extent, set him apart from other producers within the film industry at the time – none of these women became a major figure within the movement. In addition, few women were employed during the latter part of the movement, from 1940 onwards.[16]

Few conclusions can be drawn from this other than that the lack of women in the movement reflected the general picture concerning women's entry into professional life during the period. One other factor which may have contributed, however, was Grierson's apparent animosity towards the feminine, and the strongly masculinist nature of his ideas. In a series of articles written for American newspapers between 1925 and 1926, he defined the ethical values which he held to be the most important as 'strength, simplicity, energy, directness, hardness, decency, courage, duty and upstanding power'.[17] At the same time he defined categories such as 'sophistication', 'sentimentality', 'nostalgia' and 'excessive sexuality' as ethically negative.[18] Underlying these distinctions is a rigorously masculinist ethos which, in conjunction with the 'documentary boys'' habit of spending substantial periods of time in the local pub, and the 'monastic' culture which Grierson is said to have insisted upon, may have made it difficult for women to survive within the movement.[19]

A link to the 'old', white, British Empire is also apparent within the documentary movement. Grierson established the NFB of Canada and employed a number of Canadians and New Zealanders, including Len Lye, Evelyn Spice and Norman McLaren. Opportunities to employ people of colour may have been rare, so few conclusions can be drawn from their absence from the movement. Nevertheless, the fact remains that all the members of the movement were white. No evidence of racist remarks can be found in Grierson's writings, although he did adopt a discourse of the exotic and the primitive when discussing the representation of native peoples in films such as Flaherty's *Moana*.[20] Such an anthropological approach to the third world was common amongst white, liberal, middle-class intellectuals during the period, however. Some critics have argued that a colonialist rhetoric can be found in the films of the movement, and there is evidence to support this.[21] There is also evidence to suggest that Grierson may have been an anti-semite.[22]

The members of the documentary movement can be classified as middle-class, university educated, primarily male, exclusively white, politically liberal, and drawn mainly from the English home counties, with some from Scotland, Australia, New Zealand and Canada. None was from working-class, particularly wealthy or radicalised backgrounds. None, with the possible exceptions of Rotha, Grierson, Jennings and Cavalcanti, could really be classed as an 'intellectual'. They were employed when young and inexperienced, and, in the main, passed the greater part of their careers working for corporate sponsors making public relations films of variable quality. They developed alliances with these bureaucratic institutions, but also remained film-makers, influenced by traditions of avant-garde European film-making: a factor which led to strained relations with the corporate employers whom they depended upon for an income.

At an institutional and organisational level the documentary movement can be characterised as a set of affiliated, often loosely connected organisations, concerned primarily with film production and film distribution, but also with questions of public education and corporate publicity production. The main film production units – the EMB, GPO, Crown, Realist, Strand and Shell – were all small-scale production units, dependent on either public or corporate sponsorship. The mode of production was craft – rather than mass-production-based, and the movement had little connection with the commercial film industry.

The history of the documentary movement can be divided into a number of different phases. The first phase, from 1929 to 1936, was one of location within a single public sector organisation. The second, from 1936 to 1948, was characterised by dispersal, as parts of the movement relocated out of the state sector into commercial corporations. Three separate branches of the movement can be distinguished during this phase, each with its own experience of success and failure. In Britain, the Crown Film Unit expanded its production and produced some major films, but also lost a number of its most important film-makers to the commercial industry and to those elements of the movement outside the state system. In Canada, Grierson founded the NFB of Canada, and set about expanding documentary film production there. In contrast to these two public sector organisations, the third branch of the movement operated within the insecure and unpredictable market of the commercial corporate sector. The third phase of the movement, between 1948 and 1950, was characterised by a degree of reunification. It began in 1948, when Grierson was appointed as Controller, Film, at the COI, and ended in 1950, when he left the organisation. After 1950, the fourth and final phase of the movement was characterised by gradual disintegration. Its final point could be said to be 1972, the year of both Grierson's death and the writing of Rotha's *Documentary Diary*, with its valedictory 'Afterthought' and epilogue to the movement.[23]

What is striking about this history is the pattern of fragmentation which it reveals, particularly during the vital period of 1939–45. The movement never managed to occupy the central position within the British state that Grierson so desired, and the disparity between his original aspirations and what actually transpired was a considerable one.

THE FILMS OF THE DOCUMENTARY FILM MOVEMENT

The Empire Marketing Board Film Unit

The first two films to emerge from the documentary film movement were to be short productions on pedigree cattle and herring fishing. The film on pedigree cattle was eventually dropped, and the herring film became *Drifters* (1929).[24] However, *Drifters* was very different from the straightforward publicity film which EMB officials had expected. It was a poetic montage documentary, which drew heavily on the film-making styles of Sergei Eisenstein and Robert Flaherty, and on Grierson's understanding of avant-garde aesthetics. Grierson later described it as an 'imagist' film, because it added 'poetic reference' to 'symphonic form'.[25] This poetic, even romantic aspect of the film was further emphasised by the choice of musical accompaniment, which was drawn from nineteenth-century romantic composers such as Wagner and Rimsky-Korsakov.[26] The surprise felt by EMB officials at the outcome of this first attempt at film-making is illustrated by the fact that the EMB Film Committee initially insisted some of the more spectacular montage sequences in the film be removed. Grierson complied, but later secretly reinserted the missing sequences. *Drifters* received its premiere on Sunday 10 November 1929, when it shared the bill with Eisenstein's *Battleship Potemkin*.[27] Grierson's film was compared favourably with Eisenstein's, and remains one of the most important films in the British cinema.

Drifters was followed by *Conquest* (Grierson and Wright, 1929), a compilation film made up of footage from Hollywood films, and then by a series of short 'poster' films made by Basil Wright and Paul Rotha, with titles such as *Scottish Tomatoes* and *Butter*.[28] A number of other, relatively simple, single-reel films were also made during 1930, including *South African Fruit* (Wright and Rotha, 1930) and *Canadian Apples* (Wright and Rotha, 1930). The films produced in the following year were more advanced. Basil Wright directed *The Country Comes to Town*, on food and milk supplies brought to London from the country, and *O'er Hill and Dale*, about a sheep farm in the Scottish borders. Arthur Elton made *The Shadow on the Mountain*, about research into grass-growing techniques in Wales, and *Upstream*, on salmon breeding in Scotland. Edgar Anstey joined an admiralty expedition to Labrador and made *Uncharted Waters* and *Eskimo Village*. Marian Grierson re-edited the earlier *Lumber* to make *King Log*, on the lumber industry in Canada, and Robert Flaherty filmed *Industrial Britain*. From the spare footage from this film Marian Grierson edited a single-reel film, *The English Potter*.[29]

One of Grierson's principal strategies for circumventing restrictions on film-making within the EMB was to seek commissions from outside organisations, and the final group of films to emerge from the EMB Film Unit, some of which were completed after the Board's demise, was largely commissioned by such organisations. Stuart Legg directed the first of these, *New Generation* (1932), for the Chesterfield Education Authority. Donald Taylor made *Lancashire at Work and Play* (1933) and *Spring Comes to England* (1934) in association with the Ministries of Labour and Advertising. Marian Grierson made *So This is London* (1933) and *For All Eternity* (1934) for the Travel and Industrial Association. Evelyn Spice made a number of short films for schools on the English seasons, and Stuart Legg made two films for the GPO, *The New Operator* (1933) and *Telephone Workers* (1933). Basil Wright made *Cargo from Jamaica* (1933) and *Windmill in Barbados* (1933) for the EMB and the Orient Line, and then went on to make *Song of Ceylon* (1933–4) for the Ceylon Tea Company. Arthur Elton made *Aero-Engine* (1933) and *The Voice of the World* (1934) for the HMV company, and Harry Watt made *Six-Thirty Collection* (1934) and *BBC Droitwich* (1934) for the GPO and the BBC respectively.[30]

A number of underlying themes can be identified in these early films. There is a general concern with issues of rural and regional identity, and with representations of working-class culture and craft skills. Work, as a distinct physical activity, embedded within the social relations of the small production unit and the rituals and techniques of skilled labour, constantly emerges as a recurrent theme, particularly in *Drifters* and *Industrial Britain*. In contrast, there are few representations of large-scale industry or mass labour. Similarly, representations of metropolitan life and culture, which become more common in the films made during the late 1930s, are conspicuously absent in these early films. Where scientific research or technology is depicted it is frequently set against the natural world and the rural environment, suggesting a concern with exploring the relationship between humanity and nature, rather than between humanity and technology. This pantheistic humanism, when linked to a rural and regionalist affinity, often leads to an ambivalent attitude towards scientific development, where the latter is sometimes viewed as progressive and sometimes as disruptive of traditional mores and practices. A concern with indigenous cultures – particularly in Basil Wright's *Cargo from Jamaica, Windmill in Barbados* and *Song of Ceylon* – can also be identified in this body of films, but such concerns generally merge with representations of the local and intimate, as in *Drifters* and *Industrial Britain*.

After 1933 a change of emphasis is identifiable in the films produced by the movement, as a rhetoric of modernity encompassing representations of modern industry, technology and mass communications began to challenge the preoccupation with rural and regional experience in the early films. A similar shift of focus can be identified in relation to the types of worker depicted in these later films. A considerable variety of workers is represented in the films of the documentary movement, including postal workers, radio operators, scientists, engineers, labourers, fishermen, managers, telephone operators, sailors, lumberjacks, farmers, priests, shepherds, teachers, agriculturalists, explorers, steel workers, potters and factory workers. However, between 1929 and 1934 the focus gradually switches from manual to semi-skilled and skilled labour, and from lower-class to lower middle- class workers.

A greater appreciation of the characteristic thematic concerns of the early films can be obtained through a study of the most important produced during the EMB period, Grierson's *Drifters* (1929). *Drifters* presents an impressionistic account of the events and circumstances

Figure 1.1 Still from Drifters *(1929).*
Source: Crown Copyright (COI).

which it portrays, and subordinates descriptive detail to an evocative representation of the relationship between working fishermen and nature. The film works at the level of myth, in Grierson's own words, 'exalting' the work of herring fishing.[31] Despite this prioritisation of symbolic expression over descriptive detail, *Drifters* does, however, present a significant amount of information about working practices. It is, to some extent, a film about work and the institutions of work, and contains many sequences displaying the skills and techniques of manual labour, such as stoking a boiler, hauling in nets, and gutting and barrelling fish. *Drifters* also depicts different occupations within the fishing industry, such as deep-sea fishing, fish processing, packaging and distribution by rail and sea. Despite its representation of institutional practices, however, *Drifters* is essentially concerned with a particular kind of labour-intensive working activity, and not with the institutions which depend on that activity.

Technology is depicted as playing an integral role in the activities of the fishermen in *Drifters*. Like the fishermen, the steam winches and engines which the fishing boat relies on are sturdy and reliable. A comfortable harmony between men and machine is depicted here, exemplified by the scene in which a man stoking a boiler withdraws a shovel of coals from the furnace and casually lights his cigarette from it. The potential for modern technological development to disrupt traditional patterns of life does not arise in *Drifters*, and the film's central concern with issues of organic unity leads it to depict an overall harmony between humanity, nature and technology.

However, a significant departure from the film's concern with unity occurs when commerce and commercial institutions are represented, and the film comments on the way that labour is commodified and degraded by market forces. Grierson suggests this in one scene through the device of superimposing an image of fishing at sea over an image of fish being barrelled at market. This criticism of the way in which human activity is exploited within an economic system ruled by utilitarian values is a recurrent motif in Grierson's writings, in *Drifters*, and in other films made by the documentary movement, and reveals an anti-capitalist or anti-laissez-faire tendency within the movement.

Drifters also celebrates the consolations and gratifications of the masculine, professional group. Strength, endurance, professional ability and dexterity are all emphasised, as is the camaraderie of the working environment. The world of work on board ship is a closed, masculine world, in which the rituals of communal leisure are emphasised and the continuity of generations is accented, with young, middle-aged and older sailors working collectively. This is an image of work based on a model of traditional labour, in which knowledge is passed on through a combination of peer and kin relationships, and in which the value of the traditional, intimate and organic lower-class working community is foregrounded. The communal life on board ship also resembles family life in some respects, although it is a masculinised one, in which the feminine is excluded from the centre of events, existing only as a peripheral milieu within the fishing village.

Drifters is also primarily concerned with the representation of working-class people, and, although the film encompasses the activities of the market place, the focus is on working-class rather than middle-class or lower middle-class experience. The scenes set in the market have a quite different atmosphere and signification from those shot on the fishing boat. The latter are marked by reflection and a sense of space, or by the dramatic struggle of men against nature, whilst the market is presented in terms of bustle, chaotic movement and instrumental activity; a less moral and worthwhile social space than the communal life of the boat. Nevertheless, *Drifters'* representation of the market is not entirely negative. Although the film questions the value of the market it also emphasises the unity of manual skills and commerce necessary within modernity, showing deep-sea fishing as part of a larger system of interconnection, involving production, marketing and international distribution.

This ambivalence over the representation of commercial activity is the product of underlying contradictions within Grierson's own ideas. Whilst committed to the production of films which communicated a sense of interconnection and harmony, he was also committed to a positive portrayal of lower-class experience. These two objectives were not always fully compatible, given the existence of inequality within society, and this results in a number of tensions, contradictions and uncertainties within *Drifters* over whether or not social processes are to be described or critiqued.

Similar concerns to those found in *Drifters* can also be seen in the two other major films produced during the EMB period, *Industrial Britain* (1931) and *Song of Ceylon* (1933–4).[32] Although *Industrial Britain* looks at the steel, coal-mining, ceramic and glass-making industries, its focus is entirely on craft skills and techniques, and extensive passages depicting the operation of a furnace, the making of a ceramic pot, and the hand-blowing of glass into goblets predominate. The voice-over commentary accompanying the film celebrates these skills, but the ostentatious tone which it adopts is, to some extent, an artificial element superimposed on *Industrial Britain*'s characteristic EMB period concerns. If the editing and photography in the film are examined, and the commentary disregarded, the same concern for craft labour and working-class and regional identities found in *Drifters* becomes apparent.

The thematic concerns of Basil Wright's *Song of Ceylon* (1933–4) are also similar to those of *Drifters*. The original commission for what eventually became *Song of Ceylon* was a request to produce four short films on the tea industry in Ceylon.[33] For various reasons, primarily Grierson's insistence on fully realising the aesthetic potential of the material which had been filmed, and Cavalcanti's interest in experimenting with sound, this strategy was abandoned, and a single film emerged, divided into four sections: 'The Buddha', 'The Virgin Island', 'The Voices of Commerce' and 'The Apparel of a God'. The first and last sections are concerned with rural, traditional and religious themes, whilst the two central sections explore conflicts between the traditional and the modern. The overall focus of the film is on traditional culture, and this is reinforced by the use of a voice-over narration taken from a seventeenth-century traveller's account of the island. The tone of the film is accurately captured by Grahame Greene:

> The last reel, 'The Apparel of a God', returns by way of the gaudy gilded dancers in their devils' masks to the huge images on the mountain, to a solitary peasant laying his offerings at Buddha's feet, and closes again with the huge revolving leaves, so that all we have seen of devotion and dance and the bird's flight and the gentle communal life of harvest seems something sealed away from us between the fans of foliage. We are left outside with the bills of lading and the loudspeakers.[34]

Just as *Drifters* elevates the communal world of traditional labour over the commodified world of the market, *Song of Ceylon* elevates traditional culture, with its organic beliefs and values, above the commercial infrastructure of dockyards and warehouses. Traditional themes structure both films, and the persistence of these preoccupations indicates the presence of a dominant paradigm within the early period of the documentary film movement.

The GPO Film Unit

Most of the films produced at the GPO between 1934 and 1939 were short, two-reel films dealing with aspects of the Post Office and its communication systems. *Cable Ship* (Legg, 1933) dealt with the repair and maintenance of submarine telephone cables. *Weather Forecast* (Spice, 1934) depicted the collection and dissemination of weather information. *Six-Thirty Collection* (Anstey and Watt, 1934) dealt with the collection, sorting and dispatch of mail at a major London sorting office. *Under the City* (Elton and Shaw, 1934) dealt with the maintenance of telephone cables, and *Droitwich* (Watt, 1934), with the erection of a radio station mast. *We Live in Two Worlds* (Cavalcanti, 1937), *Line to Tschierva Hut* (Cavalcanti, 1937) and *Four Barriers* (Cavalcanti, 1937) all concerned aspects of national and international communications systems, and the best-known film of the period, *Night Mail* (Wright, Watt,

Figure 1.2 Still from Song of Ceylon *(1934).*
Source: Crown Copyright (COI).

Anstey and others, 1936) examined the Royal Mail railway delivery service.[35] In these films the shift from representations of the regional, the rural and the traditional to those of the modern and the metropolitan becomes more marked. This is particularly apparent in important films like *Night Mail* and *BBC Voice of Britain,* but lesser films, such as *Under the City* and *Droitwich,* also indicate an increasing turn away from the underlying concerns of *Drifters, Industrial Britain* and *Song of Ceylon.*

Two films which reinstate many of the central concerns of the EMB period are *Coal Face* (Cavalcanti and others, 1935), and *Spare Time* (Jennings, 1939).[36] *Coal Face,* although furnishing general information on coal production, dwells in more detail on working conditions within the mines and on the individual experience of miners. *Spare Time* is similar in that it too concentrates on the lifestyle and leisure cultures of the workers it portrays within the coal-mining, steel and textile industries, rather than on the industries within which they work. Like *Coal Face, Spare Time* also emphasises the particularity of gesture and visual appearance.

Both films mark a return to a concern with cultural identity and popular experience which was characteristic of the EMB period, even though they differ markedly from each other in the stylistic strategies which they employ. Whereas *Coal Face* employs modernist montage and overlapping atonal sound effects, *Spare Time* uses ciné-vérité techniques. Both films, in their differing approaches, accentuate one or other of the two central categories of Grierson's original formula for documentary film-making: the categories of actuality footage and montage editing. The use of these categories in *Drifters* and *Song of Ceylon* was derived from Grierson's early position on the way that naturalism was to be used in conjunction with montage. However, *Coal Face* and *Spare Time* take these categories beyond the levels implied by Grierson's 1929 model.

In fact, the early Griersonian model of documentary film did not survive the EMB period, and was gradually superseded by others, based on the story documentary and the didactic, journalistic film. In many respects this early model can be regarded as a product of the silent cinema, and of the concern with visual orchestration and symbolic expression which characterised much silent film theory, from German Expressionism to the theories of Balazs and Arnheim.[37] It should be remembered that, although the sound film arrived in 1927, it was not commonplace in the British film industry until 1929, or available to the documentary film movement until 1934.[38] The continuation of the poetic montage approach from *Drifters* up to the time of *Song of Ceylon*, and its gradual abandonment after that, must, therefore, be related to the growing influence of the sound film.

One of the key documentary films of the GPO period is *Night Mail* (1936).[39] This is an account of the operation, over the course of a single day and night, of the Royal Mail train delivery service, showing the various stages and procedures of that operation, and the interactions between employees and managers. The film begins with a voice-over commentary describing how the mail is collected and made ready for transit. Then, as the train proceeds along the course of its journey, we are shown the various regional railway stations at which it collects and deposits mail. Inside the train the process of sorting goes on, and we see procedures such as the pick-up of mail bags at high speed. As the train nears its destination there is a sequence – the best known in the film – in which the poetry of W. H. Auden and the music of Benjamin Britten are superimposed over montage images of racing train wheels.

Figure 1.3 Still from Spare Time *(1939).*
Source: © The Post Office, 1998. Reproduced by kind permission.

Finally, an emotive voice-over, narrated by Grierson, emphasises the importance of the mail to national communication.[40]

Although the narrative architecture of *Night Mail* is concerned with issues of national communication and distribution, its thematic centre is linked to representations of regional accents, forms of behaviour, place names and environments. The railway and mail service are represented not as a modern, national communication system, but as a set of institutional practices based within traditional and regional milieus. This elevation of the regional above the national in the film is further reinforced by the depiction of the railway as separate from the metropolitan environment. The only images of the city which appear are those shot in railway stations, and little attempt is made to link the railway and its workers with the city.

Night Mail also channels representations of mass technology, speed, power and volume of mail away from an account of the industry and organisation of postal delivery, and into an imagistic study of the train as a powerful image of technology, in its natural element speeding freely into the countryside, away from the dark city stations. The emphasis here, as in *Drifters* and *Industrial Britain*, appears to be on the relationship between technology and natural forces, rather than on that between technology and the commercial. *Night Mail* mobilises a metaphor of the speeding train, disseminating communication, and uniting the regional and the national, the technological and the rural. However, the imperative of describing mundane postal services fits uneasily with this more abstract project, and the film's ostensible mission is further undermined by its inclination towards one side of the opposition between the regional–rural–cultural and the national–industrial–organisational.

One of the reasons why *Night Mail* lacks the symbolic potency or narrative conviction of *Drifters* and *Song of Ceylon* is that its attempt to integrate the concern with regionalism and symbolic expression found in those films with more administrative, national concerns is, ultimately, unsuccessful. In this respect *Night Mail* can be regarded as a miscon-strued and half-realised attempt to draw upon the model of documentary film initially proposed by Grierson. It can also be regarded as one of the last, as no 'montage' documentary was made after 1936.

After *Night Mail* film-making at the GPO Film Unit adopted an increasingly naturalistic approach to continuity editing, voice-over commentary and visual narrative. One film which provides a good illustration of the more conventional production which emerged from the GPO Film Unit during this period is Cavalcanti and Elton's *The City* (1939), which looks at the difficulties caused by traffic congestion in London.[41] The film's narrative structure is comprehensive, covering the history and growth of London, the problems of the inner cities, and the inconveniences experienced by suburban commuters. *The City* also employs the metaphor of traffic in order to conduct a study of the ways in which social and cultural behaviour are fashioned by the car.

The City begins with a voice-over commentary in local idiom which invokes a symbolism of community and integration through a charac-terisation of London as the commentator's 'local village'. The film then examines the issue of commuting through a depiction of scenes from suburban commuter life, and through a discursive account of the growth of suburbia. After this we are shown examples of inner-city depriva-tion, and, finally, the affluence and privilege of the Royal Borough of Westminster. These different social environments are presented as constituting a diverse but interconnected society containing areas of

disadvantage, and although social inequality is not explicitly represented as an issue, but rather as a fact, the film does, indirectly, stress
the need to respond positively in order to help the disadvantaged
working classes in the inner city.

This opening section is followed by two parallel sequences depicting
work routines in organisations associated with different social class
positions. In the first sequence we are shown a number of scenes
portraying the lower middle-class white-collar workforce which was
expanding rapidly during the 1930s. In a large office building, young
female clerks are shown sitting in rows, processing commercial and
official correspondence. The overall impression is of an over-regulated
environment in which work is repetitive and monotonous. However,
this impression is contradicted by the appearance and disposition of the
clerks, who appear smart, poised and assured. *The City*'s representation
of this metropolitan clerical labour is, therefore, ambivalent, in that it is
depicted as both oppressive and fulfilling.

This sequence is followed by its counterpart, a scene shot in the
sorting room of a major London post office. Here, there is a similar
emphasis on large numbers working within an extensive open space,
and dealing with repetitive work. Like the lower middle-class female
clerical workers, these male working-class postal workers seem self-
possessed, and, although they do not display the composed assurance
of the clerical workers, they exhibit an energetic vigour which indicates
that their working environment is less constrained. There is less
ambiguity, and a more positive representation of this type of work in
The City than is the case with the earlier type, and this bias towards
manual as opposed to administrative or managerial work is also characteristic of the documentary movement as a whole.

The City employs a conventional and naturalistic style of visual
expression and narrative construction and, as such, is typical of the
style adopted in the films of the late GPO period. Apart from films like
The City, the major direction which film-making at the GPO Film Unit
took during the late thirties was in the development of the story
documentary, the most important of which was *North Sea* (Watt, 1938),
a film which, in many respects, completely abandoned Grierson's early
model of documentary.[42] The synthesis of documentary and the feature
film in *North Sea* was influenced by Watt and Cavalcanti, both of whom
had become convinced that the future of documentary lay in a closer
relationship to the commercial cinema. In addition, Cavalcanti had

always disagreed with Grierson's conception of documentary, and had argued instead for a broader definition of realist cinema which could accommodate a variety of film-making styles.

The Realist, Shell and Strand Film Units

Between 1935 and 1939 the film units outside the GPO made films for corporate sponsors on a variety of subjects. Many of these were routine commissions, and included films such as Stuart Legg and Evelyn Spice's *Zoo Babies* (Strand, 1938), one of a series of six films commissioned by the Royal Zoological Society.[43] Others included Ralph Keene's *Rooftops of London* (Strand, 1936), commissioned by MGM in order to meet their obligations under the Quota Act of 1927. The overwhelming majority of films made by the Strand and Shell film units were of this type: educational and publicity films, generally lacking much critical content or aesthetic innovation. There were some exceptions to this general rule, however, including Donald Alexander's *Eastern Valley* (Strand, 1937), and Paul Rotha's *Today We Live* (Strand, 1937).

The most important of these units was Realist, which, in addition to more routine commissions, made a number of films on issues such as education, pollution, housing policy, nutrition and unemployment. These included *Housing Problems* (Elton and Anstey, 1935), *Enough to Eat* (Anstey, 1936), *The Fourth Estate* (Rotha, 1940), *Children at School* (Wright, 1937), *The Smoke Menace* (Taylor and Grierson, 1937) and *Workers and Jobs* (Elton, 1935).[44] The Realist Film Unit also contributed films to the most important production programme supervised by Film Centre. This was commissioned by the Films of Scotland Committee, established by the Scottish Development Council in order to commission films for screening at the 1938 Empire Exhibition. The films were shown at the Exhibition cinema over a six-month period and, after commercial release, were seen by an audience of over twenty-two million. Seven films were produced in 1938, the most important of which were *Wealth of a Nation* (Strand, Alexander and Legg, 1938), on economic regeneration, and *The Face of Scotland* (Realist, Wright, 1938) on aspects of Scottish national identity.[45]

Taken as a group, the films made by the Realist, Strand and Shell Film Units are more sociological and less concerned with formal experimentation than some of the other films made by the documentary movement. In general, they adopt a journalistic approach, conveyed through a voice-over commentary which was, in some cases, influenced by the narrational style of the American 'March of Time' newsreel series.[46] These films also illustrate the forms of compromise which the documentary movement was forced to adopt when making commissioned films for sponsors. In almost all of these films the subject matter available provided considerable opportunities for critical enquiry to take place. However, the film-makers had to conform to the agendas of the sponsors, whose aspirations were rarely as progressive or critical as the film-makers would have liked. For example, although the films made for the Films of Scotland Committee were concerned with important social problems, they were obliged to present a generally optimistic account of the steps being undertaken to resolve those problems. The overall tone of the films is one not of critical enquiry, but of an optimistic exposition of faith in the ability of the nation to surmount its problems.

The film most often cited as disclosing the sorts of compromise which the documentary movement was forced to make is *Housing Problems*, a film sponsored by the gas industry and the London County Council (LCC).[47] The direct predecessor of *Housing Problems*, *Workers and Jobs* (Elton, 1935), employed location shooting and direct sound-recording techniques in transcribing the views of people in an unemployment exchange office. These techniques were further refined in *Housing Problems*, although the bulky technology then available still made it difficult to shoot and interview on location. This difficulty was compounded by the fact that, even by 1935, the film-makers within the documentary movement had relatively little experience of sound film production.

The historical importance of *Housing Problems* lies in the way that, in some sequences, it sets aside the conventional technique of voice-over commentary to present an account of conditions within the slums given by those who lived there. As a consequence, the stories of poor health and child mortality which emerge are rich in anecdotal detail and vivid in impact. However, the issue upon which critics of the documentary movement have fastened is that, in the film, an often strongly conveyed critique of privation is subsumed within a discourse which primarily functions to further the interests of the institutions which sponsored the film. At the time, faced with a degree of critical concern over its house-building policies, the LCC wished to publicise the view that it was dealing effectively with the problem of slum poverty.

Consequently, *Housing Problems* was obliged to assert that the 'problem of the slums' was being addressed and resolved by the construction of 'new and fine housing', and this undermined the implicit demands for reform contained within the location-shot ciné-vérité sequences in the film.

The Crown Film Unit 1941–52

During the war period the divisions which had begun to emerge within the documentary movement from 1936 onwards deepened. The two most important film-makers at the Crown Film Unit, Cavalcanti and Watt, left in 1940 and 1942 respectively, whilst those who had left the GPO Film Unit in the late 1930s, including Grierson, Wright, Anstey and Rotha, were deliberately excluded from high-level participation in the wartime propaganda system.[48] This context of division, the loss of experienced film-makers and other factors eventually led to a drop in the quality of the films produced at Crown, particularly after 1943, and this decline continued until the film unit's abolition in 1952.[49]

Government film production during the war was organised through the Films Division of the MOI, and took the form of both theatrical and non-theatrical exhibition. The latter was largely organised through the MOI's system of mobile film display units, which arranged screenings in factories and rural locations. By 1942, 130 such units were in operation[50] and over 1,000 such displays were taking place each week.[51] Non-theatrical film production was largely undertaken by independent producers and those elements of the documentary movement outside Crown. The films were made in relation to closely specified propaganda campaigns, and this limited the film-makers' opportunities to experiment, or to engage with issues critically.

Despite these constraints, however, the sheer volume of films made for non-theatrical distribution provided the film-makers with occasional opportunities to cover subjects such as post-war reconstruction more critically.[52] In this respect, films such as *Tyneside Story* (1943), about social problems and prospects for post-war change in Newcastle, carried on the tradition of *Enough to Eat* and the other social documentaries of the 1930s. Such scope for critical analysis was, however, limited, and in general the non-theatrical films produced during the war were clear and directive, rather than critical. According to Helen Forman, second in charge of non-theatrical film distribution at the MOI during the war, the films made had 'uncomplicated soundtracks and clear commentary throughout'.[53]

In addition to the non-theatrical film system the MOI also produced short films for screening alongside feature films in commercial cinemas. These films, which were made by Crown and other documentary film units, fell into two main categories: the five- and fifteen-minute film schemes, introduced in 1940 and 1942 respectively.[54] Because they were intended for theatrical exhibition the films produced within these schemes were made, in theory at least, with 'entertainment' as well as propaganda value. They include films such as *Britain Can Take It* (Watt, Jennings, 1940), *Builders* (Jackson, 1940), *Men of the Lightship* (Cavalcanti, 1940), *Squadron 999* (Watt, 1940), *Heart of Britain* (Jennings, 1941) and *Listen to Britain* (Jennings, 1941).

In addition to these short films, the Crown Film Unit also produced a small number of expensive, feature-length story documentaries during the war. The policy of developing this type of film was strongly supported by Watt and Cavalcanti, but it was also encouraged by officials within the MOI, who had been impressed by the commercial success of Watt's *North Sea* (1938) and Cavalcanti's *Men of the Lightship*.[55] The first of the war-time story documentaries, and the most commercially successful, was Harry Watt's *Target for Tonight* (1941). This was followed by *Coastal Command* (J. B. Holmes, 1942), *Fires Were Started* (Jennings, 1943), *Close Quarters* (Lee and Holmes, 1943) and *Western Approaches* (Pat Jackson, 1944). These films focused on routine service activities, showing how such activities were planned and executed, but they also employed dramatic development, characterisation and humour, in order to draw the audience into an emotional identification with the characters within them. These relatively expensive productions accounted for only about 10 per cent of the MOI's output during the war, but consumed a large part of its budget.[56]

Although the feature-length story documentaries were by far the most popular films made by the documentary movement during the war, they were, with the exception of Jennings's *Fires Were Started*, by no means the most aesthetically successful of the movement's films. The documentarists lacked experience in assembling long, complex film narratives, and that inexperience is apparent in the awkward and stilted narrative construction and use of dialogue in these films. In general, plot development is predictable and unimaginative, and the build-up of dramatic suspense falls well below the standards set by some of the commercial feature films being produced in Britain at the time. Despite possessing better resources than they had ever enjoyed in the 1930s, those available to the film-makers at Crown were still considerably inferior to those available to most film-makers in the commercial feature-film industry, and this was inevitably reflected in the low production values found in the films. The use of 'social actors', with limited or non-existent acting skills, also restricted opportunities for the films to capture the emotional involvement of the audience.

The feature-length story documentary was a transitory product of the war period, and did not survive beyond 1945. Nevertheless, during the war these films provided realistic accounts of important wartime activities for an audience which clearly required such representations. Their use of characterisation and dramatic structure in delivering these also proved more effective than the didactic techniques employed by other documentaries of the period. One film from this group, Humphrey Jennings's *Fires Were Started*, can, in addition, be compared with the more important of the earlier films made by the documentary movement. Yet, despite its many good qualities, Jennings's film is still tainted by the awkward dialogue and characterisation inherent within the story documentary form. There is also evidence to suggest that Jennings was persuaded to make the film by Harry Watt and Ian Dalrymple, both of whom questioned the value of the poetic montage style adopted by Jennings in films such as *Listen to Britain*.

Listen to Britain, possibly Jennings's most influential film, employs symbolic oppositions which are unified through juxtaposition, suggesting that beneath the appearance of difference an underlying reality of national unity exists. The oppositions employed are powerful, and include those of country/town, feminine/masculine, old/new, popular culture/high art, local/national and lower-class/upper-class. As the film progresses these oppositions are mobilised with increasing intensity, reaching a climax in the final scenes of the film. Within this highly charged symbolic structure Jennings deploys ciné-vérité images of ordinary people and public figures apparently caught unawares, giving the impression that this depiction of national unity has been objectively witnessed, rather than constructed for propaganda purposes. *Listen to Britain* also mobilises some of the key thematic motifs of the EMB period, such as that of the local, the regional and the intimate, and its combination of these with images of national interconnection is far more effective than that attempted in films such as *Night Mail*.

The Documentary Movement and the National Film Board of Canada

In 1938 Grierson was approached by officials from the Canadian High Commission in London and asked to prepare a report on the development of government film-making in Canada.[57] The report, submitted in June of that year, formed the basis of what was to become the NFB of Canada, and Grierson was then offered the position of Film Commissioner at the new organisation.[58] When he eventually arrived to take up his post he brought with him other members of the documentary movement, including Stuart Legg, Stanley Hawes, J. D. Davidson, Evelyn Spice, Raymond Spottiswood and Basil Wright.[59] These more experienced film-makers then trained young Canadian apprentices such as James Beveridge, Louis Applebaum, Tom Daly and Norman Mclaren.[60] Beginning with an initial complement of only five, the staff at the NFB expanded throughout the war period until, by 1945, almost eight hundred people were employed.[61]

The NFB was by far the largest film-making organisation which Grierson had ever worked in, and he also enjoyed considerably more autonomy there than he had in Britain. Not only was he responsible for the co-ordination of all government film-making in Canada, but he had also ensured that the NFB was not directly subject to the Canadian Civil Service, thus avoiding the constraints experienced at the EMB and GPO Film Units. However, Grierson's response to this promising situation was not to encourage his film-makers to be creative or imaginative, but, on the contrary, to impose a tightly regulated regime, based upon the mass production of standardised, formulaic propaganda films. As one of Grierson's young Canadian recruits, Louis Applebaum, recalled, the object of film-making at the NFB was to make films which contained 'realistic war-time propaganda messages' with 'no room for improvisation'.[62]

The film-making model which Grierson drew on in order to put his ideas on documentary and propaganda into practice in Canada was the compilation film. This type of film had first been used within the documentary movement as early as 1930, in *Conquest*. After that the films made within the movement continued to use compilation footage in conjunction with newly shot material, and the compilation footage used was generally taken from other films made within the movement, rather than from external sources as was the case with *Conquest*. The compilation film did not, therefore, become the dominant model of film-making within the British documentary movement, although, under Grierson's insistence, it did become so in Canada.[63] Grierson adopted the compilation film format because it allowed more rigorous control to be exercised over the articulation of propaganda messages than was the case with other types of documentary film-making. Such films could be made quickly and inexpensively, and all stages of the production process could be monitored and supervised from within the studio.

Grierson combined this approach to film-making with a labour model based on threshold specialisation. Inexperienced apprentices would be trained to master aspects of film-making to a satisfactory level, then moved on to other areas. Although the film-makers became familiar with different areas of film-making, none developed specialist skills or expertise. This model of collaborative film-making had been introduced into the documentary movement by Grierson in the 1930s, but it was only in Canada that he insisted on applying it rigorously and pervasively.[64]

Two major programmes of films, 'Canada Carries On' and 'World in Action', each with its own distinctive perspective, emerged from this context of 'factory-based' film production at the NFB during the war. Sixty-two films were made within the 'Canada Carries On' series, which was primarily concerned with Canada's role within the war effort, whilst thirty films were made for 'World in Action', which dealt with international relations, and included films such as *The War for Men's Minds* (1943), on the role of government propaganda, and *Food-Secrets of the Peace* (1943), on food scarcity within Europe. Like the 'Canada Carries On' series, these films were inspirational and didactic in tone, but they also focused on the idea of the 'interdependency of nations', elevating this international perspective above purely Canadian concerns.[65]

These films obtained theatrical distribution during the war but, in addition to this, Grierson also established systems of non-theatrical distribution. One of these was the rural circuit scheme, in which travelling projectionists screened NFB films in schools, village halls and other public sites across Canada. One hundred and seventy such projectionists were eventually employed – more than the MOI employed in Britain – and, by the end of 1941, they were reaching an audience of a quarter of a million per month.[66] These audiences were shown a standard slate of films which conveyed the idea of a diverse but united Canada, and debates, based on lecture notes supplied by the NFB, were encouraged after the screenings.

It should be made clear that the rural circuit schemes had an instrumental purpose, and were not primarily designed to promote the free exchange of critical debate. Grierson, and others at the NFB, attempted to manage the schemes as much as possible, closely supervising the activities of the projectionists in order to ensure that propaganda objectives were met. Although some have argued that audience response data from the circuits allowed the film-makers to respond better to the needs of the audience,[67] such information was, on the whole, primarily used to develop more effective propaganda campaigns.[68] Nevertheless, the schemes were intrinsically difficult to control from the centre because of the geographical distances involved. Open debate often broke out around issues raised in the films shown, and the screenings also functioned as social events, allowing local, as opposed to national, concerns to be aired.

The films produced by Grierson during this period were made for specific purposes, rather than to endure, and, consequently, they have not lasted. There is also evidence to suggest that, both inside and outside Canada, considerable opposition existed to Grierson's approach. In 1941, for example, Cavalcanti made *Film and Reality*, an aesthetic study of the documentary film, as a riposte to Grierson's more instrumental approach (Grierson hated the film). Jack Beddington, the head of film propaganda within the MOI, found the films produced by Grierson to be too crudely propagandistic[69] and, in Canada, a number of government officials thought Grierson's views on propaganda film-making and information management too authoritarian. Some of the young Canadian film-makers recruited by Grierson also objected to his approach to film-making,[70] and there is evidence to suggest that the audiences in the rural circuits sometimes reacted negatively to the prescriptive and didactic tone of the films they watched. Even film-makers involved in the making of these films later took a dim view of them. Basil Wright has described them as 'rough', James Beveridge as 'derivative', Paul Rotha as 'ephemeral', and Stuart Legg as 'mundane', 'ordinary', and an unsuitable model for the future development of documentary.[71]

THE HISTORICAL CONTEXT OF THE DOCUMENTARY FILM MOVEMENT

The documentary film movement was a product of the inter-war period, and in order to understand the movement fully it is important to appreciate its relationship to the constellation of ideologies and circumstances which characterised that complex and rapidly changing period. The 1930s, in particular, were a paradoxical time, which has given rise to contradictory interpretations, some of which have endowed the decade with an almost mythic character. This characterisation has also influenced accounts of the documentary film movement, which has become identified in some quarters with both the achievements and the failures of this legendary decade.

Although radical political movements and ideologies did expand their sphere of influence during the 1930s, in general the period was dominated by conservative beliefs, and by Conservative-controlled National Governments. Although some parts of Britain suffered severe economic recession during this period, other parts of the country enjoyed increasing economic prosperity. Whilst the decline of coal, steel and textile manufacturing during the period did create areas of significant unemployment, the rate of overall national economic growth was comparable to that of any other period in the history of British capitalism.[72] Although the 1930s were characterised by the growth of unemployment, then, they were also distinguished by the growth of suburbia, the rapid expansion of London, the rise of corporate capitalism, and the creation of a new lower- middle-class workforce.[73] Auden's 'dark dishonest decade' of mass poverty and political appeasement was also that of Betjeman's tennis-playing suburban belles.

The condition of Britain in the 1930s was a complex and uneven one in which circumstances and experience differed significantly from region to region. This fast-changing environment was also inherently difficult to understand at the time because the mass media were unwilling or unable to convey objective or critical analysis on the condition of the nation. National newspapers were used as platforms for the personal prejudices of press barons such as Beaverbrook or Northcliffe, radio was heavily regulated, and the cinema, dominated by Hollywood, was unable to, in Stephen Tallents' words 'project England'.[74] As a consequence, politicians, public figures, artists and intellectuals were often poorly informed about the circumstances surrounding them. Orwell, for example, did not expect conditions to be as bad as he found them in the deprived areas, and many of the social surveys of national nutrition and health carried out during the 1930s exposed a degree of deprivation which startled the social scientists conducting the research.[75] Similarly, the work of writers such as J. B. Priestley and Julian Symons conveys an impression of attempting to connect an ambiguous mosaic of divergent social experiences together, reinforcing the impression that the political, cultural and social topography of the nation was unclear at the time.[76]

It is important to bear this context in mind when considering the documentary film movement. The movement was influenced by the same uncertainty and indecisiveness which affected many middle-class intellectuals during the period, and this was reflected in the rather vague political views expressed by Grierson and other members of the movement. Although one of the myths associated with the movement is that it was 'left-wing', in fact Grierson was opposed to any radical or Marxist transformation of society, and, despite some claims to the contrary, the other film-makers did not generally perceive themselves to be left-wingers.[77] These factors, and others, help to explain – although, in the eyes of some critics, not excuse – why liberal–centrist rather than radical attitudes took root within the documentary film movement.

The ideological discourse of the documentary film movement during the 1930s can be positioned to the left of dominant conservatism, to the right of Marxist and socialist opinion, and within a constellation of centrist ideologies associated with currents of social democratic reform. These ideologies were diverse and heterogeneous, but they shared a common core of agreement on the value of established social institutions, the need for public regulation of market forces, and the need to reject both Communism and Fascism.[78] This social democratic consensus transcended traditional party political boundaries during the period. For example, in 1936, the Conservative politician Harold Macmillan attempted to establish a new political party under the leadership of the Labour politician Herbert Morrison. Macmillan's aim, as set forth in his influential book *The Middle Way* (1938), was to 'obtain a fusion of all that is best in left and right'.[79]

The documentary movement can be associated with this emerging and diverse movement of social democratic reformism. However, beyond this broad association it is difficult to identify the movement with any particular political party or ideology, because the movement consistently refused to associate itself with party political activities. There was one occasion, however, when Grierson came close to clarifying his political position, and, typically, he did so by referring to the influences on him in his youth. Writing in 1952, in the Preface to Paul Rotha's *Documentary Film*, Grierson argued that:

> The Clydeside cult was the most humanist in the early socialist movement. This was its deep political weakness, as Lenin himself pointed out, and men like James Maxton came practically to demonstrate. But while recognising this, as one must, the overriding humanist factor did not thereby lose its ultimate validity. It has seemed to me, on the other hand, to assume more and more validity as the harder forces of political organisation have taken control of the thoughts we had and the sympathies we urged. For myself, I shall only say that what I may have given to documentary – with the working man on the screen and all that – was simply what I owed to my masters, Keir Hardie, Bob Smillie, and John Wheatley.[80]

The 'Clydeside cult' which Grierson refers to here, and which is more generally referred to as the Red Clydeside movement, was made up of a number of left-wing organisations, including the Independent Labour Party, the British Socialist Party, the Socialist Labour Party, and the Communist Party of Great Britain. These organisations, and individuals such as James Maxton, whom Grierson refers to, were involved in one of the most important upsurges of radical politics in modern British history.[81] However, in the quotation above, Grierson explicitly identifies himself with the more moderate figures of Keir Hardie and John Wheatley, rather than with Maxton, or with Marxists such as John McLean, who were active at the centre of the Clydeside revolt.

Hardie, an important figure in the history of labour politics, was influenced by the same idealist tradition which had influenced Grierson. His socialism was based on moral premises derived from the Bible, and he believed socialism to be the 'embodiment of Christianity in the industrial sphere'.[82] Similarly, Wheatley, an Irish Catholic, also wished to make religious morality the foundation of political and social life. He founded the Catholic Socialist Society in 1906, and went on to become a member of the first Labour Party government of 1923–4.[83] The 1952 Preface makes it clear, therefore, that it is to the moderate, religiously derived reformism identified with figures such as Hardie and Wheatley, rather than to the communist, socialist or guild-socialist positions of McLean, Maxton and others, that Grierson's political position must be associated.

The documentary movement can also be associated with a number of centre–progressive pressure groups which emerged following the sizeable defeat of the Liberal Party in the general election of 1931. The primary objective of these groups was to promote the development of a reformed, progressive, corporate state in Britain, and to define the parameters of post-laissez-faire society. One of these groups, Political and Economic Planning (PEP), which argued for greater public regulation of the economy, typified the concern with corporate- and reform-oriented planning which Grierson advocated, and which films such as *Housing Problems*, *The City* and *Roadworks* embodied. In their report on the state of the short film industry in Britain, *The Factual Film* (1947), PEP explicitly endorsed the positions on public subsidy advocated by the documentary movement,[84] and, in the final paragraph of their report on the feature film industry, *The British Film Industry* (1952), they also advocated the type of government involvement which Grierson had always urged:

> If the public considers it desirable for political, cultural or economic reasons that British films should be produced, then it must be prepared for the government not only to protect the industry indefinitely, but also to aid it financially for as far ahead as can be seen.[85]

Another important cultural trend which appeared during the inter-war period, and to which the documentary movement must be related, is that of the growth of a naturalistic, documentary aesthetic. The origins of this can be traced back to World War I, when films such as *The Battle of the Somme* (1916) had a considerable impact. A number of written documentary accounts of the war also appeared in the 1920s, including Robert Graves's *Goodbye to all That* (1929) and Siegfried Sassoon's *Memoirs of a Foxhunting Man* (1928).[86] Other works based on a documentary format which appeared in the 1930s included Walter Greenwood's *Love on the Dole* (1933), J. B. Priestley's *English Journey* (1934), George Orwell's *The Road to Wigan Pier* (1937) and *Down and Out in Paris and London* (1933) and Christopher Isherwood's *Goodbye to Berlin* (1939).

One of the central features of this concern with documentary representation, particularly during the 1930s, was a desire to bring working-class experience within the sphere of representation. Grierson's *Drifters* was, in many respects, a pioneer of this within the British cinema, and, although *Drifters* was not a Marxist film, its representation of working-class experience was seen as a genuinely radical intervention. As Montagu Slater, writing in *Left Review* in 1935, argued, describing the 'ordinary world of people' was a 'revolutionary act in itself'[87] and, because of this, documentary naturalism was widely regarded as an important part of progressive cultural practice. However, the excessive use of naturalism was also seen as problematic. Marxist theory, in particular, drew a distinction between naturalism, which describes immediate appearances, and realism, which goes beyond appearances to describe more abstract realities. Writing in 1932, a spokesman for the Workers'Theatre Movement argued that:

> The naturalistic form, namely that form which endeavours to show a picture on the stage as near to life as possible, is suitable for showing things as they appear on the surface, but does not lend itself to disclosing the reality which lies underneath. And it is just this reality, lying just beneath the surface of capitalist society, that the worker's theatre must reveal.[88]

An overly naturalistic approach was, therefore, insufficient, because it could not represent abstract realities, or offer sufficient scope for social and political comment. Beyond this, naturalism was also problematic because it paid insufficient attention to questions of aesthetic form. The critical success of Soviet films such as *Potemkin* and *Earth* was largely due to the fact that they had achieved a successful integration of naturalism, formalism and political statement, and, as a result of this, they became important models on which to base a radical cultural practice. To a lesser extent the same was also true of the films made by the documentary movement, which were seen in some quarters as having achieved the same synthesis of naturalism, formalism and social content: 'Perhaps the nearest equivalent of what is wanted already exists in another form in the documentary film . . . We may stumble on the solution in the effort of trying to create the literary equivalent of the documentary film.'[89]

The documentary movement did, therefore, provide a model for progressive cultural practices in the 1930s, and Grierson encouraged this by establishing contacts with a wide range of artists and intellectuals, including Benjamin Britten, W. H. Auden, J. B. Priestley, Graham Greene, H. G. Wells and Julian Huxley. The house journals of the movement, *Cinema Quarterly* (1932–6), *World Film News* (1936–8) and *Documentary Newsletter* (1940–7), also published articles from authors as diverse as Ivor Montagu, George Bernard Shaw, Somerset Maugham and Aldous Huxley. Although the extent to which the documentary movement influenced the cultural life of the period is difficult to gauge, the evidence suggests that its impact was not inconsiderable.

GRIERSON'S THEORY OF DOCUMENTARY FILM

The final context within which Grierson and the documentary movement must be situated is idealism, a philosophical system which provided the foundation for many of Grierson's ideas. Philosophical idealism achieved its most systematic expression in Germany during the eighteenth and nineteenth centuries, when, in returning to the intellectual atmosphere of the Middle Ages, it made Germany a focal point for metaphysical and anti-materialist ideologies, and developed into 'a philosophy of contempt for empirical reality, based on the timeless and the infinite, the eternal and the absolute'.[90] Idealism also functioned, particularly under Hegel, as an ideological support for German feudalism and, to that extent, can be considered as a conservative response to the emergence of modernity and capitalism within western Europe. However, although idealism looked back to the Middle Ages in an attempt to defend feudal social structures, it also offered a sceptical and critical response to unregulated laissez-faire capitalism, and it is here . that its progressive dimension can be located.

As idealism grew in importance in Britain after 1860 it developed into a movement which advocated state regulation of capitalism in the interests of the nation.[91] British idealism combined elements from both right and left into an often contradictory ideology which emphasised themes such as social duty, reform, spirituality, rule by 'enlightened' elites, and the need to return to the social relations of pre-industrial England.[92] As a radical middle-class and lower- middle-class response to the social problems created by capitalism, idealism was progressive in that it advocated a more equitable distribution of wealth and resources, and conservative in that it was often derived from a perception of the need to preserve the position of the professional middle classes.[93]

British idealism reached the zenith of its influence between 1880 and 1914, after which it declined in importance, and was absorbed into theories concerned with the role of the mass media and popular education in fostering national unity. Here, the earlier idealist proposition that a 'clericy' of intellectuals should co-operate with politicians, in communicating national objectives to the people, became assimilated into theories on how new mass communications technologies could create channels of communication and consensus between the state and the public. A concern with social communication and civic education was, therefore, central to idealist thought and, after 1918, many idealists became involved in the establishment of a public service role for the new social media of radio and film; John Grierson founded the documentary film movement, whilst John Reith helped to establish the public service and educational profile of the BBC. Idealists such as these were, to varying degrees, reformers, but they also employed mass communication in a directive way, in order to help create a more unified society. In this respect, their attitude towards mass communication and 'civic education' was more authoritarian than libertarian.[94]

This is the context from which Grierson emerged. He was not an isolated thinker, but the product of a tradition of idealism which influenced many areas of intellectual life in Britain between the 1880s and 1939. Grierson first gained access to idealist thought through his father, Robert, who introduced him to the work of Carlyle, Byron and Ruskin.[95] After this he studied idealist philosophy at Glasgow University, reading Plato, Kant and Hegel, and becoming influenced by the neo-Hegelian philosopher F. H. Bradley and the idealist–socialist philosopher A. D. Lindsay.[96] Grierson derived a number of beliefs from these influences which remained with him throughout his life, including those in the value of the state and corporate institutional structures, in the existence of organic unities within society, in the value of non-cognitive aesthetic experience, and in gradualist, as opposed to radical, political reform.[97]

One of the central concepts within the philosophical discourse of idealism was that of organic totality. Grierson rejected the idea that fundamental divisions existed within society, and argued instead that social life was characterised by a 'matrix of inter-dependent relations' and, consequently, that societies and institutions which were highly integrated were superior to those which were not.[98] These views led him to place considerable emphasis on the role of the state in ensuring

social unity. According to Grierson, when the state constrained individualism or sectarianism in the interests of social unity, it was exercising
'good totalitarianism':

> You can be 'totalitarian' for evil and you can also be 'totalitarian'
> for good ... So, the kind of 'totalitarianism' I am thinking of,
> while it may apply to the new conditions of society, has as deep a
> root as any in human tradition.[99]

Grierson's position seems, at first sight, to be explicitly authoritarian
here. However, that appears less so when his particular conception of
the state is taken into account. Grierson conceived of the state not as a
centralised agency, but as an assembly of corporate institutions which
regulated and administered social life for the national good.[100] His
theory of the state was a corporate, idealist one, based on notions of
social responsibility, rather than a totalitarian one, based on centralising
authoritarian principles.

Grierson also drew a distinction between the institutions and the
agents of the state, and argued that the former could be subverted by
its agents for sectarian purposes. Under these circumstances, film-
makers could pursue a more critical agenda. This distinction provided
a rationale for the emergence of a critical film-making practice within
the documentary movement. However, according to Grierson, such a
practice must be premised on an understanding of the imperative need
to sustain the central institutions of state, and this also effectively ruled
out fundamental criticism of the establishment.

In addition to his influence by idealist conceptions of the state,
Grierson was also influenced by a number of idealist aesthetic positions
founded on intuitionist and expressive premises. He was particularly
influenced by Kant's assertion that the basis of aesthetic experience lay
in the perception of complex unities and harmonies, and argued that
the role of art was to present such harmonies to the spectator, so that
they would symbolise the harmonised 'relations of life' which the
individual sought.[101] Another important influence on Grierson was F.
H. Bradley's conviction that the existential complexity of underlying
reality could only be experienced intuitively, and not through conceptual reason.[102] This meant that, in order to communicate effectively, art
must employ generalised and symbolic rather than didactic or peda-
gogic modes of expression.[103] These beliefs on symbolic expression and

social communication were also influenced by theories of mass communication and public cognition which Grierson encountered whilst
in America in the 1920s. He was particularly influenced by Walter
Lippmann's argument that public communication had to adopt an
impressionistic and generalised form in order to be effective.

From these various influences Grierson arrived at a definition of the
principal function of the documentary film as that of representing the
interdependence and evolution of social relations in a dramatic, descriptive and symbolic way. This function was simultaneously sociological
and aesthetic: it was sociological in that it involved the representation
of social relationships, and it was aesthetic in that it involved the use of
imaginative and symbolic means to that end.[104] Furthermore, Grierson
argued that the documentary film was ideally suited to represent the
interconnected nature of social relationships because it was 'the medium
of all media born to express the living nature of inter-dependency . . .
[it] outlined the patterns of interdependency more distinctly and more
deliberately than any other medium whatsoever'.[105] Examples of such
interdependency can be found in most of the major early films made by
the documentary movement. In *Drifters*, montage is used to illustrate
the way that all parts of the process of deep-sea fishing are interconnected. In *Song of Ceylon*, the links between the traditional and the
modern, the religious and the secular, are emphasised, whilst in *Night
Mail*, the nation is shown as bound together through its communication
processes. In all these films, descriptive information about particular
working processes is combined with, and often dominated by, impressionistic, symbolic techniques whose function is to express a poetic
sense of unity.

Grierson's first systematic elaboration of his theory of documentary
film appeared in an EMB memorandum written in 1927, entitled 'Notes
for English Producers'.[106] In the second part of this memorandum,
headed 'English Cinema Production and the Naturalistic Tradition',
Grierson postulated two different categories of film production, one
consisting of films between seven and nine reels in length, the other of
films around four reels in length. The first of these categories was based
on the theory of 'epic cinema' which he had elaborated in America in
the mid-1920s, in which films featuring individual dilemmas, preoccupations and relationships would also contain representations of social
and national institutions.[107]

Although Grierson's theory of epic cinema could be described as a form of cinematic realism, it could not be described as a form of critical cinematic realism. The approach advocated by Grierson would neither give a critical account of contemporary reality, nor cultivate the critical faculties of the spectator. Instead, the spectator's understanding would be directed into a recognition of the essential underlying unity of society; what Grierson referred to as the 'continuing reality'.[108] Grierson's model of epic cinema also drew on particular conceptions of spectatorial identification and human nature when he argued that such films should contain reassuring representations of contemporary social realities. He believed that the 'popular mind was disposed towards optimistic representations of the social world', and would not identify with negative or unfamiliar representations.[109] This view of the popular mind, when combined with a directive stance on social representation, further emphasises the fact that Grierson's theory of epic cinema was considerably more directive than critical.

Grierson's model of epic cinema bore little relation to the limited budget and resources available to the EMB, however, and so in the second part of his 1927 memorandum he defined a form of cinema more appropriate to those modest circumstances. This second category of film production would consist of shorter films, whose principal objective would be to represent 'social interconnection in both primitive cultures and modern industrial society'. Grierson believed that these films would mark a 'new phase in cinema production', and that they would have, of necessity, to be superior to and different from existing actuality film genres:

> if these pictures are to avoid the fate of industrial commercial and so-called educational pictures of the past and if they are to be really effective for educational and propaganda purposes they will have to be made on entirely original lines. They [previous actuality films] have gone frequently about the business of regarding some scene or other without the first regard to the value of tempo, rhythm and composition: indeed without realising that, even where a story is absent, intensely exciting effects can be gained by exploiting movement in masses in a dramatic way.[110]

In these films the visual features of prosaic subject matter 'could be orchestrated into cinematic sequences of enormous vitality' through a sophisticated use of montage editing and visual composition.[111] Such an approach would involve the abandonment of both rudimentary documentary naturalism and the processes of narrative construction common to the commercial feature film, and this positions Grierson's early theory of documentary film within a clearly modernist paradigm.

Although this original definition of the 'Griersonian' documentary explicitly emphasised formative editing technique, the actuality content of the documentary image remained an important factor for Grierson, as is illustrated by a distinction he drew between the 'real' and the 'actual'. Writing about *Drifters* shortly after it was made, Grierson argued that the empirical content (the actual) of its documentary images were organised so as to express general truths (the real), which existed at a level of abstraction beyond the empirical, and could not themselves be directly represented.[112] Grierson's definition of the real is rather nebulous, but was essentially based on the Hegelian notion of *Zeitgeist*, or 'spirit of the age'. The real consisted of general determining factors and predispositions specific to a particular time and place, and Grierson argued that the documentary imagery should be so organised as to express these.

Grierson's first definition of documentary film was based on the revelation of the real through the manipulation of documentary footage by formative editing technique. Grierson argued that the documentary image was able to signify the real more profoundly than the image produced within the artificial environment of the film studio because it registered and transcribed the 'phenomenological surface of reality', and because, for Grierson, an existential relationship existed between the phenomenal (the actual) and the real.[113] Grierson's reference to phenomenology here is also significant: one of the major influences on him at the time was the Hungarian theorist Bela Balazs, who argued that film could express a poetic reality which existed beyond the empirical, but which could only be reached through the empirical. There is a considerable resemblance between Balazs's belief that 'The artist could represent . . . the soul's bodily incarnation in terms of gesture or feature' and Grierson's belief that documentary could represent 'the characteristic gestures and features which time has worn smooth'.[114] Both formulations reveal an emphasis on the ability of the naturalist image to signify abstract realities.

In addition to the influence of Balazs, Grierson's ideas were also influenced by a more general concern with the visual which permeated European film theory during the silent period. This critical discourse on the cinema included the work of Kracauer, Arnheim and Balazs, and was characterised by a concern for non-cognitive and irrationalist forms of expression. Within these critical writings cinema was regarded as a site of visual pleasure, and as a redemptive instrument through which the 'real' could be made visible.[115] The visual was considered to be a primal mode of communication which pre-dated the rise of conceptual reason, and the cinema was thought to offer the possibility of a return to lost sensory experience.[116]

In addition to an emphasis on the visual, this early critical discourse also stressed the importance of concrete immediacy as a means of 'seeing' the world through the veil of ideology and convention. Cinema's ability to represent the concrete, including gesture and facial expression, was, therefore, regarded as particularly important and, like the visual in general, gesture and facial expression were regarded as a kind of primeval language, capable of transcending national, class and gender divisions, and the manipulative operations of language.[117]

Grierson's early theory of documentary film consisted of three principal elements: (1) a concern with the content and expressive richness of the actuality image; (2) a concern with the interpretative potential of editing; and (3) a concern with the representation of social relationships. All these can be found in his early film theory and in some of the films produced by the documentary movement between 1929 and 1935. After that date the poetic montage style of films such as *Drifters* and *Song of Ceylon* gradually gave way to a more didactic, journalistic style, whilst the earlier concern with philosophical aesthetics was increasingly superseded by a discourse grounded in issues of propaganda and instrumental 'civic education'.

The preoccupations and concerns of this later period are most clearly expressed in the collection of Grierson's essays published in *Grierson on Documentary* (1946).[118] Readers encountering the essays in this book generally agreed with critics such as Andrew Tudor, who argued that Grierson had advocated an approach in which 'purposive cinema emphasises the purposiveness at the expense of the cinema . . . and in which film was only of significance as an instrument of social persuasion'.[119]

The essay in *Grierson on Documentary* which embodies this attitude most uncompromisingly is 'The Documentary Idea', written in 1942. Here, Grierson talks about 'bang[ing films] out one a fortnight . . . with a minimum of dawdling over how some poor darling happens to react to something or other'.[120] He goes on to argue that the 'documentary idea was not basically a film idea at all . . . the medium happened to be the most convenient', and that the documentary movement was an 'anti-aesthetic movement'.[121] An excessive and immoderate attitude prevails throughout this essay. For example, Grierson boasts that he 'used' the aesthetes within the movement, describing Flaherty and Cavalcanti as 'fellow travellers': a loaded terminology, implying self-interest and untrustworthiness. Film-makers who did not make the 'banged-out', mass-produced instrumental films which he advocated were described as 'the old . . . left alive to feel sorry for themselves and make "beautiful" pictures about it'.[122] Rather startlingly, he also looked back with regret to the production of the 'social documentaries' of the 1930s, claiming that, after Munich, he became determined to abandon the concern with the local and the particular within these films, and, thereafter, to only produce films about 'world forces'.[123]

The word 'beautiful' receives particular abuse within this essay, and is defined in terms of decadence and 'culture without action'. Bizarrely, Grierson also applauds Goering's infamous saying, 'when anyone mentions the word culture, I reach for my gun', as a 'successful recognition' of the need to replace beauty with action, and, in the new 'era of action', to give 'law' to the 'wilderness' of inaction which contemporary culture had become.[124] This use of excessive language is also accompanied by an unrealistic assessment of Grierson's own achievements, as, for example, when he asserts that 'in a decade of spiritual weariness it [the documentary film movement] reached out, almost alone among the media, towards the future'. The essay concludes with a denunciation of commercial cinema and public taste:

> So the long, windy openings are out and the cathartic finishes in which a good, brave, tearful, self-congratulatory and useless time is had by all. The box office – pander to what is lazy, weak, reactionary, sentimental and essentially defeatist in all of us – will, of course, instinctively howl for them. It will want to make 'relaxation', if you please, even out of war. But that way leads nowhere.[125]

The tone of the 1942 essay could be interpreted as an uncharacteristic aberration, provoked by Grierson's sense of injustice at his exclusion from the British wartime propaganda system, and by the rejection of his approach to documentary film-making by the film-makers at Crown. In some respects the essay was a manifesto, which set out Grierson's beliefs concerning the basic principles of the documentary film at the time. It was first published in a 1942 edition of *Documentary Newsletter* as a response to the appearance of Cavalcanti's *Film and Reality* (1942), a compilation film which looked back over the history of the documentary film, emphasising the aesthetic qualities and achievements of the genre. Cavalcanti's film was, in part, intended to be an overt and deliberate rejection of the model of didactic, civic education documentary then being promoted by Grierson and his supporters. The 1942 essay was designed to criticise the approach being developed at Crown under Cavalcanti's leadership, and to re-establish Grierson's model of the documentary film as the hegemonic one within the documentary movement.

It has been suggested that not only the 1942 essay but most of Grierson's writings during the war should be considered as uncharacteristic of his true position, and as a temporary and strategic response to the demands of the time. Such an argument is, however, undermined by the fact that what is particularly striking about Grierson is that his general ideology remained largely unchanged from the 1920s to the 1970s. This unusual degree of continuity makes it unlikely that any 'epistemological shift' occurred during the war period, and demonstrates the importance of understanding the ideological continuity which underlay Grierson's pre- and post-1937 positions on the relationship between the aesthetic and the sociological.

The source of that ideological continuity was philosophical idealism, and, rather than an epistemological shift occurring in Grierson's post-1940 ideas, authoritarian tendencies which were always implicit in his ideology, but which were, prior to 1936, dialectically linked with more progressive tendencies, became increasingly dominant. This is clearly illustrated in many of the post-1940 essays in *Grierson on Documentary*, where an illiberal and authoritarian approach to the management of social communication processes prevails. Within these parameters the vocation of the film-producer/educator becomes one of preaching the creed of social interconnection and 'good propaganda', rather than of encouraging discursive pluralism, and the type of documentary film to emerge from this renewed conservative idealism can only be described as functional and instrumental, and explicitly opposed to categories such as art and authorship.

The radical change of style and emphasis from the pre-1936 to the post-1936 period can also be explained in terms of a shift from a concern with the phenomenological naturalism of the image to a more directive style always implicit in Grierson's notion of the creative interpretation of reality. In the later period this more directive approach became increasingly allied to the cardinal objective of representing unified social relationships, whilst the earlier aesthetic of the image is increasingly discarded.

Grierson's later approach to documentary film is problematic on both ethical and aesthetic grounds, and would appear to have little to offer those wishing to develop viable forms of documentary theory and practice. However, there is evidence to suggest that, towards the end of his life, he returned to his earlier concerns, and increasingly emphasised the importance of the aesthetic dimension within documentary. In *I Remember, I Remember*, the film which he made for BBC TV in 1970, he described documentary almost entirely in tems of art, and abandoned the instrumental discourse which characterised his middle period. This indicates that the dialectical tension between the aesthetic and the sociological, which was always implicit in his ideology, and which was skewed decisively in one direction during the 1937–67 period, had reverted once again to the kind of balance which had characterised the 1929–36 period.

THE CRITICAL DEBATES ON THE DOCUMENTARY FILM MOVEMENT

A substantial body of critical writing and commentary on the documentary movement has accumulated since 1929. Critical writings during the 1930s focused on issues such as the quality of the films and the nature of the movement's aesthetic and political intervention. Some critics argued that the films of the movement were insufficiently radical or critical, others that Grierson's insistence on group film-making and the employment of inexperienced trainees led to a dearth of technical and professional expertise within the movement. Yet another criticism was that the policy of rejecting key aspects of the feature film meant that the films made by the movement were unsuitable for a mass audience. On the more positive side, the aesthetic achievements of films such as *Song of Ceylon* and *Drifters* were frequently praised, and the affirmative representation of the working class in such films was also considered to be an important development.

One way of acquiring an overall picture of opinion during the period is to examine the critical response to the most commercially successful film produced by the movement during the 1930s, *North Sea* (1938). *North Sea* provides a good illustration of the constituent elements within this discourse on the movement because it was one of the few films to obtain widespread theatrical distribution in the 1930s, and was, therefore, seen by a correspondingly larger number of critics and reviewers. *North Sea* was also made in 1938, a year in which debates on documentary and British cinema took place against the context of the passage of the 1938 Films Act. The critical commentary on *North Sea* reflects and illuminates this more general context.

Most contemporary reviewers of *North Sea* praised the film. Robert Flaherty argued that if such films were made in any quantity they would soon establish a mass audience.[126] Trade journals such as *Kinematograph Weekly* and *Picturegoer* also approved of the film, describing it as a 'brilliant achievement', and asserting that 'there is one department in which Britain rules the world, and that is in the pro- duction of documentaries'.[127] However, Basil Wright, whilst approving of the film, argued that its description of work processes was inade- quate,[128] whilst other members of the Grierson camp, writing in *World Film News* and *Documentary Newsletter*, also voiced the concern that *North Sea* contained insufficient information, and was, therefore, an inappropriate model for the future development of documentary film. In similarly critical vein, the journal *Life and Letters Today* argued that the film contained nothing about the social conditions of the fisher- men it depicted,[129] whilst reviews in the trade press complained about the film's lack of feminine or romantic interest.

Critics generally felt that *North Sea* represented working-class people in a dignified and sympathetic way. For example, the *Spectator* argued that the film was 'a proper comment on our nature and our being',[130] whilst the *New Statesman* praised the film for allowing working-class characterisation to emerge.[131] The film's realism was also commented on widely, as was its employment of 'entertainment devices' absent from more conventional documentaries. The *Spectator* argued that documentary was a 'cold, hard . . . and inadequate' word, and that *North Sea* succeeded because of its rejection of such aspects of the documentary.[132] *North Sea*'s formal qualities were also praised. *Picturegoer* regarded the film as 'a major formal breakthrough' because of its synthesis of representational conventions from both documentary and the feature film,[133] whilst other critics admired the film for its integration of formal experimentation and realist representation.

Such attitudes can be extrapolated to the films of the documentary movement in general during the 1930s. Although some critics argued that the films were insufficiently radical, analytical or artistic, the majority of critical opinion held that they played an important role in building a progressive, oppositional film culture. This view was shared not only by liberal intellectuals, but also by those associated with left-wing organisations such as the Communist Party.

Up to 1945 critical commentaries on the documentary film movement largely appeared in periodicals such as the movement's own house journals, *Cinema Quarterly*, *World Film News* and *Documentary Newsletter*, and in journals such as *Artwork*, *Life and Letters Today*, *Tit-bits*, *New Britain*, the *New Statesman*, the *Spectator*, the *Land*, the *Realist* and *Sight and Sound*. Newspapers such as the *Manchester Guardian*, the *Glasgow Herald* and *The Times* also reviewed the activities of the movement. The major exception to this context of periodical publication was Paul Rotha, who published two books prior to 1945, *The Film Till Now* (1930) and *Documentary Film* (1936). The former was a general 'survey of world cinema' up to 1930, with an emphasis on the documentary tradition. In the section on 'The British Film', for example, Rotha argued that 'Without exception there is one production that is pre-eminent in the British cinema, Grierson's film of the herring fleet [*Drifters*].'[134] Rotha's second book, *Documentary Film*, was concerned with the theory and practice of documentary film-making, and it was here that he made the now much-quoted claim that the documentary film movement was 'this country's most important contribution to the cinema as a whole'.[135]

Rotha's *Documentary Film*, together with his later *Rotha on the Film* (1958) and *Documentary Diary* (1973), provide excellent biographical material on the documentary movement, but sometimes show insufficient understanding of the historical context from which the movement emerged, or of Grierson's ideology.[136] Other writings offering similar perspectives on the documentary movement to that offered by Rotha include historical surveys, autobiographies, and collections of interview material on or by major figures within the movement. These include Steven Tallents's *The Projection of England* (1932), *Cinema* (1945) and

'The Birth of British Documentary' (1968), Basil Wright's *The Long View* (1974), Elizabeth Sussex's *The Rise and Fall of British Documentary* (1975), Harry Watt's *Don't Look at the Camera* (1974), Eva Orbanz's *Journey to a Legend and Back* (1977), the John Grierson Project's *John Grierson and the NFB* (1984), and James Beveridge's *John Grierson: Film Master* (1979, 2nd edition 1986). Grierson's official biographer, H. Forsyth Hardy, has also published two edited collections of Grierson's writings, *Grierson on Documentary* (1946) and *Grierson on the Movies* (1981), as well as an authorised biography, *John Grierson: A Documentary Biography* (1979). This body of writings contributes to an understanding of the documentary movement by providing important biographical and empirical information. However, the writings of Hardy, Watt, Tallents, Wright and others often embody an uncritical belief in the stature and authority of the movement, whilst the edited reminiscences in Orbanz, Beveridge and the Grierson Project book reinforce the 'heroic' conception of the movement.[137]

Other works written between the 1940s and the 1970s which present a positive image of the documentary movement include *The Factual Film* (Political and Economic Planning and the Arts Enquiry, 1947) and *The British Film Industry* (Political and Economic Planning, 1952). More recent works which, whilst not being explicitly committed to a positive representation of the movement, nevertheless accept the intrinsic value of its realist and progressive credentials include *The Documentary Tradition* (Lewis Jacobs, 1971), *Non-Fiction Film* (Richard Barsam, 1974), *Film and Reality* (Roy Armes, 1974), and *Documentary: A History of the Non-Fiction Film* (Eric Barnouw, 1974).

Of all the work within the tradition which celebrates the achievements of the documentary movement, by far the most historically important has been Forsyth Hardy's edited collection of Grierson's writings, *Grierson on Documentary*, which has been published in three editions since 1946. However, *Grierson on Documentary* is a highly selective account of Grierson's ideology, because the majority of papers within it reflect the position on the socially purposive and educational function of the documentary film which he adopted after 1937. Fourteen of the twenty-two articles in the book were written between 1937 and 1947, whilst only six were written before 1937, and only two after 1947. The construction of Grierson and the documentary movement which emerges from this, is, therefore, strongly slanted towards Grierson's post-1937 position. Moreover, a study of all Grierson's writings, from his youth to his final years, makes it clear that what is crucially missing from the Hardy collections are writings which reveal Grierson's influence by philosophical idealism and avant-garde aesthetics.

Grierson on Documentary provided the basis for many of the critical writings on the documentary movement which appeared during the 1970s and early 1980s, when major reassessments of the movement were taking place. Throughout this period new forms of film theory were emerging in Britain, influenced by continental critical theory, and by translations of Eisenstein, Vertov, Brecht and other avant-garde theorists. This eventually precipitated the emergence of a critical paradigm within film studies which, when applied to the documentary movement, took issue with Grierson's ideas on documentary realism, instrumental film-making and consensualism. Bill Nichols, for example, argued that Grierson's ideas on filmic representation amounted to an untenable naive realism,[138] whilst Andrew Tudor claimed that Grierson only considered film in terms of its use as an instrument of social persuasion.[139] Reflecting another central criticism of the documentary movement, Paul Willeman argued that the documentary movement had become enshrined by 'official film culture' as the 'high point of the British cinema',[140] whilst Claire Johnstone expressed a similar point of view in claiming that the documentary movement was a conservative institution, which both reinforced the ideological status quo, and obstructed the development of more radical documentary practices.[141]

This critical discourse justifiably exposed some of the inadequacies present within previous writings on the documentary movement, and raised pertinent questions concerning Grierson's ideology and the role played by the movement in the institutionalisation of naturalistic, consensual film-making in Britain. However, some of this work was also undermined by *a priori* assumptions that the documentary movement was part of the establishment, and therefore a necessarily reactionary institution. One consequence of this was that the relationship between the documentary movement and its historical context was not sufficiently understood and this led, during the 1980s, to the emergence of more empirical historical forms of enquiry into the movement.

This historical work was, in general, founded on the conviction that primary source material, such as that held in archives, constituted a better, more objective evidential basis for arriving at an adequate understanding of the movement. Paul Swann took this approach in two papers published within the *Historical Journal of Film, Radio and Television* in 1983 and 1984, and in *The British Documentary Film Movement 1926–1946* (1989), whilst Nicholas Pronay has also dealt with the subject in an important reassessment of Grierson in an edition of the *Historical Journal*.[142] This body of work has been extremely valuable in bringing academic, historiographical technique to bear on a study of the documentary movement. The close study of archival material has illuminated the movement's relationship to institutional constraints, and has had a demythologising impact. However, the reliance on archival material has also led to a particular type of interpretation of the documentary movement emerging: one in which Grierson and his film-makers are accused of damaging their own cause through political ineptitude, in-fighting, and the flouting of official rules and procedures.

Although there is considerable truth in the argument that the documentary film-makers, and Grierson in particular, brought about their own downfall by engendering opposition within the institutions which employed them, there are also a number of difficulties associated with this account of the movement. First, the reliance on archival documentation written by junior civil servants and politicians has led to greater credence being given to the views expressed by officials than to those expressed by members of documentary movement, and this has resulted in an imbalance in the final interpretation of the movement. Second, although the approach to the study of film history adopted within this work has been particularly successful in terms of its empirical analysis of the documentary movement, it has been less effective in examining the movement's relationship to important theoretical and contextual issues. Finally, neither Grierson's ideology nor the aesthetic qualities of the films made by the movement have been as adequately explored within this body of work as they might have been.[143]

The shift from high theory to more empirical approaches to the study of film history which occurred in the late 1970s and early 1980s was not, in general, marked by a repudiation of abstract theoretical analysis. The issue was one of incorporating theoretical and empirical enquiry within an appropriate model, so that theory neither colonised the evidence nor disappeared beneath a welter of empirical information. Writing in 1983, for example, Raymond Williams argued that film history should be explored within a theoretical framework consisting of theories of modernism, popular and establishment culture, and institutional determination.[144] Leaving aside the question of the value of these particular categories, Williams's model clearly indicates the kind of synergy of theoretical and empirical methodology which film theorists were seeking at the time.

However, the historical work which appeared on the documentary movement was generally drawn not from these debates within film studies, but from more traditional approaches to historiography, based upon empirical methodology. Whilst such methods provided profitable accounts of the documentary movement, accounts which remain amongst the most useful and solid explorations carried out so far, they did not allow the wider network of historical determinations, or the influence of such factors as philosophical idealism and avant-garde aesthetics, to be explored fully.

Another group of critical writings on the documentary movement which has appeared from the late 1960s onwards has taken an exploration of the origins, development and content of Grierson's ideas as its central objective. In their *Studies in Documentary* (1972), Alan Lovell and Jim Hillier attempted to trace the origins of Grierson's ideas within traditions of philosophical idealism which he encountered at Glasgow University during the 1920s. However, although Lovell and Hillier's work has helped to illuminate the philosophical basis of Grierson's ideas, it has also advanced an argument which has had a dubious influence on subsequent studies of Grierson.

In relating Grierson to philosophers such as T. H. Green and Bernard Bosanquet, Lovell and Hillier argued that Grierson could be associated with the neo-Hegelian ideas identified with these philosophers. However, Grierson was, in fact, far more profoundly influenced by the philosopher F. H. Bradley, who was not a Hegelian in the strict sense of the word, and by A. D. Lindsay, who was a neo-Kantian social democrat. Grierson's neo-Hegelianism was, then, heavily mediated by other influences, and his general ideology can be defined as a neo-Kantian social-democratic version of Bradley's absolute idealist philosophy. This means that Grierson's ideology cannot be characterised as 'Hegelian' in any simple sense; in fact he was sometimes strongly critical of Hegelianism, referring to it as 'the old ideology which led to the conservatism of death, and to the atrocities of the Great War'.[145] Although the charge of Hegelianism was not used by Lovell and Hillier to depict Grierson as an extreme right-winger, later writers have taken up this cue, and have associated him with right-wing or proto-Fascist ideologies.

Explorations into the influence of philosophical idealism on Grierson have also been carried out by Jack C. Ellis. His 'The Young Grierson in America 1924–1927' (1968) and 'Grierson at University' (1973), together with his 'John Grierson's Relation with British Documentary in World War Two' (1984) and *John Grierson: A Guide to References and Resources* (1986), have been seminal in helping to establish the origins and substance of Griesons's ideas. My own work, including 'Grierson, Idealism and the Inter-war Period' (1989), and *Film and Reform* (1990), has followed on from Ellis in attempting to understand the philosophical idealist roots of Grierson's ideas.

In addition to exploring Grierson's ideas, *Film and Reform* also adopted an inclusive model of historical enquiry, which drew on the work of Eric Hawbsbawm, Ernst Mandel and the French Annales School, in attempting to relate Grierson and the documentary movement to the context of the inter-war period. The influence of a network of factors, including the rise of left-wing movements in Scotland, the emergence of the public relations and publicity industries, the development of a naturalist aesthetic tradition, and the absorption of philosophical idealist thought into post-war ideas on mass communication and social information, were considered in the book, in an attempt to situate Grierson and the documentary movement within a broad-based network of determinations.

Further explorations into the nature and value of Grierson's ideology have also taken place in the work of North American writers such as Peter Morris and Joyce Nelson, and much of this has concentrated on the question of Grierson's 'Hegelianism' and elitism. Peter Morris has argued that Grierson's ideas were derived from continental theories closely aligned with the development of Fascism during the inter-war period,[146] whilst Joyce Nelson has argued that Grierson's attitude to the development of film culture in Canada was essentially a colonial and authoritarian one.[147] Much of this work is illuminating, but the authors often fail to appreciate fully that Grierson's ideology must be related to social-democratic as well as neo-Hegelian ideologies. Other considerations of Grierson's ideas by North American scholars have been primarily concerned with Grierson's role in shaping Canadian national film culture. The work of Gary Evans has been seminal in this respect, particularly his *John Grierson and the National Film Board*

(1984), but other North American scholars, such as Ian Jarvie, Andrew Rodger, Peter Morris, D. B. Jones and Robert Macmillan, have contributed to this debate as well.

A concern with the issue of national identity has also characterised recent writing on the documentary film movement in Britain. Much of this work has emerged in conjunction with a reappraisal of the role of realism within 'official' British film culture. Echoing earlier criticisms by Johnstone, Willeman and others, Andrew Higson has argued that the documentary tradition has come to define British cinema, and that this has led to the marginalisation of other genres, such as the 'gothic, the fantastic, the melodramatic' and the experimental. Higson also argues that the dominant 'documentary-realist' tradition within British cinema has played a significant role in the management of the British public sphere, and in the establishment of a hegemonic 'liberal-humanist morality and social-democratic politics' in Britain.[148]

Writing in 1996, Philip and Kathryn Dodd reiterate many of Higson's ideas, and have no hesitation in rejecting Paul Rotha's 1936 declaration that the documentary film movement is 'this country's most important contribution to the cinema as a whole'. The Dodds assert that 'no one now shares Paul Rotha's judgement' and, like Higson, go on to argue that the gothic tradition within British cinema is 'more resonant for both young film-makers and critics'.[149] A closely related approach to realism and the melodrama is also adopted within the work of writers such as Pam Cook, who argue that the realist cinema is associated with a dominant 'masculinist', middle-class culture, whilst the melodramatic tradition reflects popular and female taste more directly and genuinely.[150]

CONCLUSIONS

'The modern-day prophet of cinema.'[151]

Many of the debates over the documentary film movement revolve around the role played by Grierson, and around the ideas, personality and actions of this unusual, strange and difficult individual. Of the various accusations levelled against Grierson, by far the most damaging has been that he himself was largely responsible for the ultimate collapse of the documentary film movement. How true is this claim?

Grierson was a self-taught amateur and pioneer, obsessively influenced by a combination of ideas which he had encountered in his youth, and which, he believed, provided definitive answers to contemporary problems of democratic accountability and social unity. The evangelical sense of certainty which he derived from these ideas was reflected in the conviction with which he expounded them, and in the abstract and rhetorical language which he employed in order to baffle his opponents and endow himself with a mystique of erudition and consequence. However, as a strategy for influencing opinion, this approach often misfired, as civil servants and others failed to take it seriously, interpreting its opacity and conviction as a reflection of confused or esoteric thinking, rather than insight. Grierson's unswerving belief in the veracity of his convictions also led him to adopt strategies which ultimately proved counterproductive. Although prepared to work in accordance with established rules and procedures when these suited his purposes, he often disregarded them when they did not. Such manoeuvring, however justified it may have appeared to Grierson and his associates at the time, was bound to disconcert civil servants charged with managing organisations like the GPO, the COI and the NFB.

It has been argued here that Grierson's decision to resign from the GPO Film Unit in 1936 led to the fragmentation of the movement. The reasons for his decision have always been unclear. At the time, he argued that he left in order to develop the documentary movement outside the state system. However, as Harry Watt and Paul Rotha have argued, he could easily have done this whilst remaining at the GPO. Nicholas Pronay has argued that Grierson was actually forced to leave the GPO by officials who had finally had enough of his maverick ways.[152] However, although there may be some truth in this, Pronay does not present enough evidence to back up his case. More convincing is Harry Watt's claim that Grierson left because he sought new converts elsewhere: 'he was an evangelist for the documentary idea'.[153]

Grierson's vagueness over his reasons for leaving the GPO may have been to do with the fact that he knew that GPO and government officials had 'blackballed' him, as Pronay puts it, and he may have wanted to keep this knowledge to himself. But his behaviour here also fits a common pattern of leaving to seek new opportunities elsewhere when things began to go against him. A major reorganisation of the GPO Film Unit management structures was to take place in 1937, a reorganisation which would have significantly clipped Grierson's wings. Although he may genuinely have believed that his departure would

create a more secure environment for the GPO Film Unit, evidence
from the archives of the Post Office suggests that the real reason he left
was that he could not countenance such clipping, believing, as he did,
that his way was best.

The critical and disputatious approach which Grierson adopted
between 1936 and 1939 led him to be excluded from the setting up of
the MOI in 1939, and from involvement in the British wartime information system. By 1945, he had succeeded in alienating a number of
senior officials in Canada, effectively ending his career there, whilst, at
Group 3, he quickly fell out with his co-producer, John Baxter. Such
abrasive and confrontational behaviour, when combined with political
naivety and his repeated failure to form permanent alliances with his
superiors, marked him out as unsuitable, in the eyes of the powerful,
for the positions of authority and influence he coveted.

By 1946, Grierson's evangelical approach to propaganda was also
out of step with a post-war cultural climate characterised by demands
for greater freedom of information and broader critical debate. In such
a climate, his equation of propaganda with education appeared increasingly anachronistic. There is also evidence from within the documentary
movement to suggest that, by 1946, the movement had already entered
a period of intellectual decline. Writing in 1975, Stuart Legg has argued
that Grierson had passed his creative peak in Canada, and that when
he returned to England in 1948 there was no more 'spark'.[154] Similarly,
Basil Wright has expressed the belief that, by 1946–7, the documentary
movement was 'over the peak', and 'the documentary idea had run its
course'.[155] Cavalcanti puts the beginning of the decline even earlier, in
1943.[156]

However, if it is accepted that Grierson and his film-makers must
bear some, perhaps considerable, responsibility for the decline of the
documentary movement, it must also be accepted that the possibilities
for success and achievement during the period were significantly circumscribed. Many of Grierson's actions may have proved counterproductive,
but they were carried out in a context of retrenchment and hostility. In
the 1930s, government film-making was opposed by both the commercial industry and the Treasury, and closely regulated by a variety of
official organisations. Even after Grierson had left the GPO in 1936,
attempts to close it down continued unabated, and, when the unit was
transferred to the MOI in 1940, it was informed that it would be abolished within six months of the end of the war.[157]

Similar problems were experienced at the COI, and it is worth concentrating, for a moment, on the COI period, because it provides many of the clues which explain why the documentary movement fell into such terminal decline. Nicholas Pronay has argued, fairly uncompromisingly, that the failure of the Crown Film Unit was largely the fault of Grierson:

> the fact was that, having been brought in by the government with the title and the powers he himself had stipulated, Grierson had totally failed to achieve his or the government's objective; that is the re-vitalisation, re-orientation and establishment of the public service documentary. Once again he created his own opportunity, mesmerised and enthused people with his plans, but when it came to it he failed to carry them through.[158]

But Pronay is being either deliberately provocative or just unfair, and the reasons behind the failure of Crown are far more complex, involving both Grierson and the context of the post-war Labour Government. Some of the blame can certainly be placed on Grierson's shoulders. When he returned from Canada he set about reorganising Crown in order to reproduce the centralised control which he had introduced at the NFB, separating film-making into a number of different strands, and creating specialist production units. As was the case with the NFB, this 'specialisation' had the effect of restricting the emergence of auteurs from within Crown and the production of ambitious films such as *Night Mail* or *North Sea*. Grierson also restarted the Canadian 'World in Action' series at the COI under the editorship of Stuart Legg. Unsurprisingly, the importation of the 'banged-out film' model did not lead to an improvement in production quality.

Grierson's belief in 'the documentary idea' – the notion that documentary film-makers should work closely with civil servants and politicians in order to produce 'educational' material for the public – also lead to a dead end after 1948. Encouraged to work closely with public officials, Grierson's film-makers found that when they did so they were rendered powerless as a result. The Labour Government was far more interventionist than the pre-war conservative National Governments had been and, consequently, the film-makers enjoyed less autonomy than they had experienced during the 1930s. Labour were also concerned that they should not be seen to use the COI films machinery for party political purposes, and one consequence of this was an insistence that the films coming out of the COI should be as politically neutral as possible. Finally, the new government, although radical in a number of ways, also wished to demonstrate its loyalty to the civil service machinery which it depended on. The consequence of this was that supervisory and budgetary controls over Crown became far tighter than those which had affected the GPO Film Unit. Given all this, Grierson's belief in the necessity of close collaboration between film-makers and officials was bound to result in the production of anodyne and over-cautious films.

There was, in fact, little possibility of producing innovative films of aesthetic quality at the COI. Although a relatively high level of film production continued at Crown after 1945, the post-war context of tight budgetary control ruled out the production of both the expensive story documentaries made during the war, and the less expensive experimental montage films made during the 1930s. In addition, the COI was a service, as opposed to a policy formation department, and was dominated by other government departments, which were able to dictate terms for the films they commissioned.

Other factors made it unlikely that the COI period would mark a new dawn for the British documentary movement. By 1945 many of the most talented film-makers had left Crown to join the commercial industry. Crown's location within what Pronay describes as 'the largest and most modern of British studios – Beaconsfield' also turned out to be an unmitigated disaster. The studio, which had been used as an aircraft hanger during the war and was being rebuilt during the period when Crown was based there, has been described as an 'absolute ruin' in 1946.[159] The decision to locate Crown at Beaconsfield turned out to be a colossal mistake. The studio was not officially opened until 1 April 1949, and, when it did open, Crown found that they simply could not cover the costs of running the studio, or make sufficient films to use up its floor space. However, the decision to move to Beaconsfield cannot be blamed on Grierson. The decision, an administrative blunder which eventually led to the Crown operation at Beaconsfield being closed down in May 1950, was taken by his superiors.

One result of all these problems was that the quality of films produced at Crown slumped precipitously. When the Director General of the COI asked for a review of Crown's longer films in May 1949, his response to the films he saw was that they were 'ghastly', 'feeble' and 'total distribution flops'.[160] When the crisis eventually arrived Grierson reverted to his usual pattern of behaviour. Rather than seeking to find productive ways of managing this unpropitious environment he attempted to extricate himself by seeking new employment elsewhere, and by going on frequent 'research' trips abroad. As Pronay has argued, during this period Grierson worked flat out to become head of Group 3, the new film production organisation created by the government, from the moment he heard about the post's availability.[161] From 1949 on his absences abroad also escalated to the point where he had only minimal involvement in the bulk of films produced.[162] All this was going on, as Pronay correctly argues, whilst Grierson was still 'Controller, Film' at the COI, 'supposedly providing it with the revitalising creative leadership it had lacked before his arrival'.[163]

The same combination of contextual difficulties and eccentric behaviour was evident during the Group 3 project. Group 3 was a branch of the National Film Finance Corporation, established in 1949 by the Labour Government to promote the development of the British film industry. The corporation lent money to support film production in Britain but it also established a production company in 1951, Group 3, which was given a mandate to produce a limited number of high-quality, low-budget films. Grierson was placed in charge of the project, as head of production, but, because of concerns about his management abilities, administrative control was placed in the hands of John Baxter, the director of *Love on the Dole* (1941). However, Group 3 was closed down in July 1955, after only four years of operation and having produced twenty-two films, of which only one, *The Brave Don't Cry* (1952), could be considered a success. As a whole, the project lost over half a million pounds and has been described as 'one of the worst disasters in the history of the British film industry'.[164]

In many respects, Grierson must be held partly responsible for the collapse of Group 3. Although he initially committed himself to the project with great energy, he quickly found that his lack of experience in developing feature films made it difficult for him to bring projects to fruition.[165] In addition, by as early as 1952 he had managed to fall out with Baxter and, later, Michael Balcon, the Chief Executive of Group 3. He resigned as executive producer in late 1952 and, thereafter, continued to work intermittently and irregularly. Although his often erratic behaviour during this period can be partly explained by the fact that he was seriously ill for a while, his actions also fit a pattern, evident from the 1930s onwards, of initial commitment to a project, followed by subsequent dissipation of energy and sense of direction.

Nevertheless, the failure of Group 3 cannot be entirely attributed to Grierson. Group 3 films depended on the commercial film industry for distribution and exhibition, but the industry was unhelpful, regarding the project as an unacceptable intrusion by government into the commercial market. In the end, it was the lack of effective distribution and exhibition for Group 3 films which finally killed the project. In addition to Grierson's lack of direction and his inability to take hold of the project, the failure of Group 3 must, then, also be attributed to the same hostility to government-funded film-making which the documentary movement had experienced during the 1930s.

Beyond this, the failure of Group 3 illustrates the existence of a fundamental problem within the British film industry, and one which the documentary film movement had initially been founded in order to help resolve. The commercial monopolies of the period effectively killed off this experiment in social realist film-making because they could not control it, and because it fell outside their own commercial concerns. The failure of Group 3 illustrates a continuing problem within the British cinema of finding adequate funding, distribution and exhibition for independent, innovative or experimental films.

During the late 1940s much concern was expressed about the 'crisis of documentary' in Britain. Was that crisis inevitable? Was there a way forward which would have led to a reinvigorated documentary movement that could have reclaimed Rotha's title of 'Britain's outstanding contribution to the film'? The answer may have been provided by Cavalcanti in the late 1930s,[166] when he argued that the whole concept of documentary should be abandoned in favour of the concept of 'realist' film-making. However, two events which occurred during the 1940s illustrate why this could not have taken place within the documentary film movement, and how unfortunate Grierson's influence on documentary in Britain was during this period.

The first of these events concerned the attempt by the documentarists to establish an international organisation of documentary film-makers called the World Union of Documentary. When Basil Wright returned from a conference of the Union held in Eastern Europe he was enthusiastic about what he had experienced there:

We learned that in most countries the pattern of nationalisation was nearer to our own BBC . . . we saw many imaginative and experimental films which no power on earth could have persuaded some of our more staid government departments to sponsor.[167]

The World Union of Documentary represented one way forward for the British documentary movement. However, Grierson chose to sabotage the project. Since his problems in Canada in 1944, when he was implicated in a Soviet spy scandal and was refused an entry visa into the United States, Grierson had been very careful to distance himself from any suggestion that he was associated with eastern European organisations. He became anxious that the World Union of Documentary had a number of eastern European members, and decided to discredit it by implying that it was a Communist front organisation.[168] This led to an exodus of members from British Documentary, the British arm of the World Union, which had been established by one of Grierson's most loyal allies, John Taylor. Grierson's actions effectively destroyed the World Union in Britain, and eventually led to Taylor's resignation from Crown.

The second major development of the 1940s which could have reinvigorated British documentary in the way suggested by Cavalcanti was the emergence of Italian neo-realism. The films of Rossellini, Visconti, De Sica and others had a considerable impact upon post-war European film culture. However, the documentary movement failed to incorporate the achievements of neo-realism because, in the end, Grierson, whose ideas had been formed in the twenties, was unwilling to be influenced by new developments. As with the World Union of Documentary, Grierson rejected the model of independently produced realist films offered by neo-realism, and insisted, instead, that documentary films must be made in close relation to the needs of government departments, and to the imperatives of 'civic education'.

The lack of attention paid to Italian neo-realism is also indicative of another factor which contributed to the decline of the documentary movement after 1945. During the early post-war period British film culture became increasingly preoccupied with the emergence of a critical European art cinema. Periodicals such as *Sequence* and *Sight and Sound* adopted this concern, and, at the same time, distanced themselves from the ideas of the documentary movement. Against this context of the emergence of European art cinema, and auteurs such as Rossellini,

Fellini, Cocteau, Ophuls and, later, Bergman and Antonioni, Grierson's insistence that the film director must subordinate his or her creative inclinations to the needs of government departments appeared increasingly anachronistic.

The critical stance adopted by journals such as *Sequence* must also be understood against the context of the failure of the Group 3 experiment, and the emergence of English auteurs such as David Lean, Laurence Olivier, Michael Powell, Emeric Pressburger and Carol Reed, all of whom moved away from Grierson's documentary realist model to embrace theatrical, melodramatic and epic forms. However, even the Free Cinema movement of Lindsay Anderson and Karel Reisz, which carried on the documentary realist tradition into the 1950s, made clear distinctions between film-makers such as Jennings, whom they admired, and the more conservative ideas of the Grierson camp: the 'documentary boys', the 'Soho Square gang'.

It is indicative of the insularity of Grierson and his associates, and of their apparent inability to accept models other than their own, that they made no attempt to embrace Free Cinema. Lindsay Anderson accuses the 'Grierson people', who, he says, occupied good positions within the documentary industry, of being 'jealous and antagonistic' towards the Free Cinema film-makers, and of not offering them film commissions (Anderson makes an exception of Basil Wright, whom he regards as having been friendly).[169] Anderson goes on to describe Grierson's contribution in Britain after the war as 'disastrous', and depicts Rotha as 'sad, bitter, excluded ... and unable to work with other people'.[170] Like Anderson, Karel Reisz also associates Free Cinema with the work of Jennings, rather than Grierson, Wright or Rotha, and describes Jennings's *Fires Were Started* as the 'source film for Free Cinema'.[171]

It would seem that Grierson, and most of the other members of the documentary film movement, were unable to respond to the challenges offered by the new generation of critics and film-makers which emerged during the post-war period. Grierson's position was too fixed and inflexible and, between the late 1930s and early 1960s, too hostile to the notion that documentary films could be substantially concerned with questions of aesthetics. This led to the critical margin-alisation of the documentary movement, as documentary film-making developed in other directions from the 1950s onwards, in the work of film-makers such as Jean Rouch, Chris Marker, Frederick Wiseman and Peter Watkins.

Finally, if a reinvigoration of British documentary could have been possible during the 1940s through the adoption of models derived from eastern European documentary and Italian neo-realist cinema, it is also possible that, today, a potentially valuable form of film-making can be discerned within the early theory and practice of the documentary film movement. This possibility has already been recognised by groups such as the Black Audio Film Collective, whose postmodern *Handsworth Songs* (Akomfrah, 1986) is, they claim, influenced by the Griersonian tradition. The early 'Griersonian' documentary was characterised by a phenomenology of the image, formative use of montage editing, and an indeterminate, impressionistic and symbolic style. It is summed up in what Grierson called the 'imagist' documentary. It is beyond the scope of this introduction to draw up the parameters of a revitalised, 'imagist', realist film tradition, but it is perhaps here, in Grierson's *Drifters*, and in some of the films of Wright, Cavalcanti and Jennings, that future studies of the documentary movement may be fruitfully directed.

NOTES

1. Pronay, Nicholas, 'John Grierson and the Documentary – 60 Years on', *Historical Journal of Film, Radio and Television*, 9:3 (1989), p. 238.
2. Aitken, Ian, *Film and Reform: John Grierson and the British Documentary Film Movement* (London, Routledge, 1990), p. 2.
3. Forsyth Hardy, H. *John Grierson: A Documentary Biography* (London, Faber & Faber, 1979), p. 31.
4. Aitken (1990), op. cit., pp. 52–3.
5. Ibid., pp. 90–1.
6. Forsyth Hardy (1979), op. cit., p. 71.
7. Aitken (1990), op. cit., p. 136.
8. Pronay (1989), op. cit., pp. 243–4.
9. The biographical material covered here is drawn from a number of sources, including Orbanz, Eva (ed.), *Journey to a Legend and Back: The British Realistic Film* (Berlin, Edition Volker Spiess, 1977); Rotha, Paul, *Documentary Diary* (London and New York, Hill & Wang, 1973); and Forsyth Hardy (1979), op. cit.
10. Forsyth Hardy (1979), op. cit., pp.57–8.
11. In Orbanz (1977), op. cit., pp .172 and 193.
12. Grierson, John, 'Letter to Renwick' (1926), unpublished letter, Grierson

Archive G1.7; and Watt, Harry, *Don't Look at the Camera* (London, Elek, 1974).

13. Such references are sprinkled throughout his writings. The existence of tensions between Grierson and some of the gay members of the movement came up during an interview with Forsyth Hardy, carried out by me in Edinburgh, May 1986. See also Aitken (1990), op. cit., p. 60.

14. Grierson, John, 'Letter to Francis Strauss', 7 September 1927 (Grierson Archive Papers, Grierson–Strauss Correspondence 1927–34), G21A. Quoted in Aitken (1990), op. cit.

15. Biographical data in Orbanz (1977), op. cit., pp. 179–80.

16. Nelson, Joyce, *The Colonized Eye: Rethinking the Grierson Legend* (Toronto, Between the Lines, 1988), p. 76.

17. Grierson, John, *Chicago Evening Post* articles on modern painting (Grierson Archive Papers), G1A.3.1–G1A.3.10, and 'Better Popular Pictures', *Transactions of the Society of Motion Picture Engineers*, IX:29 (August 1926), p. 234.

18. Grierson, John, 'The B.B. Lollipop Company Incorporated' (Grierson Archive papers 1898–1927), G1A.3.1.

19. Nelson (1988), op. cit., p. 77; and Sussex, Elizabeth, *The Rise and Fall of British Documentary* (Berkeley, Los Angeles and London, University of California Press, 1975), p. 86.

20. Grierson, John, 'Flaherty', in Forsyth Hardy, H. (ed.), *Grierson on Documentary* (Faber & Faber, 1946), pp. 29–34. There were other editions in 1966 and 1979.

21. Nelson (1988), op. cit., *passim*.

22. Anti-semitic references are not widespread in Grierson's writings, and mainly appear in his unpublished correspondence.

23. Rotha (1973), op. cit. ('Afterthought' is reprinted below, Chapter 3.)

24. *Drifters* (Grierson, EMB, 1929, silent, four-reel, 3,631 ft). Full production and exhibition details are in Aitken (1990), op. cit., p. 104.

25. Grierson, John, 'First Principles of Documentary', in Forsyth Hardy (1979), op. cit., p. 42 (reprinted below, Chapter 2).

26. Draft music score for *Drifters* (Grierson Archive Papers 1898–1927), undated, G1.2.4.

27. Forsyth Hardy (1979), op. cit., p. 54.

28. Rotha (1973), op. cit., p. 49.

29. Forsyth Hardy (1979), op. cit., p. 65.

30. Ibid., p. 68.

31. Grierson, John, 'New Worlds for Old' (typescript for an unpublished manuscript on the use of film in education and by the church; Grierson Archive papers 1927–1933), G2.21.5, p. 16.

32. *Industrial Britain* (direction and photography Robert Flaherty, production and editing John Grierson and Edgar Anstey, EMB, 1931); *Song of Ceylon* (direction Basil Wright, production John Grierson and Alberto Cavalcanti, photography Basil Wright and John Taylor, music and sound track Walter Leigh, narration by Lionel Wendt, EMB, 1933–4), winner of the Prix du Gouvernement Belge at the Brussels Film Festival 1935.

33. Rotha (1973), op. cit., p. 125.
34. Ibid., pp. 125–6. First published in the *Spectator* (1934). Reprinted in Cooke, Alistair, *Garbo and the Nightwatchmen* (London, Cape, 1937).
35. Further details for these films are in Aitken (1990) op. cit., pp. 142–5.
36. *Coal Face* (GPO, sound and direction Alberto Cavalcanti, production John Grierson, verse W. H. Auden, music Benjamin Britten, GPO, 1935); *Spare Time* (direction Humphrey Jennings, production Alberto Cavalcanti, GPO, 1939).
37. See Barthrick, David, Elsaesser, Thomas, and Hansen, Miriam (eds), 'Weimar Film Theory, Special Issue', *New German Critique*, 40 (Winter 1987), and Hake, C. S., *The Cinema's Third Machine: Writing on Film in Germany 1907–1933* (Nebraska, University of Nebraska Press, 1993).
38. Rotha (1973), op. cit., p. 73.
39. *Night Mail* (direction Harry Watt, editing Basil Wright and Alberto Cavalcanti, production John Grierson, with contributions from Stuart Legg, W. H. Auden (verse) and Benjamin Britten (music), GPO, 1936, distributed by Associated British Film Producers).
40. Rotha (1973), op. cit., is critical of Grierson's intervention here, describing his narration as 'sob-throated' and 'sentimental' (p. 133).
41. *The City* (direction Ralph Elton, production Alberto Cavalcanti, editing R. Q. Mcnaughton and J. Chambers, GPO, 1939, filmed in London) features a talk by Sir Charles Bressey, urban planner, on the history and growth of London.
42. *North Sea* (direction Harry Watt, production Alberto Cavalcanti, GPO, 1938).
43. Rotha (1973), op. cit., p. 159.
44. Low, Rachel, *Documentary and Educational Films of the 1930s* (London, Allen & Unwin, 1979), pp. 122–3.
45. Sherrington, Jo, *To Speak its Pride: The Work of the Films of Scotland Committee 1938–1982* (Glasgow, Scottish Film Council Publication, 1996), p. 9.
46. The 'March of Time' series was founded by Louis de Rochemont in 1945. It had a considerable impact upon the documentary film movement, and a number of figures within the movement worked for the organisation from time to time. Its style was abrupt, dramatic and staccato. Rotha (1973), op. cit., pp. 274–5, has described the style of the series as 'strident' and 'powerful', but also superficial, and he has also argued that the 'March of Time' had a 'bad influence' on the documentary movement.
47. *Housing Problems* (direction and production Edgar Anstey and Arthur Elton, photography John Taylor, Realist, 1935, commissioned by the Gas, Light and Coke Company).
48. Pronay (1989), op. cit., p. 237.
49. Swann, Paul, *The British Documentary Film Movement 1926–1946* (Cambridge, Cambridge University Press, 1989), p. 164.
50. Ibid., p. 169.
51. Ibid.

52. Ibid., p. 168.
53. Forman, Helen, in John Grierson Project, *John Grierson and the* NFB, papers presented at a conference held at McGill University, Montreal, Quebec (Montreal, ECW Press, 1984), p. 228.
54. Swann (1989), op. cit., p. 159.
55. *Men of the Lightship* (direction David Macdonald, production Alberto Cavalcanti, GPO/Crown, 1940). This film was more financially successful than any other documentary film made during the war, with the sole exception of Harry Watt's *Target for Tonight*.
56. Swann (1989), op. cit., p. 158.
57. Rodger, Andrew, 'Some Factors Contributing to the Formation of the National Film Board of Canada', *Historical Journal of Film, Radio and Television*, 9:3 (1989), p. 259.
58. Forsyth Hardy (1979), op. cit., p. 101.
59. Evans, Gary, *John Grierson and the National Film Board: The Politics of War-Time Propaganda* (Toronto, Buffalo and London, University of Toronto Press, 1984), p. 55.
60. Applebaum, Louis, 'The NFB in the 1940s', in John Grierson Project (1984), op. cit., p. 10.
61. Evans, Gary, *In the National Interest: A Chronicle of the National Film Board of Canada from 1949 to 1989* (Toronto, Buffalo and London, University of Toronto Press, 1991), p. 6.
62. Applebaum (1984), op. cit., p. 11.
63. Nelson (1988), op. cit., p. 63.
64. This is referred to in Nelson (1988), op. cit., and more detail is provided by Daly, Tom, 'The Growth of my Craft: My Debt to Legg and Grierson', in John Grierson Project (1984), op. cit.
65. Evans (1984), op. cit., p. 223.
66. Ibid., p. 151.
67. Ibid., p. 163.
68. Nelson (1988), op. cit., p. 131.
69. Wright, Basil, 'An Innocent in Canada', in John Grierson Project (1984), op. cit., p. 122.
70. Nelson (1988), op. cit, p. 75.
71. In Sussex (1975), op. cit., pp. 180–1; and Rotha (1973), op. cit., p. 276.
72. Aldcroft, D. H., *The Inter-War Economy* (London, Batsford, 1970), p. 64.
73. Aldcroft, D. H., *The British Economy Between the Wars* (Oxford, Philip Allen, 1983), p. 53.
74. Tallents, S., *The Projection of England* (London, Faber & Faber, 1932).
75. See Orwell's *The Road to Wigan Pier* (London, Gollancz, 1937) and *Down and Out in Paris and London* (London, Gollancz, 1933); and see for example Sir John Boyd Orr, *Homes, Food and Income* (London, HMSO, 1936), which provided the basis for Edgar Anstey and Arthur Elton's film *Enough to Eat* (1936).
76. Priestley, J. B., *English Journey* (London, Heinemann, 1934); and Symons, Julian, *The Thirties* (London, Faber & Faber, 1960).
77. Interview between the author and Alberto Cavalcanti, Paris, May 1983.

78. Marwick, Arthur, 'Middle Opinion in the Thirties', *English Historical Review*, 79 (1964), p. 296.
79. Cited in Addison, Paul, *The Road to 1945* (London, Quartet, 1977), p. 43.
80. Grierson, John, 'Preface', in Rotha, Paul, *Documentary Film* (London, Faber & Faber, 1952), pp. 22–3 (reprinted below, Chapter 2). There were other editions in 1936, 1939, 1966.
81. For more information on the Red Clydeside movement see Aitken (1990), op. cit., pp. 29–37; Middlemas, R. K., *The Clydesiders* (London, Hutchinson, 1965); and Gallacher, William, *Revolt on the Clyde* (London, Lawrence & Wishart, 1936).
82. Dickson, Tony, *Scottish Capitalism* (Lawrence & Wishart, 1980), p. 342.
83. Cole, G. D. H., and Postgate, Raymond, *A History of the Common People 1746–1936* (London, Methuen, 1938), pp. 568–70.
84. Political and Economic Planning and the Arts Enquiry, *The Factual Film* (London, PEP, 1947).
85. Political and Economic Planning, *The British Film Industry* (London, PEP, 1952), p. 293.
86. Mowat, C. L., *Britain Between the Wars, 1918–1940* (London, Methuen, 1955), p. 537.
87. Slater, Montagu, *Left Review* (May 1935), pp. 364–5.
88. Cited in Laing, Stuart, 'Presenting Things as They Are', in Gloversmith. F. (ed.), *Class, Culture and Social Change* (London, Harvester Press, 1980), p. 158.
89. Jameson, Storm, *Fact*, 4 (1937), p. 18.
90. Hauser, Arnold, *Roccoco, Classicism and Romanticism: The Social History of Art vol. 3* (London, Routledge and Kegan Paul, 1951), p. 105.
91. Williams, Raymond, *Culture and Society 1780–1950* (London, Chatto & Windus, 1958), pp. 123–8.
92. Hobsbawm, Eric, *The Age of Revolution* (London, Cardinal, 1962), pp. 299–305.
93. Ibid., p.299.
94. The basic distinction between a libertarian and an authoritarian system is that, in the former, the organs of mass communication are independent of and able to criticise the state, whereas, in the latter, they are closely connected to the state and act as its instruments.
95. See Aitken (1990), op. cit., pp. 24–6.
96. Ibid., pp. 41–7.
97. Ibid., pp. 43–7.
98. Grierson, John, 'The Challenge to Peace', in Forsyth Hardy, (1979), op. cit., p. 176.
99. Grierson, John, 'Education and the New Order', in Forsyth Hardy (1979), op. cit., p. 130 (reprinted below, Chapter 2).
100. Grierson, John, 'Answers to a Cambridge Questionnaire', *Granta* (Cambridge, Cambridge University Press, 1967), p. 10 (reprinted below, Chapter 2).
101. Grierson, John, 'The Social Relationships of Cinema' (Grierson Archive Papers), G3.9.4, p. 1.

102. Bradley, F. H., *Essays on Truth and Reality* (London, Clarendon Press, 1914), p. 175.
103. Grierson, John, 'The Contribution of Poetry to Religion' (Grierson Archive Papers), G1.5.2, p. 2.
104. Grierson (1967), op. cit.
105. Grierson, John, 'The Challenge to Peace', in Forsyth Hardy (1979), op. cit., p. 178.
106. Grierson, John, 'Notes for English Producers' (1927) (Public Records Office BT 64/86/5511/28).
107. Grierson (1926), op. cit., pp. 227–49.
108. Grierson (1952), op. cit., p. 16.
109. Grierson (1926), op. cit., p. 13.
110. Ibid., p. 21.
111. Ibid.
112. Grierson, John, untitled, undated article beginning 'Against this background some indication of the part of cinema is possible' (Grierson Archive Papers), G2.8.7, p. 1.
113. Ibid.
114. Grierson, John, 'Flaherty, Naturalism and the Problem of the English Cinema', *Artwork* (Autumn, 1931), p. 124.
115. Kaes, Anton, 'Literary Intellectuals and the Cinema: Charting a Controversy', in Barthrick *et al.*(1987), op. cit., p. 24.
116. Koch, Gertrud, 'Bela Balazs: The Physiognomy of Things', *New German Critique*, 40 (Winter, 1987), p. 177.
117. Hake, Sabine, 'Towards a Philosophy of Film', in Hake (1993), op. cit., p. 132.
118. Forsyth Hardy (1946), op. cit.
119. Tudor, Andrew, *Theories of Film* (London, Secker & Warburg, 1974), p. 75.
120. Grierson, John, 'The Documentary Idea', in Forsyth Hardy (1979), op. cit., pp.111–12 (reprinted below, Chapter 2).
121. Ibid., p. 112.
122. Ibid.
123. Ibid., p. 115.
124. Ibid., p. 121.
125. Ibid.
126. *Sight and Sound* (Summer, 1938), p. 62.
127. *Kinematograph Weekly* (5 May 1938), p. 13.
128. *World Film News* (August 1938), pp. 170–1.
129. *Life and Letters Today* (Autumn, 1938), p. 26.
130. *Spectator* (6 March 1938), p. 42.
131. *New Statesman* (25 June 1938).
132. *Spectator* (1938), op. cit., p. 42.
133. *Picturegoer* (17 September 1938), p. 9.
134. Rotha, Paul, *The Film Till Now: A Survey of World Cinema* (London, Jonathan Cape, 1930; this edition London, Spring Books, 1967), p. 318.
135. Rotha, Paul, *Documentary Film* (London, Faber & Faber, 1936; this edition London, Faber & Faber, 1968), p. 97.

136. Rotha attempted to address these problems in the excellent 'Afterthought' in his *Documentary Diary* (1973), op. cit. (reprinted below, Chapter 3).

137. It should be made clear that these books have many other qualities. Elizabeth Sussex's *Rise and Fall of British Documentary*, for example, provides considerable insight into the problems faced by the documentary movement. Similarly, Eva Orbanz's *Journey to a Legend and Back* contains important biographical information, plus commentaries by leading film scholars.

138. Nichols, Bill, 'Documentary Theory and Practice', *Screen*, 17:4 (Winter, 1976–7), p. 34.

139. Tudor (1974), op. cit., p. 75.

140. Willeman, Paul, 'Presentation', in Macpherson, D. (ed.), *British Cinema: Traditions of Independence* (London, BFI, 1980), p. 1.

141. Johnston, Claire, in Macpherson (1980), op. cit., p. 18.

142. Pronay (1989), op. cit., pp. 227–46.

143. This final point is not really a criticism of this body of work, as the writers involved could quite justifiably claim that neither of these issues was amongst their primary concerns.

144. Williams, Raymond, 'British Film History, New Perspectives', in Porter, Vincent, and Curran, James (eds), *British Cinema History* (London, Weidenfeld & Nicholson, 1983), p. 12.

145. Grierson, John, 'The Character of an Ultimate Synthesis' (Grierson Archive Papers), G1.2.6, p. 12 (reprinted below, Chapter 2).

146. Morris, Peter, 'Re-thinking Grierson: The Ideology of John Grierson', in Verronneau, P., Dorland, M., and Feldman, S. (eds), *Dialogue Canadian and Quebec Cinema* (Montreal, Mediatexte, 1987), pp. 24–56.

147. Nelson (1988), op. cit.

148. Higson, Andrew, 'Britain's Outstanding Contribution to the Film: The Documentary Realist Tradition', in Barr, Charles (ed.), *All Our Yesterdays* (London, BFI, 1986), p. 83.

149. Dodd, Philip, and Dodd, Kathryn, 'Engendering the Nation: British Documentary Film 1930–1939', in Higson, Andrew (ed.), *Dissolving Views: Key Writings on British Cinema* (London, Cassell, 1996), p. 38.

150. Cook, Pam, 'Neither Here nor There: National Identity in Gainsborough Costume Drama', in Higson (1996), op. cit., pp. 51–65.

151. Evans (1991), op. cit., p. 3.

152. Rotha (1973), op. cit., p. 283; Pronay (1989), op. cit., p. 236.

153. Watt (1974), op. cit., p. 189.

154. Legg, Stuart, quoted in Sussex (1975), op. cit., p. 168.

155. Wright, Basil, quoted in ibid., p. 176.

156. Cavalcanti, Alberto, 'The Producer', in Blakeston, Oswell, *Working for the Films* (London, Focal Press, 1947), p. 66.

157. Aitken (1990), op. cit., p. 148.

158. Pronay (1989), op. cit., p. 241.

159. Sussex (1975), op. cit., p. 165.

160. Hogenkamp, Bert, 'The British Documentary Film Movement and the 1945–51 Labour Government', unpublished Ph.D. thesis (1991), p. 137.

161. Pronay (1989), op. cit., p. 242.
162. Badder, David, and Baker, Bob, 'John Grierson', *Film Dope* 21 (October 1988), pp. 17–28.
163. Pronay (1989), op. cit., p. 243.
164. Ibid.
165. MacCann-Dyer, Richard, 'Subsidy for the Screen, Grierson and Group 3/1951–55', *Sight and Sound*, 46:3 (Summer, 1977), p. 170.
166. Sussex, Elizabeth, 'Cavalcanti in England', *Sight and Sound*, 44:4 (Autumn, 1975), p. 208 (reprinted below, Chapter 4).
167. Hogenkamp (1991), op. cit., p. 138.
168. Ibid.
169. Anderson, Lindsay, quoted in Orbanz (1977), op. cit., p. 40.
170. Ibid., p. 41.
171. Reisz, Karel, quoted in Orbanz (1977), op. cit., p. 54.

Chapter 2

JOHN GRIERSON (1898–1972)

COMMENTARY

This selection of writings by Grierson attempts to illustrate both the continuities and discontinuities within his ideas, from the 1920s to the 1970s. 'English Cinema Production and the Naturalistic Tradition' (1927) contains Grierson's first definition of documentary film. It is an essentially modernist definition, which places emphasis on the creative potential of editing. The extract from Grierson's university paper 'The Character of an Ultimate Synthesis' (1922) is very much a piece of undergraduate writing, but it is also characteristic of many of his other undergraduate papers, and illustrates the extent to which he was involved with philosophical idealism at the time. The untitled lecture on documentary, written between 1927 and 1933, also reveals the influence of idealism, and indicates a phenomenological approach to documentary representation, making an important distinction between 'the real' and 'the actual'. 'Drifters' (1929) continues the formative approach. Grierson talks about the need for an impressionistic and indeteminate type of documentary representation, where images take on abstract and symbolic significance. In addition to an essentially modernist approach to film form, Grierson also argues for the merits of depicting working-class communities. 'First Principles of Documentary' (1932) is a more systematic elaboration of Grierson's early film theory. Here, Grierson criticises Ruttmann's *Berlin* (1930) for saying nothing meaningful about its subject matter. Nevertheless, in this paper, Grierson places considerable emphasis on formative technique in the documentary film, and accepts the existence of a number of equally valid modernist documentary traditions, including that represented by

Figure 2.1 Portrait of John Grierson.
Source: BFI. *Copyright could not be traced, but the publishers will be happy*
to make amendments in future editions of this book.

Ruttmann. The central idea in the paper is that the conventional
'story' form is no longer able to represent the condition of modernity
within the city, and that new formal methods of depiction have to be
explored. The paper also contains his definition of *Drifters* as an 'imagist' documentary.

'Education and the New Order' (1941) shows Grierson becoming
preoccupied with issues of propaganda and civic education. He argues
that the function of education is to create social unity, rather than to
promote critical debate, and that mass education and propaganda

should be defined in religious terms, as preaching a 'faith' about the need to subsume individualism beneath collective duty. An ascetic, almost puritan discourse of self-sacrifice and hostility to individualism pervades the paper, which also contains Grierson's controversial notion of 'good totalitarianism'. 'The Documentary Idea' (1942) represents Grierson's attempt to reimpose his own vision on the documentary movement in Britain. He is critical of British propaganda production, and advocates the mass production of 'banged-out', journalistic films. The tone throughout is excessive, sometimes vituperative, as Grierson insists that the documentary film should uncompromisingly depict a 'background of faith and destiny'.

In the Preface (1951) to Paul Rotha's *Documentary Film*, Grierson worries about the centralising tendencies of the new post-war government in Britain. He argues that the role of documentary film is to express the unity in diversity of the nation, rather than the unity represented by central instititutions. He continues to argue, however, that documentary film-makers should not be 'radical beyond their time'. The Preface is also important for indicating the early political influences on Grierson stemming from the Red Clydeside movement. In 'Art and Revolution' (1966) Grierson reveals his enthusiasm for America and the modern, whilst Europe is equated with the old and the dark. Individualism is again seen as an unfortunate product of the Enlightenment, which is no longer appropriate to the needs of the twentieth century. Grierson argues that the 'will to order' is fundamental and that, beneath the perception of social contradiction, real order can be found, and must be sought. Grierson also argues here that abstract art is 'realist' because its form reflects the abstract condition of modernity.

In 'Answers to a Cambridge Questionnaire' (1967) Grierson reinstates his interest in the aesthetic, talking about the 'secret aesthetic intention' which should pervade documentary film. The paper does, in many respects, return to the positions expressed in the *Drifters* essay of 1929, and is far removed from the positions expressed in the essays of the mid-1940s. Whilst referring to his usual intellectual sources here, i.e. Kant and Hegel, he also mentions Lévi-Strauss and Barthes. Finally, in '*I Remember, I Remember*' (1970), Grierson defines the documentary film in almost entirely aesthetic terms. The word 'beautiful', so disparaged in 'The Documentary Idea' (1942), becomes a key term here. As Jack Ellis (1986: 19) has argued, '*I Remember, I Remember*' 'might almost be an anthology of the avant-garde, one that Cavalcanti could have assembled'.

ENGLISH CINEMA PRODUCTION AND
THE NATURALISTIC TRADITION (1927)

This suggests that naturalistic production needs to be of two types. The first, a seven-, eight- or nine-reel form, ought to be dramatic in the usual sense with a powerful story and clear characters carried along on the tide of a great event, a stirring adventure, or a large-scale enterprise. The second form would be in the nature of a glorified newsreel and would extend properly to two, three or four reels. In this one could afford to dispense with the powerful story and the main appeal would be quite frankly to the spectator's curiosity rather than to his emotions. In both cases, however, the classifications of a picture as a scenic ought to be feared. A picture, to be cinematically or commercially satisfactory, must have a certain coherence: and this may be the developed drama of a great undertaking or the developed account of a subject of such interest, say, as the life of an Indian village. A rambling account of more or less casual wanderings means little or nothing.

In the first or major category might be included the stories of objective authors like Kipling and all the stories of adventure from Conan Doyle's *African Tales* down to Ballantyne's *Coral Island*, though the latter of course would be less authentic and less significant for imperial purposes. The most valuable series would come from choosing stories which illustrate some specific phase of imperial achievement, and it might be even possible to create a school of Empire directors with talents moulded to the special conditions of such production. Where no story existed there would be no great difficulty in creating original scenarios round the adventures of the great explorers, round the different phases of colonial life, and round the great commercial and industrial enterprises of the time. We might, for instance, have a picture of the search for the Northwest Passage, a picture of the exploits of the Hudson Bay Company, a picture of the crossing of Canada before the railways came, a picture of the veld and migration north over the Zambezi, a picture of South African diamond mines or of western Australian goldfields, of the building of a canal, a bridge, a dam, a railway in some part of the Empire, of the fishing fleet, the building of a line on the Clyde, the passing of sailing ships on the eastern trade route or of those lost ships of England which trade up and down the coasts on the other side of the world. There is no lack of the dynamic settings on which successful cinema so absolutely depends.

Into the second category would come those subjects which do not lend themselves to major treatment. There is a place in cinema for accounts of the lives of primitive peoples and distant civilisations and a great number of pictures could be made in Africa, New Zealand, Australia, Egypt and the East, which would be cinematically fascinating; but it is doubtful, if justice is to be done to the peoples themselves and western motivation excluded, whether they ought to be long films. . . . This second series too would give those simpler accounts of modern activities in commerce, industry, research and kindred fields in which the human interest of a definite plot is not attempted. But if these pictures are to avoid the fate of industrial, commercial and so-called educational pictures of the past and if they are to be really effective for educational and propaganda purposes they will have to be made on entirely original lines.

The short features of the past have had no value whatever cinematically. They have gone frequently about the business of regarding some activity or another in some scene or other without the first regard to the value of tempo, rhythm and composition; indeed without realising that, even where a story is absent, intensely exciting effects can be gained by exploiting movement in masses in a dramatic way. A single illustration will make clear what can be done in this direction. In *Potemkin*, one entire sequence had as its solitary subject the various movements on board a ship, which is getting up steam and putting to sea. There was no story interest at all in this, no characters other than the usual engineers, seamen and officers engaged in the activity; yet this sequence stands out as the most exciting piece of cinema ever shot.

The effects were gained entirely by inspired camerawork, a sense of continuing and developing movement, and a mastery of the art of 'cutting'. The still dials of the engine room and stokehold, the gauge glasses, the ship's telegraph, the signal and answer, the first jolt of the engines, the taking up of the ladder and the fuss in the foc'sle head, the water that goes faster and faster along the clean line of the ship's side, the plunging of the engines, the still swifter movement of the auxiliaries, the feather at the bow, the streaming smoke at the funnels: all are used as themes, repeated, stepped up to the racing intensity and smashing solidity of full speed.

The ship becomes alive and and the spectator feels it in the way any seaman might feel it, as a dramatic entity of final and absorbing interest. The effect of this passage on New York audiences was so strong that it was greeted night after night with universal cheering, a spectacle utterly unknown in cinema before. If the directors of the short films could understand something of this, the present status of commercial, indus- trial and educational films would be altogether changed, and their propaganda value would become enormous. The secret of success is to realise that, even where there is no story, the visual aspects of a seem- ingly prosaic subject can be orchestrated into a cinematic sequence of enormous vitality.

The need for greater cinema skill cannot be overemphasised, and there is every reason to believe that industrial and commercial films require an even greater consideration of visual effects than the average dramatic film. They have indeed little else on which to subsist. At the present time when many of the possible effects in cinema are ignored and their box office value hardly realised, it ought to be possible to produce a series of short glorified newsreelers, which will not only accomplish whatever propaganda ends they set themselves, but mark a new phase in cinema production.

A mastery of tempo and visual composition generally is essential, but there is every opportunity too at the present time to improve on the photography of the average commercial production. Even now panchromatic film is not widely used and, where it is used, it is not always handled with care and skill. Yet in outdoor scenes and, given proper lighting arrangements, in indoor scenes too, panchromatic film allows for an enormous advance on the photography of the past. It gives the blue of the sky and the white of the clouds in their proper colour gradation, whereas the old film blanches them both to a paper white; it gives reds and greens in their proper gradation, whereas the old film makes them black; it keeps the natural lustre and luminosity of objects; and it can with the aid of filters cater to the natural preference of the human eye for reds and yellows; it gives something more of the depths of things and by enabling actors to do without make-up and by transcribing accurately such surface effects as reds of a western face and bronzes of a Polynesian body, it gives to cinema the added life of natural texture and natural character. The old type film in fact is colour blind. This other corrects its errors and improves in every way the camera's feelings for the world about it. . . . And these films must stand as films, for their dramatic value within their own special limits, whatever their underlying propaganda and educational values may be.

THE CHARACTER OF AN ULTIMATE SYNTHESIS (1922)

The demand of the mind indeed is for a coherent whole. Its every activity of imagination (using the word in its Kantian sense) implies it; its every activity of conception and judgement assumes it. We perceive no individual thing except as a determination within the infinite wholes of time and space. It is in the name of a unity which pervades particular objects that we form our every concept . . . The process of thought is seen as a constant differentiation of an initial whole whose unity pervades its particulars. Experience, that is, is a constant self-articulation of reality, and we do in reasoning move towards a final grasping of the ultimate. For as each field of experience approaches internal coherence, it does become more and more real in the only sense in which we can logically conceive of reality. In this way the notion of a coherent whole is implicit in all our thinking. . . .

It is only when we have accepted these things (and we must if we are to go on talking at all – even if we offer a prefatory gesture of disdain) that the real difficulties of the problem arise. For, granted that the notion of a unity in difference is the presupposition of all our thought, it has still to be shown how it is at the same time a vital whole. Is it true, for example, that we can know reality and live in reality? . . . From the initial outline of the coherence view it does appear that we have only to proceed in patience for all things to be one day revealed to us, that thought is so clearly the principle of reality that all things are possible to it. It is, however, necessary to emphasise that the reality – the ideal underlying thought – is not in principle the thought which reveals it. Presupposing thought it is yet different in kind from thought, and finally unattainable in thought. Such a conclusion is based on a consideration that the ideal of thought is, of its essence, a unity in difference which is immediate. And thought by its very nature cannot claim such immediacy. Its characteristic activity of judgement must always, as Bradley points out, involve a separation of the ideal from the real. . . .

There is no final imperative, in fine, except towards what harmony is in our power. We may call that the 'pull' of the absolute, if we like – and in that sense the absolute does deeply and fundamentally concern us. In another and equally definite sense, however, it cannot. For we are wrapped up inevitably in a world which is our world – a world where goodness and beauty and truth are the only Trinity. We may bow afar to the Absolute, in fact we do bow afar to the Absolute, in our every action and every thought – good or evil, true or false. But it is indirectly in the name of the Absolute harmony – very, very directly in the name of our own intellectual and life harmony that we seek the true and the good.

UNTITLED LECTURE ON DOCUMENTARY (1927–33)

With this lecture I want to take you away from the studios into the full air of cinema itself – away from the stories and the fancifications of stories, acting and the fancifications of acting, away from artificial buildings, artificial streets and artificial roles to real buildings and real people. I want to take you into the world of documentary.

But before I do I must give you one warning. Do not be confused by the word 'real'. When documentary people like myself talk about the superiority of the world outside the studios and tell you how much more genuine our world is than the other worlds, it is wise to remember the philosophic meaning of reality. In documentary we deal with the actual and in one sense with the real. But the really real, if I may use that phrase, is something deeper than that. The only reality which counts in the end is the interpretation which is profound. It does not matter whether that interpretation comes by way of the studio or by way of documentary or for that matter by way of music hall. The important thing is the interpretation and the profundity of the interpretation. Ballet is artificial, the post-impressionist painting is artificial, the abstractions of music are artificial, but do not charge them contemptuously with artifice and say they are less profound because of that. The sentiments of Shakespeare, as you know, are often as not expressed in blank verse, an artificial form of utterance – but the sum effect of them is as you know near reality – philosophic reality – as material utterance can reach.

So when we come to documentary we come to the actual world, to the world of the streets, of the tenements and the factories, the living people and observation of living people, but I charge you to remember that the task of reality before you is not one of reproduction but of interpretation. We have to give creative shapes to it, we have to be profound about it before our documentary art is as good or better than the art of the studio. In other words it is not sufficient to say that documentary is a greater art because material is the real thing. It is only good if its interpretation is a real interpretation, that is to say one which lights up the fact, which brings it alive, which indicates precisely and deeply our human relation to it.

But documentary does start with certain advantages. In the first place it has direct contact with material which has been denied the other arts. It cannot only observe the living material of the world, it can also reproduce it. It can bring clearer before you the living lineaments of human endeavour, human achievement and human emotion, it can bring you those nuances of action and reaction which we see about us every day, which are sometimes the despair of the artist or the writer. A world of material never before available to creative art, or never in the same sense available to creative art, is open to the cinema; and it is a world of material peculiarly necessary to our minds and our imaginations at the present.

I have tried to suggest to you, and I have probably insisted too much on the point, that our imaginations are out of step with the world we live in. My suggestion has been that we have lost contact with the actual, and because we have lost contact with the actual, we have lost the power of interpreting it. That is to say, we have lost the knowledge of reality in the deeper sense and lost those arts which come with a knowledge and operation in terms of reality.

You have only to look at the scattered efforts of the other arts to appreciate how true this is. Our writers are concentrating on the studies of individual idiosyncracies. They have, with few exceptions, no interest in general affairs and give no sweeping account of them. Our papers are engaged for the most part in studio leap-frog. Our poets are engaged in the more genteel preciosities of language and syllogism and persuade you to no emotion, because they have no simple, straightforward emotion to communicate.

DRIFTERS (1929)

Drifters is about the sea and about fishermen and there is not a

Piccadilly actor in the piece. The men do their own acting, and the sea does its – and if the result does not bear out the 107th Psalm, it is my fault. Men at their labour are the salt of the earth; the sea is a bigger actor than Jannings or Nitikin or any of them; and if you can tell me a story more plainly dramatic than the gathering of the ships for the herring season, the going out, the shooting at evening, the long drift in the night, the hauling of nets by infinite agony of shoulder muscle in the teeth of a storm, the drive home against a head sea, and (for finale) the frenzy of a market in which said agonies are sold at ten shillings a thousand, and iced, salted and barrelled for an unwitting world – if you can tell me a story with a better crescendo in energies, images, atmospherics and all that make up the sum and substance of cinema, I promise you I shall make my next film of it forthwith.

But, of course, making a film is not just the simple matter of feeling the size of the material. If that were so every fool who fusses over a nondescript sunset, or bares his solar plexus to the salt sea waves on his summer holiday, would be an artist. I do not claim the brave word, though I would like to, but I think I know what it mostly means. It has very little to do with nondescript enthusiasm, and a great deal to do with a job of work.

In art, as in everything else, the gods are with the big battalions. You march on your subject with a whole regiment of energies: you surround it, you break in here, break in there, and let loose all the shell and shrapnel you can (by infinite pushing of your inadequate noddle) lay hands on. Out of the labour something comes. All you have to do then is to seize what you want. If you have really and truly got inside, you will have plenty – of whatever it is – to choose from.

So in this rather solid adventure of the herring fishery I did what I could to get inside the subject. I had spent a year or two of my life wandering about on the deep-sea fishing-boats, and that was an initial advantage. I knew what they felt like. Among other things they had developed in me a certain superior horsemanship which was proof against all bronco-buckings, side-steppings and rollings whatsoever. I mention this because the limiting factor in all sea films is the stomach of the director and his cameramen. It is a super fact, beyond all art and non-art. Of my cameramen one also was an ex-seaman. The other, for all his bravery, was mostly unconscious.

In this matter I was altogether to blame. What I know of cinema I have learned partly from the Russians, partly from the American westerns, and partly from Flaherty, of *Nanook*. The westerns give some notion of the energies. The Russians give you the energies and the intimacies both. And Flaherty is a poet.

The net effect of this cinematic upbringing was to make me want a storm: a real storm, an intimate storm, and if possible a rather noble storm. I waited in Lowestoft for weeks till the gale signal went up, and I got it. So did the cameramen. The wild Arabian breeze of the drifter's bilges did not help matters.

Taking the film as a whole I got the essentials of what I wanted. I got the most beautiful fishing-village in the world – I found it in the Shetlands – for a starting point. I staged my march to the sea preparations, the procession out. I ran in detail of furnace and engine room for image of force, and seas over a headland for image of the open. I took the ships out and cast the nets in detail: as to the rope over the cradle, the boy below, the men on deck against the sea; the rhythm of the heaving, the run on the rollers, the knotted haul of each float and net; as to the day and approaching night; as to the monotony of long labour. Two miles of nets to a ship: I threw them in a flood of repetition against a darkening sky.

The life of natural cinema is in this massing of detail, in this massing of all the rhythmic energies that contribute to the blazing fact of the matter. Men and the energies of men, things and the function of things, horizons and the poetics of horizons: these are the essential materials. And one must never grow so drunk with the energies and the functions as to forget the poetics.

I had prepared against that as best I knew how. Image for this, image for that. For the settling of darkness, not darkness itself, flocks of birds silhouetted against the sky flying hard into the camera repeated and repeated. For the long drift in the night, not the ship, not the sea itself, but the dark mystery of the underwater. I made the night scene a sequence of rushing shoals and contorting congers. For the dawn, not a bleary fuss against the sky (which in cinema is nothing), but a winding slow-rolling movement into the light. Then a bell-buoy. Then a Dutch lugger rolling heavily into the light. Three images in a row.

You can never have your images too great, and I think there are none of us poets enough to make cinema properly. It is in the end a question of suggesting things, and all the example of Shakespearian metaphor is there to tell you how short we stand of the profundities.

The most solid scene, I would say, was the spectacle of the hauling.

Camera and cameraman were lashed on top of the wheelhouse, and the nets came up through the heavy sea in great drifts of silver. We got at it from every angle we could and shot it inside-out with the hand camera; and, put together, it made a brave enough show. But even then the fact of the matter, however detailed, however orchestrated, was not enough. The sea might lash over the men and the ship plunge, and the haul of the nets tauten and tear at the wrists of the men: it was still not enough. This business of horizons had to be faced over again. By fortune a whale came alongside to clean the nets, and I used it for more than a whale. I used it for a ponderous symbol of all that tumbled and laboured on that wild morning. It adds something, but it is possible that something else, had I but felt it properly, would have carried the scene still further to that horizon I speak of. Images, images – details and aspects of things that lift a world of fact to beauty and bravery – no doubt half a hundred passed under my nose, and I did not see them.

So through the procession into harbour, and the scenes in the market place at Yarmouth – fact joined to fact and detail to detail. But here, of course, because of the size and variety of the scene, rather greater possibilities in the matter of orchestration. The gathering procession of buyers and sellers on the quayside, the procession of ships through the harbour mouth: the two processions interwoven. The selling itself, the unloading, the carrying: mouth work and shoulder work interwoven, made complementary to each other, opposed to each other as your fancy takes you. Rivers of fish, being slid into a ship's hold, cartfuls of baskets, girls gutting, barrels being rolled: all the complex detail of porterage and export dissolved into each other, run one on top of the other, to set them marching. It is the procession of results. Cranes and ships and railway trains – or their impressionistic equivalents – complete it.

The problem of images does not arise so plainly here, for cinematic processions, if you bring them off, are solid affairs that carry their own banners. Two, however, I did try. As the labour of the sea turned to the labour of the land, I carried forward a wave theme. It is played heavily for accompaniment as the ships ride in; but as life on one quayside takes charge of the picture, it is diminished in strength until it vanishes altogether. Through breaking waves the buyers and sellers go to their business. Count that, if you will, for an image of opposition. It is a far cry from the simple and solid labour of the sea to the nepman [sic] haggling of the market place.

The last was of a similar type. As the catch was being boxed and barrelled I thought I would like to say that what was really being boxed and barrelled was the labour of men. So as the herring were shovelled in, and the ice laid on, and the hammer raised to complete the job, I slid back for a flash or two to the storm and the hauling. The hammer is raised on mere fish: it comes down on dripping oilskins and a tumbling sea. This notion I kept repeating in flashes through the procession of barrels and the final procession of railway trucks. The barrels of the dead pass for a second into the living swirl of a herring shoal, in and out again; the smoke in a tunnel dissolves for a moment into the tautened wrist of a fisherman at the net-rope.

I cannot tell you what the result of it all is. Notions are notions and pictures are pictures, and no knowledge of cinematic anatomy can guarantee that extra something which is the breath of life to a picture. If I raise this matter of images it is rather to give you some idea of how the movie mind works. It has to feel its way through the appearances of things, choosing, discarding and choosing again, seeking always those more significant appearances which are like yeast to the plain dough of the context. Sometimes they are there for the taking; as often as not you have to make a journey into a far country to find them. That, however, is no more difficult for cinema than for poetry. The camera is by instinct, if not by training, a wanderer.

FIRST PRINCIPLES OF DOCUMENTARY (1932)

Documentary is a clumsy description, but let it stand. The French who first used the term only meant travelogue. It gave them a solid, high-sounding excuse for the shimmying (and otherwise discursive) exoticisms of the Vieux Colombier. Meanwhile documentary has gone on its way. From shimmying exoticisms it has gone on to include dramatic films like *Moana, Earth* and *Turksib*. And in time it will include other kinds as different in form and intention from *Moana* as *Moana* was from *Voyage au Congo*.

So far we have regarded all films made from natural material as coming within the category. The use of natural material has been regarded as the vital distinction. Where the camera shot on the spot (whether it shot newsreel items or magazine items or discursive 'interests' or dramatised 'interests' or educational films or scientific films proper or *Changs* or *Rangos*) in that fact was documentary. This array of species is, of course, quite unmanageable in criticism, and we shall have to do something about it. They all represent different qualities of observation, different intentions in observation, and, of course, very different powers and ambitions at the stage of organising material. I propose, therefore, after a brief word on the lower categories, to use the documentary description exclusively of the higher.

The peacetime newsreel is just a speedy snip-snap of some utterly unimportant ceremony. Its skill is in the speed with which the babblings of a politican (gazing sternly into the camera) are transferred to fifty million relatively unwilling ears in a couple of days or so. The magazine items (one a week) have adopted the original 'Tit-Bits' manner of observation. The skill they represent is a purely journalistic skill. They describe novelties novelly. With their money-making eye (their almost only eye) glued like the newsreels to vast and speedy audiences, they avoid on the one hand the consideration of solid material, and escape, on the other, the solid consideration of any material. Within these limits they are often brilliantly done. But ten in a row would bore the average human to death. Their reaching out for the flippant or popular touch is so completely far-reaching that it dislocates something. Possibly taste; possibly common sense. You may take your choice; those little theatres where you are invited to gad around the world in fifty minutes. It takes only that long – in these days of great invention – to see almost everything.

'Interests' proper improve mightily with every week, though heaven knows why. The market (particularly the British market) is stacked against them. With two-feature programmes the rule, there is neither space for the short and the Disney and the magazine, nor money left to pay for the short. But by good grace, some of the renters throw in the short with the feature. This considerable branch of cinematic illumination tends, therefore, to be the gift that goes with the pound of tea; and like all gestures of the grocery mind it is not very liable to cost much. Whence my wonder at improving qualities. Consider, however, the very frequent beauty and very great skill of exposition in such UFA shorts as *Turbulent Timber*, in the sports shorts from Metro-Goldwyn-Mayer, in the 'Secrets of Nature' shorts from Bruce Woolf, and the Fitzpatrick travel talks. Together they have brought the popular lecture to a pitch undreamed of, and even impossible, in the days of magic lanterns. In this little we progress.

These films, of course, would not like to be called lecture films, but this, for all their disguises, is what they are. They do not dramatise, they do not even dramatise an episode: they describe, and even expose, but in any aesthetic sense, only rarely reveal. Herein is their formal limit, and it is unlikely that they will make any considerable contribution to the fuller art of documentary. How indeed can they? Their silent form is cut to the commentary, and shots are arranged arbitrarily to point the gags or conclusions. This is not a matter of complaint, for the lecture film must have increasing value in entertainment, education and propaganda. But it is as well to establish the formal limits of the species.

This indeed is a particularly important limit to record, for beyond the newsmen and the magazine men and the lecturers (comic, interesting or exciting or only rhetorical) one begins to wander into the world of documentary proper, into the only world in which documentary can hope to achieve the ordinary virtues of an art. Here we pass from the plain (or fancy) descriptions of natural material, to arrangements, rearrangements, and creative shapings of it.

First principles. (1) We believe that the cinema's capacity for getting around, for observing and selecting from life itself, can be exploited in a new and vital art form. The studio films largely ignore this possibility of opening up the screen on the real world. They photograph acted stories against artificial backgrounds. Documentary would photograph the living scene and the living story. (2) We believe that the original (or native) actor, and the original (or native) scene, are better guides to a screen interpretation of the modern world. They give cinema a greater fund of material. They give it power over a million and one images. They give it power of interpretation over more complex and astonishing happenings than the studio mind can conjure up or the studio mechanician recreate. (3) We believe that the materials and the stories thus taken from the raw can be finer (more real in the philosophic sense) than the acted article. Spontaneous gesture has a special value on the screen. Cinema has a sensational capacity for enhancing the movement which tradition has formed or time worn smooth. Its arbitrary rectangle specially reveals movement; it gives it maximum pattern in space and time. Add to this that documentary can achieve an intimacy of knowledge and effect impossible to the shim-sham mechanics of the studio, and the lily-fingered interpretations of the metropolitan actor.

I do not mean in this minor manifesto of beliefs to suggest that the studios cannot in their own manner produce works of art to astonish the world. There is nothing (except the Woolworth intentions of the people who run them) to prevent the studios going really high in the manner of theatre or the manner of fairy tale. My separate claim for documentary is simply that in its use of the living article, there is also an opportunity to perform creative work. I mean, too, that the choice of the documentary medium is as gravely distinct a choice as the choice of poetry instead of fiction. Dealing with different material, it is, or should be, dealing with it to different aesthetic issues from those of the studio. I make this distinction to the point of asserting that the young director cannot, in nature, go documentary and go studio both.

In an earlier reference to Flaherty, I have indicated how one great exponent walked away from the studio: how he came to grips with the essential story of the Eskimos, then with the Samoans, then latterly with the people of the Aran Islands: and at what point the documentary director in him diverged from the studio intention of Hollywood. The main point of the story was this. Hollywood wanted to impose a ready-made dramatic shape on the raw material. It wanted Flaherty, in complete injustice to the living drama on the spot, to build his Samoans into a rubber-stamp drama of sharks and bathing belles. It failed in the case of *Moana*; it succeeded (through Van Dyke) in the case of *White Shadows of the South Seas*, and (through Murnau) in the case of *Tabu*. In the last examples it was at the expense of Flaherty, who severed his association with both.

With Flaherty it became an absolute principle that the story must be taken from the location, and that it should be (what he considers) the essential story of the location. His drama, therefore, is a drama of days and nights, of the round of the year's seasons, of the fundamental fights which give his people sustenance, or make their community life possible, or build up the dignity of the tribe.

Such an interpretation of subject matter reflects, of course, Flaherty's particular philosophy of things. A succeeding documentary exponent is in no way obliged to chase off to the ends of the earth in search of old-time simplicity, and the ancient dignities of man against the sky. Indeed, if I may for the moment represent the opposition, I hope the neo-Rousseauianism implicit in Flaherty's work dies with his own exceptional self. Theory of naturals apart, it represents an escapism, a wan and distant eye, which tends in lesser hands to sentimentalism. However it be shot through with vigour of Lawrentian poetry, it must always fail to develop a form adequate to the more immediate material of the modern world. For it is not only the fool that has his eyes on the ends of the earth. It is sometimes the poet: sometimes even the great poet, as Cabell in his *Beyond Life* will brightly inform you. This, however, is the very poet who on every classic theory of society from Plato to Trotsky should be removed bodily from the Republic. Loving every time but his own, and every life but his own, he avoids coming to grips with the creative job in so far as it concerns society. In the business of ordering most present chaos, he does not use his powers.

Question of theory and practice apart, Flaherty illustrates better than anyone the first principles of documentary. (1) It must master its material on the spot, and come in intimacy to ordering it. Flaherty digs himself in for a year, or two maybe. He lives with his people till the story is told 'out of himself'. (2) It must follow him in his distinction between description and drama. I think we shall find that there are other forms of drama, or, more accurately, other forms of film, than the one he chooses; but it is important to make the primary distinction between a method which describes only the surface values of a subject, and the method which more explosively reveals the reality of it. You photograph the natural life, but you also, by your juxtaposition of detail, create an interpretation of it.

This final creative intention established, several methods are possible. You may, like Flaherty, go for a story form, passing in the ancient manner from the individual to the environment, to the environment transcended or not transcended, to the consequent honours of heroism. Or you may not be so interested in the individual. You may think that the individual life is no longer capable of cross-sectioning reality. You may believe that its particular belly-aches are of no consequence in a world which complex and impersonal forces command, and conclude that the individual as a self-sufficient dramatic figure is outmoded. When Flaherty tells you that it is a devilish noble thing to fight for food in a wilderness, you may, with some justice, observe that you are more concerned with the problem of people fighting for food in the midst of plenty. When he draws your attention to the fact that Nanook's spear is grave in its upheld angle, and finely rigid in its down-pointing bravery, you may, with some justice, observe that no spear, held however bravely by the individual, will master the crazy walrus of international finance. Indeed you may feel that individualism is a Yahoo tradition largely responsible for our present anarchy, and deny at once both the hero of decent heroics (Flaherty) and the hero of indecent ones (studio).

In this case, you will feel that you want your drama in terms of some cross-section of reality which will reveal the essentially co-operative or mass nature of society: leaving the individual to find his honours in the swoop of creative social forces. In other words, you are liable to abandon the story form, and seek, like the modern exponent of poetry and painting and prose, a matter and method more satisfactory to the mind and spirit of the time.

Berlin or the Symphony of a City initiated the more modern fashion of finding documentary material on one's doorstep: in events which have no novelty of the unknown, or romance of noble savage on exotic landscape, to recommend them. It represented, slimly, the return from romance to reality.

Berlin was variously reported as made by Ruttmann, or begun by Ruttmann and finished by Freund: certainly it was begun by Ruttmann. In smooth and finely tempo'd visuals, a train swung through suburban mornings into Berlin. Wheels, rails, details of engines, telegraph wires, landscapes and other simple images flowed along in procession, with similar abstracts passing occasionally in and out of the general movement. There followed a sequence of such movements which, in their total effect, created very imposingly the story of a Berlin day. The day began with a processional of workers, the factories got under way, the streets filled: the city's forenoon became a hurly-burly of tangled pedestrians and street cars. There was respite for food: a various respite with contrast of rich and poor. The city started work again, and a shower of rain in the afternoon became a considerable event. The city stopped work and, in further more hectic processional of pubs and cabarets and dancing legs and illuminated sky-signs, finished its day.

In so far as the film was principally concerned with movements and the building of separate images into movements, Ruttmann was justified in calling it a symphony. It meant a break away from the story borrowed from literature, and from the play borrowed from the stage. In *Berlin* cinema swung along according to its own more natural powers: creating dramatic effect from the tempo'd accumulation of its single observations. Cavalcanti's *Rien que les Heures* and Leger's *Ballet Mecanique* came before *Berlin*, each with a similar attempt to combine images in an emotionally satisfactory sequence of movements. They were too scrappy and had not mastered the art of cutting sufficiently well to create the sense of 'march' necessary to the genre. The symphony of Berlin City was both larger in its movements and larger in its vision.

There was one criticism of *Berlin* which, out of appreciation for a fine film and a new and arresting form, the critics failed to make; and time has not justified the omission. For all its ado of workmen and factories and swirl and swing of a great city, *Berlin* created nothing. Or rather if it created something, it was that shower of rain in the afternoon. The people of the city got up splendidly, they tumbled through their five million hoops impressively, they turned in; and no other issue of God or man emerged than that sudden besmattering spilling of wet on people and pavements.

I urge the criticism because *Berlin* still excites the mind of the young, and the symphony form is still their most popular persuasion. In fifty scenarios presented by the tyros, forty-five are symphonies of Edinburgh or of Ecclefechan or of Paris or of Prague. Day breaks – the people come to work – the factories start – the street cars rattle – lunch hour and the streets again – sport if it is Saturday afternoon – certainly evening and the local dance hall. And so, nothing having happened and nothing positively said about anything, to bed; though Edinburgh is the capital of a country and Ecclefechan, by some power inside itself, was the birthplace of Carlyle, in some ways one of the greatest exponents of this documentary idea.

The little daily doings, however finely symphonised, are not enough. One must pile up beyond doing or process to creation itself, before one hits the higher reaches of art. In this distinction, creation indicates not the making of things but the making of virtues.

And there's the rub for tyros. Critical appreciation of movement they can build easily from their power to observe, and power to observe they can build from their own good taste, but the real job only begins as they apply ends to their observation and their movements. The artist need not posit the ends – for that is the work of the critic – but the ends must be there, informing his description and giving finality (beyond space and time) to the slice of life he has chosen. For that larger effect there must be power of poetry or of prophecy. Failing either or both in the highest degree, there must be at least the socio-logical sense implicit in poetry and prophecy.

The best of the tyros know this. They believe that beauty will come in good time to inhabit the statement which is honest and lucid and deeply felt and which fulfils the best ends of citizenship. They are sen-sible enough to conceive of art as the by-product of a job of work done. The opposite effort to capture the by-product first (the self-conscious pursuit of beauty, the pursuit of art for art's sake to the exclusion of jobs of work and other pedestrian beginnings) was always a reflection of selfish wealth, selfish leisure and aesthetic decadence.

This sense of social responsibility makes our realist documentary a troubled and difficult art, and particularly in a time like ours. The job of romantic documentary is easy in comparison: easy in the sense that the noble savage is already a figure of romance and the seasons of the year have already been articulated in poetry. Their essential virtues have been declared and can more easily be declared again, and no one will deny them. But realist documentary, with its streets and cities and slums and markets and exchanges and factories, has given itself the job of making poetry where no poet has gone before it, and where no ends, sufficient for the purposes of art, are easily observed. It requires not only taste but also inspiration, which is to say a very laborious, deep-seeing, deep-sympathising creative effort indeed.

The symphonists have found a way of building such matters of common reality into very pleasant sequences. By uses of tempo and rhythm, and by the large-scale integration of single effects, they capture the eye and impress the mind in the same way as a tattoo or a military parade might do. But by their concentration on mass and movement, they tend to avoid the larger creative job. What more attractive (for a man of visual taste) than to swing wheels and pistons about in ding-dong description of a machine, when he has little to say about the man who tends it, and still less to say about the tin-pan product it spills? And what more comfortable if, in one's heart, there is avoidance of the issue of underpaid labour and meaningless production? For this reason I hold the symphony tradition of cinema for a danger and *Berlin* for the most dangerous of all film models to follow.

Unfortunately, the fashion is with such avoidance as *Berlin* represents. The highbrows bless the symphony for its good looks and, being sheltered rich little souls for the most part, absolve it gladly from further intention. Other factors combine to obscure one's judgement regarding it. The post-1918 generation, in which all cinema intelligence resides, is apt to veil a particularly violent sense of disillusionment, and a very natural first reaction of impotence, in any smart manner of avoidance which comes to hand. The pursuit of fine form which this genre certainly represents is the safest of asylums.

The objection remains, however. The rebellion from the who-gets-who tradition of commercial cinema to the tradition of pure form in cinema is no great shakes as a rebellion. Dadaism, expressionism, symphonies are all in the same category. They present new beauties and new shapes; they fail to present new persuasions.

The imagist or more definitely poetic approach might have taken our consideration of documentary a step further, but no great imagist film has arrived to give character to the advance. By imagism I mean the telling of story or illumination of theme by images, as poetry is story or theme told by images: I mean the addition of poetic reference to the 'mass' and 'march' of the symphonic form.

Drifters was one simple contribution in that direction, but only a simple one. Its subject belonged in part to Flaherty's world, for it had something of the noble savage and certainly a great deal of the elements of nature to play with. It did, however, use steam and smoke and did, in a sense, marshal the effects of a modern industry. Looking back on the film now, I would not stress the tempo effects which it built (for both *Berlin* and *Potemkin* came before it), nor even the rhythmic effects (though I believe they outdid the technical example of *Potemkin* in that direction). What seemed possible of development in the film was the integration of imagery with the movement. The ship at sea, the men casting, the men hauling, were not only seen as functionaries doing something. They were seen as functionaries in half a hundred different ways, and each tended to add something to the illumination as well as the description of them. In other words the shots were massed together, not only for description and tempo but for commentary on it. One felt impressed by the tough, continuing, upstanding labour involved, and the feeling shaped the images, determined the background and supplied the extra details which gave colour to the whole. I do not urge the example of *Drifters*, but in theory at least the example is there. If the high bravery of upstanding labour came through the film, as I hope it did, it was made not by the story itself, but by the imagery attendant on it. I put the point not in praise of the method but in simple analysis of the method.

The symphonic form is concerned with the orchestration of movement. It sees the screen in terms of flow and does not permit the flow to be broken. Episodes and events, if they are included in the action, are integrated in the flow. The symphonic form also tends to organise the flow in terms of different movements, e.g. movement for dawn, movement for men coming to work, movement for factories in full swing, etc., etc. This is a first distinction.

See the symphonic form as something equivalent to the poetic form of, say, Carl Sandburg in 'Skyscraper', 'Chicago', 'The Windy City' and 'Slabs of the Sunburnt West'. The object is presented as an integration of many activities. It lives by the many human associations and by the moods of the various action sequences which surround it. Sandburg says so with variations of tempo in his description, variations of the mood in which each descriptive facet is presented. We do not ask personal stories of such poetry, for the picture is complete and satisfactory. We need not ask it of documentary. This is a second distinction regarding symphonic form.

These distinctions granted, it is possible for the symphonic form to vary considerably. Basil Wright, for example, is almost exclusively interested in movement, and will build up movement in a fury of design and nuances of design; and for those whose eye is sufficiently trained and sufficiently fine will convey emotion in a thousand variations on a theme so simple as the portage of bananas (*Cargo from Jamaica*). Some have attempted to relate this movement to the pyrotechnics of pure form, but there never was any such animal. (1) The quality of Wright's sense of movement and of his patterns is distinctively his own and recognisably delicate. As with good painters, there is character in his line and attitude in his composition. (2) There is an overtone in his work which – sometimes after seeming monotony – makes his description uniquely memorable. (3) His patterns invariably weave – not seeming to do so – a positive attitude to the material, which may conceivably relate to (2). The patterns of *Cargo from Jamaica* were more scathing comment on labour at twopence a hundred bunches (or whatever it is) than mere sociological stricture. His movements – (a) easily down; (b) horizontal; (c) arduously 45° up; (d) down again – conceal, or perhaps construct, a comment. Flaherty once maintained that the east–west contour of Canada was itself a drama. It was precisely a sequence of down, horizontal, 45° up, and down again.

I use Basil Wright as an example of 'movement in itself' – though movement is never in itself – principally to distinguish those others who add either tension elements or poetic elements or atmospheric elements. I have held myself in the past an exponent of the tension category with certain pretension to the others. Here is a simple example of tension from *Granton Trawler*. The trawler is working its gear in a storm. The tension elements are built up with emphasis on the drag of the water, the heavy lurching of the ship, the fevered flashing of the birds, the fevered flashing of faces between waves, lurches and spray. The trawl is hauled aboard with strain of men and tackle and water. It is opened in a release which comprises equally the release of men, birds and fish. There is no pause in the flow of movement, but something of an effort as between two opposing forces has been recorded. In a more ambitious and deeper description the tension might have included elements more intimately and more heavily descriptive of the clanging weight of the tackle, the strain on the ship, the operation of the gear under water and along the ground, the scuttering myriads of birds laying off in the gale. The fine fury of ship and heavy weather could have been brought through to touch the vitals of the men and the ship. In the hauling, the simple fact of a wave breaking over the men, subsiding and leaving them hanging on as though nothing had happened, would have brought the sequence to an appropriate peak. The release could have attached to itself images of, say, birds wheeling high, taking off from the ship, and of contemplative, i.e. more intimate, reaction on the faces of the men. The drama would have gone deeper by the greater insight into the energies and reactions involved.

Carry this analysis into a consideration of the first part of *Deserter*, which piles up from a sequence of deadly quiet to the strain and fury – and aftermath – of the strike, or of the strike sequence itself, which piles up from deadly quiet to the strain and fury – and aftermath – of the police attack, and you have indication of how the symphonic shape, still faithful to its own peculiar methods, comes to grip with dramatic issue.

The poetic approach is best represented by *Romance Sentimentale* and the last sequence of *Ekstase*. Here there is description without tension, but the moving description is lit up by attendant images. In *Ekstase* the notion of life renewed is conveyed by a rhythmic sequence of labour, but there are also essential images of a woman and child, a young man standing high over the scene, skyscapes and water. The description of the various moods of *Romance Sentimentale* is conveyed entirely by images: in one sequence of domestic interior, in another sequence of misty morning, placid water and dull sunlight. The creation of mood, an essential to the symphonic form, may be done in terms of tempo alone, but it is better done if poetic images colour it. In a description of night at sea, there are elements enough aboard a ship to build up a quiet and effective rhythm, but a deeper effect might come by reference to what is happening under water or by reference to the strange spectacle of the birds which, sometimes in ghostly flocks, move silently in and out of the ship's lights.

A sequence in a film by Rotha indicates the distinction between the three different treatments. He describes the loading of a steel furnace and builds a superb rhythm into the shovelling movements of the men. By creating behind them a sense of fire, by playing on the momentary shrinking from fire which comes into these shovelling movements, he would have brought in the elements of tension. He might have proceeded from this to an almost terrifying picture of what steel work involves. On the other hand, by overlaying the rhythm with, say, such posturing or contemplative symbolic figures as Eisenstein brought into his *Thunder over Mexico* material, he would have added the elements of poetic image. The distinction is between (a) a musical or non-literary method; (b) a dramatic method with clashing forces; and (c) a poetic, contemplative and altogether literary method. These three methods may all appear in one film, but their proportion depends naturally on the character of the director – and his private hopes of salvation.

I do not suggest that one form is higher than the other. There are pleasures peculiar to the exercise of movement which in a sense are tougher – more classical – than the pleasures of poetic description, however attractive and however blessed by tradition these may be. The introduction of tension gives accent to a film, but only too easily gives popular appeal because of its primitive engagement with physical issues and struggles and fights. People like a fight, even when it is only a symphonic one, but it is not clear that a war with the elements is a braver subject than the opening of a flower or, for that matter, the opening of a cable. It refers us back to hunting instincts and fighting instincts, but these do not necessarily represent the more civilised fields of appreciation.

It is commonly believed that moral grandeur in art can only be achieved, Greek or Shakespearian fashion, after a general laying out of the protagonists, and that no head is unbowed which is not bloody. This notion is a philosophic vulgarity. Of recent years it has been given the further blessing of Kant in his distinction between the aesthetic of pattern and the aesthetic of achievement, and beauty has been considered somewhat inferior to the sublime. The Kantian confusion comes from the fact that he personally had an active moral sense, but no active aesthetic one. He would not otherwise have drawn the distinction. So far as common taste is concerned, one has to see that we do not mix up the fulfilment of primitive desires, and the vain dignities which attach to that fulfilment, with the dignities which attach to man as an imaginative being. The dramatic application of the symphonic form is not, *ipso facto*, the deepest or most important. Consideration of forms neither dramatic nor symphonic, but dialectic, will reveal this more plainly.

EDUCATION AND THE NEW ORDER (1941)

I don't think we have done very well in education. The world has been changing about us – drastically changing – and we have not kept up with it. I suspect we have held on to concepts of education fit for the last century but no longer for this and have therefore failed to create the mental qualities and capacities our generation has needed. We face one of the deepest crises in the history of human organisation. There is no question of that, with the whole world at war. This in itself represents the failure of the human mind to order human affairs in our time; and this in turn represents a failure in understanding and capacity for ordering human affairs.

I hardly think education can be absolved from its part in that failure. Talk as you will of pursuing the highest ends of man and the service of God, the base of the pyramid is in deeds done and in results achieved. In that sense, education is surely never anything other than the process by which men are fitted to serve their generation and bring it into the terms of order. It is the process by which the minds of men are keyed to the tasks of good citizenship, by which they are geared to the privilege of making a constructive contribution, however humble, to the highest purposes of the community. Grant that in so doing education does, in man's high fancy, tune the human spirit to the music of the spheres, none the less its function is the immediate and practical one of being a deliberate social instrument – not dreaming in an ivory tower, but outside on the barricades of social construction, holding citizens to the common purpose their generation has set for them.

Education is activist or it is nothing. If that is so, the utter disorder of society in this our time does not represent a very brilliant achievement for that instrument on which society depends for understanding and guidance. We have loosed the inventions and armed the human race with brilliant physical weapons for creating a rich civilisation. But we have not known how to solve the simplest problems of economic integration – either nationally or internationally. Power has been a synonym for selfishness and possession has been a synonym for greed. I do not mean that education should be blamed for this and for the wars that have resulted as night from day. I merely mean that education is the key to the mobilisation of men's minds to right ends or wrong ends, to order or chaos; and that is what education is. If men's minds have not been mobilised aright, the educational process has not been good enough. If, on the other hand, men's minds are in the future to be mobilised aright, it means an increase in the wisdom and power of the educational process. So, looking beyond the immediate, the greatest task of our time is not one for the soldiers but one for the educators and, because of the nature of the problem, it is certainly the hardest task they have ever been set.

These changing times of ours do not represent ordinary changes. There are periods in history when the whole basis of truth is re-examined and when the operative philosophies are revolutionised and renewed. This is one of them. We had such a period before when the Middle Ages passed into the Renaissance. The key to that change was not in the rediscovery of Greece as the text-books say, but in something much deeper. It was in the discovery and development of the laws of quantitative measurement. Out of it came the philosophy of pioneering and personal acquisition – the philosophy of individualism and individual rights – which has ruled our minds to this day.

No period of history has been more spectacular. But I wonder if we have not for a long time been seeing the last phases of it. Everyone today talks of the war not as a war but as a world revolution. And I wonder if the world revolution does not lie in this: that the great days of unmitigated individualism and governmental laissez-faire are over, and the day of common unified planning has arrived.

If that is so, it means an enormous change in all our thinking and all our values. It means nothing less than a drastic spring-cleaning of the concepts we teach and the sentiments by which we govern our action. At the time of the Renaissance the bases of religion and philosophy and government were altered to accommodate and articulate the deep change in human affairs. You will remember, for example, how into painting came the study of perspective and the placing of the individual in space; and into literature came the study of personal character. Personal measurement became, in varying degrees, a principle of philosophy in Berkeley, Locke, Rousseau, Bentham and the rest of them. In religion came the Reformation with a new emphasis on conscience and individual relationship with God. The arts and the philosophies changed to give men a working vision and a working faith under the new conditions of society. They followed public necessity. The same obligation may be upon us now and I think it is. This is not a sudden development. All the years I have been watching the educational process, it has been difficult not to be conscious of it. The only difference is that the picture which was dim twenty-five years ago is today rushing into focus.

Perhaps an illustration from that earlier period may be of some interest. It goes back to the small Scots village in which I was brought up and where my father was a schoolmaster. He was a good dominie of the old school. He called himself a Conservative, but his operative philosophy in education was a good sample of what a liberal Scottish education meant. He believed in the democratic process as Burns and all Scotsmen naturally and natively do. A man was a man for a' that. We were partly agriculture, partly coal mining, and it didn't matter where the boys came from. If they were lads of parts, he felt it his God-given mission to put them on their way. At 8 o'clock in the morning before school and at 5 o'clock after school, he was at work intensifying on the bright ones, so that they could win scholarships and go to high school and on to the university. Learning was power and he was taking his job seriously. It is still pleasant to think how he would trudge off miles into the country to prevail on stubborn ploughmen, who needed the extra money coming in, to give their boys a chance and not put them to work at fourteen.

The basis of his educational philosophy was certainly according to the eternal verities. It was deeply rooted in Carlyle and Ruskin and the natural rights of man. The wind of the French Revolution still blew behind it. But it was strictly individualist. Education gave men a chance in the world. It put them in good competitive standing in a grim competitive world. It fitted them to open the doors of spiritual satisfaction in literature and philosophy. But it was in the name of a highly personal satisfaction. Behind it all was the dream of the nineteenth century – the false dream – that if only everyone had the individualist

ideals that education taught, free men in a free society – each in independent and educated judgement – would create a civilisation such as
the world had never seen before.

Even when that kind of education was conscious of social relationships, the approach was on an individualist basis. Conservative as he
was, this village schoolmaster of whom I write was something of a
pioneer in the teaching of the social amenities. He pioneered school
gardens and domestic science for girls at the beginning of the century.
With a sense of bringing a wider horizon into the classroom, he
brought to that obscure village school, more than thirty years ago, the
first film show ever seen in educational circles in Scotland. He helped
to build a village institute, so that his fellow citizens would have more
literary papers on this and that, and particularly more papers on
Carlyle and Ruskin. But the prevailing idea was as always that the
individual might be more enlightened. One suspected that the end of
it all was to make every workman a gentleman in a library – perhaps
without too much leisure to be a gentleman and not too much of a
library, but still as good as any man alive in the deep pursuit of truth
and beauty.

The smashing of that idyllic viewpoint has been probably the greatest educational fact of our time; and I saw it smashed right there in my
village and I saw the deep doubt creep into the mind of that schoolmaster that everything he stood for and strove for was somewhere
wrong. That was many years ago, long before the events of today made
the dim things so much plainer.

As I have noted, one half of that village consisted of coal miners. The
every effect of the education they were given, conservative as it might
be in intention, was to make men think; and, thinking, they became
less and less satisfied with the miserable pays they received. The life
of the village became more and more affected by strikes and lock-outs.
As amalgamations were developed, the employers stood ever further
and further away and the battle for wages and safeties and securities
became the fiercer as the fight became more abstract – as decisions
came to depend on massed unions and massed corporations.

Somehow or other the educational process got to be beside the
point. What were the delights of literature when a distant judgement
by a distant corporation could throw a man into six months of
economic misery? What were the pleasures of Shakespeare and *A Mid-
summer Night's Dream* in the evening schools, when industrial conditions

were tiring the boys to death? What was the use of saying that a man was a man for a' that, when you were dealing day in day out with a war of economic forces in which only armies counted and where the motivating powers were abstract and unseen? In his local way this schoolmaster did a great deal. He started soup kitchens and got the soup-kitchen principle so well established that the miners actually in one great strike organised the feeding of their whole community. Perhaps the soup-kitchen idea was the one great educational achievement of his life. But before he finished I think the true leadership in education had passed to other shoulders. It had in fact passed to the miners themselves and the economists among them. They read their Blatchford and Keir Hardie and Bob Smillie; they attended their trade union meetings; and the day came when they elected their first Labour member of parliament, and, with so many other villages in Scotland, joined in the great drive for a socialist Britain.

At the time, I drew two conclusions from that village story. The first is that education can only, at its peril, detach itself from the economic processes and what is happening in the world. In that sense, if official education does not give realistic leadership in terms of what is happening and what is most deeply needed in the world, be assured the people will find other more realistic leadership. The second lesson was that the individualist dream in education is over and done with in a world which operates in terms of large integrated forces. There is nothing I can think of so cynical today as to teach a boy that the world is his personal oyster for the opening or talk, as Lord Birkenhead did, of the glittering prizes that fall to a flashing sword.

There is, and of course must be, a place for individual talents, but it becomes ever clearer that the heart of the matter today lies in team work and in unity. Individualism, that dream of so many centuries, has given us one of the golden ages. But what was so great a force in a simple world has become a nuisance in one more complicated. By its own bright energies, individualism has in fact created its Frankenstein. It has loosed energies and forces which it is, of all philosophies, least fitted to co-ordinate and control. We have arrived at an ironical situation. The spirit of competition which was so great a breeder of initiative yesterday has become only a disturber of the peace today. Rugged individualism, so honourable yesterday, is only rugged irresponsibility today. A philosophy in which nobody is his brother's keeper has become impossible when a decision by a board of directors hundreds of miles away will wipe out a town overnight and doom the inhabitants of a rich country to desolation and despair for years. We have seen just that, no less, in Scotland, Wales and northern England, time and again. I need not emphasise how, in international affairs, the philosophy of irresponsible competition, governmental laissez-faire, laissez-aller, and failure to plan has landed not towns but nations and continents in the deepest disaster in the history of mankind.

I want to make it eminently clear that this is not a question of blaming any particular forces. My simple point is that the values and virtues of yesterday may not be the right values or the right virtues today. My point is that in maintaining so stubbornly the old individualist, sectional, free competitive and nationalist viewpoints, we have been holding to concepts which may have, in their day, been great and glorious concepts capable of motivating men to great achievements, but which are incapable of mastering the problems of today. I regard it as foolish and unnecessary to say that financial and industrial forces have been selfish or that labour has been blind. It is similarly foolish to blame the United States for not entering the League, Britain for not supporting the Weimar Republic enough, Ottawa for making the international economic struggle inevitable in the Imperial Conference of 1932. The only real conclusion worth making is that all these events followed inevitably from the fact – as always happens in history – that we were into the new world of facts before we were out of the old world of attitudes. I am concerned to suggest that the inevitable historical process has found our operative philosophy and educative attitudes inadequate to cope with events.

To make my argument still clearer, let me say that I am not talking of the passage from capitalism to socialism. Like Professor Burnham, I do not believe that socialism as we have thought it will come at all. That surely was plain when the Workers' Soviets with all their socialist dreams of workers' control in a classless society were driven out of industrial managership in Russia and Republican Spain, and by their own leaders. They were driven out not because socialism did not represent a high ideal, but because, given the conditions of modern technocracy, workers' self-management represents an unpractical and inefficient one. My view, if any, would be that we are entering upon a new and interim society which is neither capitalist nor socialist, but in which we can achieve central planning without loss of individual initiative, by the mere process of absorbing initiative in the function of planning. I think we are entering upon a society in which public unity and discipline can be achieved without forgetting the humanitarian virtues. As one watches the implications of the New Deal and of what is happening today in the development of centralised planning at Ottawa, one sees that hope not only on a national scale but on an international one too.

But I emphasise the first and main point which is that we grasp the historical process and not bother about recriminations or moral strictures. Men are all the fools of history, even the greatest and best of them. A man or a nation that is historically wrong may not be evil. A man or a nation that is historically right may not be good. But when we come to consider the philosophy of education we have no alternative. As educators we must go the way with history and men's needs, or others will come to take the privilege of education away from us.

All this carries with it the suggestion of a drastic change in eductional outlook. I do not expect it to be popular. It is no more popular with me than with you, for like everyone of my generation I am imbued – I should more accurately say rotted through – with the old individualist ideals and cannot for the life of me be rid of them. I am still as soft as anyone to those emotional appeals that are based on concepts of personal initiative and personal right. I still find the greatest image in rhetoric is the single man against his horizon, seeking his destiny. But simply because we are so deeply imbued with these concepts and images, our effort must be the harder to change them. If they are not the key to the social future it is our duty as educators and scientists to forget our personal predilections of the past and build the concepts and images that are the key to the future.

We have no alternative, though we shall at least have the comfort that certain familiar concepts must forever remain, because they do represent the eternal verities. We may forget nationalism but still need the cohesion and spur of national tradition. Always there will be the concept of the people and the native pride in one's own people. Humanity will remain one of the essential dramatic concepts of human thought and endeavour. So will justice; so will freedom; though justice may lose its contact with the maintenance of private property rights, and freedom may return to the Platonic notion of freedom only to serve the community.

As I see it, the really hard and disagreeable task of education tomorrow is that it will have, willy-nilly, to re-examine its attitude to such

fundamental concepts as property and wealth, natural right and freedom of contract. It will have to think more cautiously when it comes to
the word 'opportunity' and the phrase 'free enterprise'. The concepts
themselves will not be obliterated. They are simply due for a sea change
which will leave them somewhat different from what they were before.

On the positive side, we shall find new concepts coming more
powerfully into our lives; and we shall find ourselves dramatising them
so that they become loyalties and take leadership of the will. We shall
talk less of the world as everyone's oyster and more about work and
jobs. We shall talk less about free enterprise and competition and more
about the state as a partner in initiative. There will be less about liberty
and more about duties: less about the pursuit of happiness and more
about the pursuit of sacrifice. Above all, there will be less about words
and more about action and less about the past and more about the
future. Already you hear the new words in the air: discipline, unity,
co-ordination, total effort, planning. They are the first swallows over
the horizon; and there are going to be more of them.

In another field, education is going to see equally drastic change.
The entire basis of comprehension and therefore of educational method
may change: in fact it is now changing. When we talk of bridging the
gap between the citizen and the community and between the classroom and the world without, we are asking for a kind of educational
shorthand which will somehow give people quick and immediate
comprehension of the highly complex forces which motivate our
complicated society. We are seeking a method of articulating society
which will communicate a sense of the corporate and a sense of
growth. No one, I hope, imagines that the new society with its wide
horizons and complex perspectives can be taught in the old ways, and
in fact we are discovering that the only methods which will convey
the nature of the new society are dramatic methods. That is why the
documentary film has achieved unique importance in the new world of
education. It does not teach the new world by analysing it. Uniquely
and for the first time it *communicates* the new world by showing it in its
corporate and living nature.

But if you add the new words together – work, unity, discipline,
activism, sacrifice, total effort, central planning and so forth – I think
you will realise where the greatest change of all is likely to happen.
Education will come out of the schoolroom and the library, the literary
circle and the undergraduate conference, into the light of day. At least

it will come out a great deal more than it has ever thought of doing in the past. It will go into the factory and the field, into the co-operatives of production and distribution. It will express itself not as thought or debate but as the positive action within the community of organised youth groups, women's groups and men's groups. One half of education, the stronger half, will lie in the organisation of active citizenship; for there can be no concept of planning without the concept of participation.

In particular we need to guard against the danger of making public guidance a matter of one-way traffic. The government has as much information and guidance to get from the people as the people from the government. The government can gain as much from local inspiration as the people from central inspiration. We should, therefore, insist that information work both ways and we should insist that new local organisations of every kind have constant and active representation at centre. It will be our fundamental safeguard against discipline and unity turning into something else.

When you deal with alterations that challenge the accepted and honoured attitudes of society, the path is always dangerous. I am not going to pretend that I do not realise how 'totalitarian' some of my conclusions seem, without the qualification I have just noted. You can be 'totalitarian' for evil and you can also be 'totalitarian' for good. Some of us came out of a highly disciplined religion and see no reason to fear discipline and self-denial. Some of us learned in a school of philosophy which taught that all was for the common good and nothing for oneself and have never, in any case, regarded the pursuit of happiness as anything other than an aberration of the human spirit. We were taught, for example, that he who would gain his life must lose it. Even Rousseau talked of transporting *le moi dans l'unité commune*, and Calvin of establishing the holy communion of the citizens. So, the kind of 'totalitarianism' I am thinking of, while it may apply to the new conditions of society, has as deep a root as any in human tradition. I would call the philosophy of individualism romantic and say we have been on a spectacular romantic spree for four hundred years. I would maintain that this other, 'totalitarian' viewpoint is classical.

There is a further point I want to make: a simple dynamic change which I foresee in educational approach. In times of crisis – particularly in times of crisis – men crave a moral imperative; and I greatly doubt if education will mean a thing or will be listened to, unless it acquires a moral imperative.

The reason is plain and I hope that we shall not be so short-sighted as to miss a fundamental psychological factor in the world situation today. Down under the surface, men have lost their faith. As the war raged across Europe and absorbed one country after another, no fact was more patent, and not least to the German propagandists. Much of their technique was built on it, and successfully so.

We all know why men have lost their faith. They have seen the world going into disorder; they have had a sense of things going from bad to worse; and nowhere have they found that leadership, mental and religious, which seemed to be taking hold of essentials and clearing the way – positively clearing the way – to the future. Now faith is a simple matter: at least simple of analysis. It is the complex of loyalties and attitudes by which men's needs are first appreciated and then fulfilled. So, if we are to help in re-creating this essential path to action and true victory, it behoves us to bind ourselves to the recognition and fulfilment of men's needs, with an unswerving loyalty which may well be called religious. For, you will remember, religion itself comes from a word which means 'a bond'. Many have recently deplored the separation of education from religion. I am making the same point, but I am also say- ing that religious power in education will only come if its recognition of men's needs is simple, fundamental, definite, activist and unswerving. If the religious reference is merely a return to the pie-in-the-sky motif, or if it is merely a return to rhetorical play with the word of God, I believe it will avail you nothing, for you will neither be talking religion nor giving the benefit of it.

Men's needs were never in our generation hard to see. They have to do with such simple matters as food and shelter and the good life for everyone and, more particularly, as a *sine qua non*, they have to do with the mobilisation of men's will to these essential ends without any deviation whatsoever. These ends may have been forgotten in sectional selfishness and private privilege; and the privileged ones may have allowed every kind of complacent, urbane, cynical and indifferent atti- tude to hide from them the primitive fact that their neighbours, national and international, have been starving and dying in their midst. Or it may be that the leadership has been depressed by the progressive difficulties of a complex world and has lost its will-power and has wearily given up the task of leadership without abandoning its privi- lege. Whatever the analysis, if education is to find its moral imperative, it must get back to the forgotten fundamentals of men's need and take upon itself the courage and the will to realise them. It will have to clear itself, in the process, of a lot of bric-à-brac so often called culture. For example, it will hardly get away with anything so easy as telling people that they are fighting for the old way of life, even if people are reminded of its unquestionable beauties and benefits. Education will not get away with it, because too many people believe in their hearts that the old way of life is the mother of chaos; and they will settle for something short of its beauties and benefits. We will have to give a plain demonstration that we have willed a new way of life and mean it. The details, even the plan, will not matter so long as the will is patent and the demonstration real; for of all men's needs the first and most principal is hope, and it is of the essence of belief that the fact must follow.

The solution is straight and simple; and in an educational world which has come perversely to worship indecision and feel honoured in unbelief, I hope I shall be forgiven my certainty. I suggest simply this, and it is the moral imperative for education as I see it. Go out and ask men to mobilise themselves for the destruction of greed and selfishness. And mean it. Ask them to forget their personal dreams and pleasures and deny themselves for the obliteration of economic anarchy and disorder all over the world. And mean it. Mean it so much that men will know that no power on earth will stop you in your tracks. Tell them that in desperate unity and before God they will give the world a greater leadership – a more humanitarian new order – than the thwarted and vengeful people of Germany can be capable of. Say with the Prime Minister of Canada that 'never again in our own land or in any other land will the gods of material power, of worldly possession and of special privilege be permitted to exercise their sway'. Mean it, and mean it so much that the people will know that, as far as human fallibility allows, the age of selfish interest is over and done with. Say it and mean it and think it and act on it. Make it your religion; which is to say, make it your bond with the people. I haven't a doubt that they will accept the new loyalties and the new attitudes of sacrifice and effort without a qualm or a question. And I haven't a doubt whatever that they will march with you till the skies open and the future is born.

THE DOCUMENTARY IDEA (1942)

The first part of our work in Canada was finished early in 1942. It produced a film organisation which suggested it could do great things for the country if it was looked after in good faith till the young people developed. Much of it was pulled off the sky. On the other hand, there are special reasons why the national use of films should have fitted so quickly and progressively into the Canadian scene. The need to achieve unity in a country of many geographical and psychological distances is only one of them and not the most important. More vital, I think, is the fact that Canada is waking up to her place in the world and is conscious, as few English-speaking countries seem to be, that it is a new sort of place in the world. A medium which tries to explain the shape of events and create loyalties in relation to the developing scene is welcome. I cannot otherwise explain the measure of support we have been given, nor the long-range hopes that have been placed in this school of projection we have set up.

Stuart Legg has been such a worker as you never saw: with one film a month in the theatre series for a couple of years, and stepping up later to two. It will be easier as the research staff grows, for the key to that sort of thing is in the first place academic. There is first-rate support in the fields of economics and international affairs. This is a characteristic of Canada and will have considerable influence on the development of the group.

The 'World in Action' series says more of what is going on in our minds. The films in this series develop in authority and command good critical attention both in Canada and in the States. We are concerned in these films primarily with the relation of local strategies to larger world ones. This is partly in reaction to what some of us regard as a dangerous parochialism in English-speaking propaganda: but also because Canada is moving as swiftly towards a world viewpoint as England in recent years has been moving away from it. The style comes out of the job. Since it is a question of giving people a pattern of thought and feeling about highly complex and urgent events, we give it as well as we know, with a minimum of dawdling over how some poor darling happens to react to something or other. This is one time, we say, when history doesn't give a good goddam who is being the manly little fellow in adversity and is only concerned with the designs for living and dying that will actually and in fact shape the future. If our stuff pretends to be certain, it's because people need certainty. If our maps look upside down, it's because it's time people saw things in relativity. If we bang them out one a fortnight and no misses, instead of sitting six months on our fannies cuddling them to sweet smotheroo, it's because a lot of bravos in Russia and Japan and Germany are banging out things too and we'd maybe better learn how, in time. If the manner is objective and hard, it's because we believe the next phase of human development needs that kind of mental approach. After all, there is no danger of the humanitarian tradition perishing while the old are left alive to feel sorry for themselves and make 'beautiful' pictures about it. Sad to say, the beating heart of the Stuarts was all they had left and so it is with vanishing politicos.

The penalty of realism is that it is about reality and has to bother for ever not about being 'beautiful' but about being right. It means a stalwart effort these days: one has to chill the mind to so many emotional defences of the decadent and so many smooth rationalisations of the ineffective. One has even to chill the mind to what, in the vacuum of daydreams, one might normally admire. In our world it is specially necessary these days to guard against the aesthetic argument. It is plausible and apt to get under the defences of any maker in any medium. But, of course, it is the dear bright-eyed old enemy and by this time we know it very well. Documentary was from the beginning – when we first separated our public purpose theories from those of Flaherty – an 'anti-aesthetic' movement. We have all, I suppose, sacrificed some personal capacity in 'art' and the pleasant vanity that goes with it.

What confuses the history is that we had always the good sense to use the aesthetes. We did so because we liked them and because we needed them. It was, paradoxically, with the first-rate aesthetic help of people like Flaherty and Cavalcanti – our 'fellow travellers' so to speak – that we mastered the techniques necessary for our quite unaesthetic purpose. That purpose was plain and was written about often enough. Rotha spent a lot of time on it. We were concerned not with the category of 'purposiveness without purpose' but with that other category beyond which used to be called teleological. We were reformers open and avowed: concerned – to use the old jargon – with 'bringing alive new materials of citizenship', 'crystallising sentiments' and creating those 'new loyalties from which a progressive civic will might derive'. Take that away and I'd be hard put to it to say what I have been working for these past fifteen years. What, of course, made documentary successful as a movement was that in a decade of spiritual weariness it reached out, almost alone among the media, towards the future. Obviously it was the public purpose within it which commanded government and other backing, the progressive social intention within it which secured the regard of the newspapers and people of goodwill everywhere, and the sense of a public cause to be served which kept its own people together.

These facts should have made it clear that the documentary idea was not basically a film idea at all, and the film treatment it inspired only an incidental aspect of it. The medium happened to be the most convenient and most exciting available to us. The idea itself, on the other hand, was a new idea for public education: its underlying concept that the world was in a phase of drastic change affecting every manner of thought and practice, and the public comprehension of the nature of that change vital. There it is, exploratory, experimental and stumbling, in the films themselves: from the dramatisation of the workman and his daily work to the dramatisation of modern organisation and the new corporate elements in society to the dramatisation of social problems: each a step in the attempt to understand the stubborn raw material of our modern citizenship and wake the heart and the will to their mastery. Where we stopped short was that, with equal deliberation, we refused to specify what political agency should carry out that will or associate ourselves with any one of then. Our job specifically was to wake the heart and the will: it was for the political parties to make before the people their own case for leadership.

I would not restate these principles merely out of historical interest. The important point is that they have not changed at all and they are not going to change, nor be changed. The materials of citizenship today are different and the perspectives wider and more difficult; but we have, as ever, the duty of exploring them and of waking the heart and will in regard to them. That duty is what documentary is about. It is, moreover, documentary's primary service to the state: to be persisted in, whatever deviation may be urged upon it, or whatever confusion of thought, or easiness of mind, success may bring. Let no one say that a few bright-eyed films or a couple of Academy awards – from Hollywood of all places! – mean anything more than that a bit of a job was done yesterday. Tomorrow it is the same grind with ever new material – some easy, some not so easy – to be brought into design; and no percentage in it for anyone except doing the rightest job of education and inspiration we know how for the people. Considering the large audiences we now reach and the historical stakes that depend on rightness of approach, it is a privilege worth a measure of personal effort and sacrifice. If there is common agreement in the 'strategy' I have indicated, differences in daily 'tactic' will not seriously affect unity.

We should see equally straight regarding the social factor in our work over the thirties. It was a powerful inspiration and very important for that period. Without *Housing Problems* and the whole movement of social understanding such films helped to articulate, I think history would have found another and bloodier solution when the bombs first rained on the cities of Britain. But that Indian summer of decent social intention was not just due to the persistence of people like ourselves and to the humanitarian interests of our governmental and industrial colleagues. It may also have marked a serious limiting of horizons. It may have been an oblique sign that England, to her peril, was becoming interested only in herself. Some of us sensed it as we reached out in every way we knew for an opportunity of wider international state-ment. We did not, I am afraid, sense it half enough and we share the guilt of that sultry decade with all the other inadequate guides of public opinion. The job we did was perhaps a good enough job so far as it went, but our materials were not chosen widely enough.

Nothing seems now more significant of the period than that, at a time so crucial, there was no eager sponsorship for world thinking in a country which still pretended to world leadership. Russia had its third International and Germany had that geopolitical brain trust which, centred in Hausofer, spread its influence through Hess to Hitler and to every department of the Reich. In the light of events, how much on the right lines Tallents was and how blind were the people who defeated his great concept! For documentary the effect was important. The EMB, which might have done so much for positive international thinking, died seven years too early; and it was hardly, as we comically discov-ered, the job for the GPO. There was the brief, bright excursion to Geneva: there was that magnificent scheme for the ILO which Winant liked but which the Rockefeller Foundation turned down: there was my own continuous and fruitless pursuit of the bluebird we miscalled the 'Empire' and the momentary hopeful stirring in the Colonial Office under Malcolm MacDonald: there was the Imperial Relations Trust, five years too late, and affected from the first by the weight of impending events. The international factor, so necessary to a realist statement of even national affairs, was not in the deal. It is, of course, more vital than ever to a documentary policy. We, the leaders of the people and of the instruments of public opinion, have been out-thought by Russia, Germany and Japan because we have been out-thought in modern international terms. Because documentary is concerned with affecting the vital terms of public thinking towards a realistic comprehension of events and their mastery, its duty is plain. To use the phrase of these present days, you can't win the war – neither 'outside' nor 'inside' – without a revision of the public mind regarding Britain's place in the world and the larger morale that goes with a sense of being on the bandwagon of history. Thumbing a ride to the future is not nearly good enough.

I look back on Munich as representing a milestone in my own outlook on documentary. From that time on the social work in which we had been engaged seemed to me relatively beside the point. Munich was the last necessary evidence of how utterly out-of-category our political thinking was and how literally our political leaders did not know what it was all about. From that point it seemed clear that we had, willy-nilly, to relate the interests of the British people to new world forces of the most dynamic sort – physical, economic and ideological. It was inevitable that our first instinct should be to put our head in the sand and in a last frantic gesture try to avoid the implications of the future; but the significance of our indecision in regard to both Germany and the Soviet Union was plain to see. World revolution had broken out on the biggest possible scale, and to the point of having people like Churchill recognise it as such. Win or lose, the economy of Britain and her place in the world were under threat of serious alteration and, however we might presently hide our eyes, people's minds had to be prepared and made fit for them if what was great and good in Britain was to survive. It was not much use concentrating on changes in a status whose quo was being challenged from every active corner of the world and apt to be blown to historical smithereens. Internal social issues were no longer enough when the deeper political issues had become the whole of realism.

This was one person's reaction. I knew it meant the exploration of a wider basis for the public instruction which documentary represented than the reactionary regime at that time allowed. But I was altogether doubtful of where the journey would lead. I hoped, vaguely I must admit, that youth and the viewpoints their world position imposed upon them would bring a measure of progressive strength from the Dominions. I did not know how that strength could ever be articulated in time to save documentary from its greatest setback: the official sponsorship of the old, the obstinate and the inept. That period, thank heaven, is over and, in the combined force which documentary has so hardly won, it should be possible to create a new strength of thought and purpose.

In spite of many difficulties and confusions in the public scene, I see no reason why documentary should not do an increasingly useful job within the limits of official sponsorship. Some of the difficulties are constantly quoted to me and particularly from England. We are, it is emphasised, far from articulating our war aims. We still insist on tolerations and freedoms which often, some say, merely disguise the 'freedom' to go back to Britain's *status quo ante* and the 'tolerance' of past stupidities. We have not yet learned to state the new creative terms which will give reality to 'freedom' and 'tolerance' in an actual future. We denounce fanaticism in others because we have not our selves discovered a shape of things-to-come to be fanatical about. We still stand bravely but vaguely between two worlds and talk the language of indecision: resting our case on hopes of Russia and the US, the bravery of our youth, and our capacity to stand up to other people's offensives. As usual, I take the position that while I believe political issues are the whole of realism, the 'agency' of correct political change is not my concern. It may come in any colour of the rainbow, and call itself the British Council or the Society of St George for England Canterbury Inc. so long as it is the midwife of correct political change. *Die tat ist alles.* To put it in its simplest and naivest form – which is still good to remember and maintain – correct political change will be that alignment of political principles and loyalties which, given the circumstances of the world today, will best serve the interests of peoples of all lands, and the British people in proportion, and actively mobilise the native heart and mind to these ends. It will be that alignment which actively eliminates the evil forces, wherever they may be, which are against such interests and all decadent forces, wherever they may be, which are not competent to control the developing scene. That is something on which all healthy elements must agree, and the unhealthy elements present events are sufficiently taking care of. War has this grim compensation that only the successful generals are considered good ones; and there is a daily measuring-stick for leaders in that most powerful quarter of public appraisal, the stomach muscles of the people.

It is also fairly plain what areas of chaos have to be reduced to order, whatever political alignment develops. The armies of the world are carving out new geographical concepts and shapes. The processes of total war are developing new economic concepts, and more modern methods of administrative control. First things are miraculously coming first, including the food and faith of the people. Though minor social changes are not major political ones and the radish may be one colour outside and another in, the present flow of social decency must lubricate the development of state planning, corporate thinking and co-operative citizenship. The most important of the British films have, of course, been those which have seized on one or other of these changes, and it is of first-rate significance that Jack Beddington should have sponsored them. Their importance is that in explaining the shape of these developments they are exploring the inevitable shapes of the future, rough and jerry-built as they may now appear. It does not matter if the films are at first not so good. The history of documentary is the history of exploring new fields of material, always with difficulty first, then easier and better. Its chief temptation has been to abandon exploration and, doing better what has been done before, pursue the comfort of technical excellence. It will be remembered that this also was one of the reasons for Russia's attack on the 'formal arts'.

The new fields of positive material are wide and we have, all of us, only scratched the surface. The field of social changes is not, *per se*, the most important of them. Kindness in a queue at Plymouth, which means so much to the BBC overseas broadcasts, does nothing about India. The important shapes are obviously those more directly related to the national and international management of industrial, economic and human forces. They are important in winning the war without. They also represent, on a longer-term view, a new way of thought which may be the deepest need of our generation. In so far as documentary is primarily concerned with attitudes of mind, this aspect of the matter is worth a great deal of attention. 'Total war' is said to require 'total effort' but this has not been easily come by in nations which still have a hangover of nineteenth-century thinking and laissez-faire. At a hundred points today wrong attitudes are still being taught: some in innocence of the dynamic change which total effort involves: some in conscious defence of the sectional and selfish interests which total effort must necessarily eliminate. This psychological fifth column is more deeply entrenched than any other and all of us have some unconscious affiliation with it as a heritage from our out-of-date education. Rotted in the old 'untotal' ways and in the personal pleasures we enjoyed under them, we have to examine every day anew what in our words and sentiments we are really saying. A critique of sentiments is a necessary preliminary to propaganda and to documentary as its critical instrument.

It will certainly take continuous teaching of the public mind before the new relationship between the individual and the state, which total effort involves, becomes a familiar and automatic one. A beginning has been made, but only a beginning. The capacity of the individual for sacrifice has already been well described and honoured. So has team work, particularly in the fighting services. So has the mastery of some of the new technical worlds which the war has opened up. So far so good, but it is the habit of thought which drives on towards the integration of all national forces for the public good which goes to the root of things. Here we come face to face with the possibility of integrating these forces in a thousand new ways; in particular in the release of co-operative and corporate energies on a scale never dreamt of before. To consider this simply as a temporary device of war is to mistake its significance and by so doing to dishearten the people; for it is what people in their hearts have been harking for and represents the fulfilment of an era. Total war may yet appear as the dreadful period of forced apprenticeship in which we learned what we had hitherto refused to learn, how to order the vast new forces of human and material energies to decent human ends. In any case, there it is, a growing habit of thought for documentary to watch and describe and instil at a hundred points: serving at once the present need of Britain and the shape of the future.

Total effort needs, in the last resort, a background of faith and a sense of destiny; but this concept of integrating all resources to an active end gives the principal pattern for a documentary approach. It will force documentary more intimately into a consideration of active ends and of the patterns of integration which best achieve them. It will also force it into a study of the larger phases of public management which may not have seemed necessary before. To take a simple example, we have an excellent film from Anstey on how to put out incendiary bombs and handle the local aspects of fire-watching; but we have had no film covering the basic revolution of strategy in anti-blitz activities which the experience of blitz inspired. Britain's discovery of the intimate relationship between the social structure and defence provides an excellent example of 'total pattern' and indicates the revolution in public viewpoint required by total effort. Consider, at the other end of the field of war, *Time*'s report from Burma:

> The Japanese fought total war, backed by political theory and strengthened by powerful propaganda. They made this total war feasible by cornering economic life in conquered areas, utilizing labour power and seizing raw materials to supply continuing war from war itself. It is a type of war thoroughly understood by the Russians and the Germans, half adopted by the Chinese, and little understood by Britain and America.

If it is 'little understood' it only means that in this aspect of activity, as in so many others, effectiveness depends on a new way of thought which we have not mastered deeply enough to practise in new circumstances. The result of peace as well as war lies in the hands of those who understand it and can teach it.

One phrase, sticking out like a sore thumb from the reports of the eastern war, reveals a further perspective. Referring to the loss of native Burmese support, we were accused of 'lacking sound political theory'. Britain's failure to understand other points of view may again be the heritage of a period in which we were powerful enough and rich enough not to have to bother about them; but that day has gone. Again new attitudes have to be created in which Britain sees her interest in relation to others. You may call it, if you like, the way of relativity. It involves an attitude of mind which can be quickly acquired, rather than a vast knowledge of what those interests are. It will mature more easily from a consideration of the patterns of real and logical relations with other countries (geopolitical and ideological) than from exchange of 'cultural' vacua. The latter have never stood the test of events; yet Britain makes no films of the former. In this field, documentary might do much to deparochialise some of our common ways of thought. There are many opportunities. Let me take an oblique example in Anstey's *Naval Operations*. Here was a neat, tight little film with that cool technical treatment which has always been the distinction of the

Shell Film Unit. But there are other fleets beside the British, including the Russian, Dutch, Australian and Canadian. They also have 'relative' importance in a total view of naval operations. So has the German. So have the American and the Japanese, for even if the film was made before Pearl Harbor, the fleet in being is also a factor in naval operations. In this film, good as it was, the relative viewpoint was not taken because the total viewpoint was not taken, and the design of it, on the theory I am urging, belonged to the past. I am not complaining of a film I like very much. I am merely indicating how various are the opportunities for the relativity approach.

Once consider that Britain is only important as it is related to other nations and its problems and developments only important as they are recognised as part of wider problems and developments, and many subjects will reach out into healthier and more exciting perspectives of description than are presently being utilised. The past lack of a sense of relativity in Britain has been responsible for a good deal that seems trivial and even maudlin to other peoples. However stern and manly the voice that speaks it, it is still the unrelative thing it is and in my view does not give an account of the reality of the people of Britain. The falsity of the impression comes from the falsity of the approach. It will not be easily cured for it derives from historical factors of the deepest sort, and even documentary is bound to reflect them, however objective it may try to be. The fact that it is being presently cured at good speed represents indeed a triumph of clear thinking in difficult circumstances. A deliberate attempt to relate British perspectives to others would help the process. It may be the key to it. Incidentally, this relativity approach, apart from being one of the guides to a logical and sure internationalism, is a necessary guide to retaining allies. It is worth noting that there is a difference between making a film of the Polish forces to flatter Poland, or making a film of a Dominion to show what that Dominion 'is doing for England', and making a film in which Britain takes her due place in a 'total' pattern.

So much for new materials and new approaches. Styles are more difficult to talk about for they must inevitably vary with countries. I think, however, that it is possible to make certain generalisations. Since events move speedily, and opportunities pass just as speedily, the tempo of production must change accordingly. A lot has to be done and done quickly if the public mind is to be tuned in time to what, amid these swift-moving changes of public organisation, is required of it. It is not the technical perfection of the film that matters, nor even the vanity of its maker, but what happens to the public mind. Never before has there been such a call for the creation of new loyalties or bringing people to new kinds of sticking points. Times press and so must production; and with it must go a harder and more direct style. A dozen reasons make this inevitable. There is the need of striking while irons are hot, and this is particularly true of front-line reporting and has its excellent examples in the German films of Poland, the West Front and Crete, and in *London Can Take It*, the Commando raids and *War Clouds in The Pacific*. There is also the need to create a sense of urgency in the public mind, and gear it in its everyday processes to the hardness and directness which make for action and decision. If there is one thing that good propaganda must not do these days it is to give people catharsis. This again, not just because 'the war has to be won', but because as far as the eye can see, we are entering an era of action, in which only the givers of order and the doers generally will be permitted to survive. Someone winced when I suggested in England that in times of great change the only songs worth writing were marching songs. This makes the same point, except that the term must be read widely to include everything that makes people think and fight and organise for the creation of order. One doesn't have to associate oneself with the German definition of order to see that their insistence on activism is an all too successful recognition of the same need. So, with a spectacular flourish, is Goering's 'when anyone mentions the word culture, I reach for my gun'. It is not peculiarly or specially a German sentiment. In the name of the inaction they call culture they have permitted a wilderness, and it will certainly not be in the name of culture that it will blossom again. In its basic meaning, culture is surely the giving of law to what is without it. That hard but truer way of culture will not go by default if we search out the design in the seeming chaos of present events and, out of the experiments in total effort now, create the cooperative and more profoundly 'democratic' ways of the future. To go back once again to Tallents's Mill quotation, the pattern of the artist in this relationship will indicate the living principle of action.

So the long, windy openings are out and the cathartic finishes in which a good, brave, tearful, self-congratulatory and useless time has been had by all. The box office – pander to what is lazy, weak, reactionary, sentimental and essentially defeatist in all of us – will, of course, instinctively howl for them. It will want to make 'relaxation', if you please, even out of war. But that way leads nowhere. Deep down, the people want to be fired to tougher ways of thought and feeling. In that habit they will win more than a war.

PREFACE TO PAUL ROTHA'S *DOCUMENTARY FILM* (1952)

With long-standing courtesy to me, Paul Rotha has asked me to do yet another preface to yet another edition of *Documentary Film*. I appreciate the privilege, because the new edition is more complete than ever before, with Richard Griffith's special consideration of work on the American continent and Sinclair Road's wide survey of the eastern hemisphere to add to Rotha's own encyclopaedic grasp of the documentary story. I have always found this very complete acquaintance with documentary work, large and little, something to wonder at, although I saw the careful and meticulous beginnings of Rotha's records long years ago. It takes some of the weight from our other critical forays, dashing as some of them may have been: and we are all beholden to the historian of a development which time will recognise as one of the most interesting emanations of social-democratic growth over a generation.

Perhaps it is because of this deep rooting of documentary in the growth of the times that I myself most appreciate the opportunities I have had to estimate its present bearings and possible future. Certainly the nature of the documentary film shifts with the times, and the old estimates, even the old theories, have to be seen anew. It is not the least so now, when again the clash of economic and political forces represents one of the great successive points of resolution. The documentary film today reflects this in its frustrations as well as in its expectations, as from its nature it must. This, of course, is the heart of all critical matter in regard to it today.

I take a recent example in a thoughtful piece in *Sight and Sound*. It describes the documentary world of the time as the Land of Pog, and it is written by one of the younger documentary men, Quentin Dobson. The analysis is just enough so far as it goes, for he correctly remembers that documentary in its early days 'was sickened with the synthetic world of contemporary cinema . . . decided to put the real world on the screen . . . was reporter and evangelist as well . . . came down heavily in favour of all that was bright, new and humanitarian'. He likewise almost correctly estimates – referring of course only to British documentary –

that he 'finds it hard to believe that his contemporaries can make a similar claim . . . and (that now) too often film makers regard ideas as an unfortunate stumbling block to an otherwise good racket; and all is spoiled in concession to the man who foots the bill'. He asks, as so many are asking – it is 1951 remember – 'whither has fled the visionary gleam . . . and is the documentary movement to fizzle quietly out, in preoccupation with technique at the expense of ideas?' He asks finally that documentarists 'turn outward, pre-occupy themselves less with the technicalities of presentation on the screen and *more with the portrayal of flesh and blood'*. The italics are mine.

This is very much what many are thinking today, and not only in the United Kingdom; and it will, I know, concern all who, reading Rotha's book, begin to match their new understanding of documentary principles with contemporary demonstration. But is it, first of all, that Mr Dobson has proved a trifle too simple in his analysis, or shall we say, not complete enough? Yes, there was the runaway from the synthetic world of contemporary cinema, but so also, as I remember, did documentary represent a reaction from the art world of the early and middle twenties – Bloomsbury, Left Bank, T. S. Eliot, Clive Bell and all – by people with every reason to know it well. Likewise, if it was a return to 'reality' it was a return not unconnected with Clydeside movements, ILP's, the Great Depression, not to mention our Lord Keynes, the LSE, PEP and such. Documentary was born and nurtured on the bandwagon of uprising social democracy everywhere: in western Europe and the United States, as well as in Britain. That is to say, it had an uprising majority social movement, which is to say a logical sponsorship of public money, behind it.

Nor should anyone miss the fundamental point that this was true even though Conservative and National Governments were actually involved. I like to put it ironically by saying that I have enjoyed a more radical conception of documentary and a richer, more imaginative, sponsorship from the Tories than I have had from those who have been thought to be my political brothers in arms. But this is not an accident, nor to be put down, altogether, to the historic preoccupation of social democratic ministers with platform techniques, nor to the inevitable overlaying of the imaginative by the new bureaucracy which socialism-in-power swept in from the suburban intelligentsia. The fact is that the first period of the social democratic urge was in the hands of the Tories and Liberals, and we had the advantage of a period in which we could develop our concern for 'reality' without disregard for the loyalty to lyricism and 'flesh and blood' which Conservative and Liberal partisans inevitably retain as almost a plank in a political platform. In that sense, *Night Mail* and *Housing Problems* were the films of a Tory regime gradually going socialist, just as *The Plow that Broke the Plains* and *The River* of Pare Lorentz were the films of that good Tory squire, F.D.R., also, though much more gradually, going socialist.

Think, however, how different it was bound to be with socialism in power. It has, like all parties, had to recognise, and insist on, its own success. Slums? The day of the slums is over. Unemployment? We have the assurance of full employment. Fair shares for all? We have them, we have them. Moreover, it is in its way true. Relatively speaking, it is true of the Clyde and Jarrow and south Wales, and that is why Herbert Morrison invokes the slogan 'Ask your Dad'. I myself hardly need to, for I was there in my youth and know. Relatively speaking, it is true if you consider the enormous social achievement which the National Health Act represents. If it is not true – and this is where social democracy was from the beginning bound to be a compromise socialism – it is when you think over to the social patterns of others elsewhere and everywhere. I write this not to complain, however, but to analyse, for it means two things, one negative and one most positive. The negative is that social democracy has enough on its local plate to withstand the naive enthusiasm of reformists, even if they are also documentarists. The positive? Let's take Quentin Dobson's question: 'Whither has fled the visionary gleam?' It is not fled at all. So far as such obvious social fronts as were occupied in the thirties are concerned, it is there, wherever the backward peoples – or as we now more sensitively call them, the underdeveloped peoples – are to be found. The young men may talk abstractedly of the return to 'flesh and blood', but it is there most obviously if they would only ease off their fat metropolitan seats and take to wherever the peoples' problems – within the practical terms of reference which social democracy in its present phase permits – are to be faced. Of this I feel sure. The sponsorship which once so easily allowed 'flesh and blood' to the handling of British social problems must progressively allow the same wider freedom to the handling of the social problems of the Colonial peoples: that is to say, their social problems up to the point of sharp economic and political issue.

If indeed I were facing the issue of sponsorship as a young man, content with the earlier dream of documentary, I would draw a conclusion

from the appearance of *Daybreak in Udi*, and its kind. Politics is the art
of the possible, and the great possible for liberal documentary sponsorship today must, I say, lie where nations have progressively to face
world opinion, progressively have to give an account of their stewardship, progressively have to consider, through Colombo Pacts and Fourth
Points, the relationship of social progress to political and economic
events. Which reminds me. The documentary film, even under Tory
sponsorship, was the first and only true art form produced by social
democracy, and did more than later socialist leaders are inclined to
allow to make their victory emotionally real: but the greatest single
force in establishing the first majority social government was, of course,
the discovery in the blitzes of the war that the social front, in its reality
and also in its promise, was in the long run the only key to effective
defence. Napoleon had said it long before. The point is basic, however
'defence' is interpreted.

All this, I know, will not satisfy the frustrations and the expectations
which Quentin Dobson expresses. Why should it? It represents only
one aspect of the contemporary problem, only one outlet for creative
effort towards the 'flesh and blood' which is missing. Moreover, it may
seem to represent an opportunist approach which will not satisfy those
who look, shall we say, to ultimate political satisfactions and feel that
to serve present social progress in certain strategic parts of the world is
to ally oneself with reaction. However that may be – and I take the
view that social progress is an end in itself – let's see what can be done
on other fronts.

One prominent level of attack on documentary today is on the
present state of sponsorship in the western world. Dobson, like all
the others, goes for it, wondering why its liberalism is declining and by
what magic we earlier operators secured its rich co-operation. Again, I
repeat, there was no miracle about it, but a true historic root, then as
now. Look at the facts. It is true that the socialist powers have a logical
interest in stemming the tide of radicalism. It is true that they have
engaged so much of their income in social reform that they have a
professional stake in economies which affect any matter which is not
of apparent political significance or justification. It is true that the new
bureaucracies, hemmed in as they must be, are not as gay or adventurous
in the courtesies of life as the old. Nor can be, for the background of
planning and security which we once preached has come to affect us
in our own estate, as sponsors increasingly secure themselves not only

against the uncertain factors in documentary film-making but against their blatantly risen costs. Finally, the conclusion from these premises is also true. They lead to the major anomaly of government film sponsorship today. In their pursuit of economy, their new ordered working of briefs, their strict concern with what is readily and publicly justifiable, they have of course lost their way to the heart of the matter. For the paradox of the film in public information is that the peculiar powers of the medium are not engaged except there is warmth of seeing: for whatever reason, lyrical or social, or, as they used to say, dramatic. If such factors are not engaged, it is as well for the briefers to spend their money on the more economical and necessarily duller media of exposition. That is precisely what they are doing.

Yet I see behind this situation something deeper than the mere dullness of mind of an overinvolved, overdriven social-democratic phase. It is noticeable in the United States, Canada, New Zealand, Australia, Denmark, Holland and the western world generally, that this tightening of the sponsorship for documentary has taken much the same course. It is a vivid irony to me that at the very time my old regime in Canada was being straitjacketed, I found myself responsible for the self-same straitjacketing of the government set-up in the United Kingdom.

Now the British have ways of doing things which are relatively mature in their sense of public presentation, but the fact of the matter may not be the warmer for that. One of the crucial decisions in the reordering of the documentary set-up in the United Kingdom was the decision to separate the authority for the production and distribution of home films from the authority for foreign-going films. It meant, if it meant anything, that international political relationships were of such an order that every word and image had to be brought under the professional control of the diplomat. *Pari passu* went the decision to bring every aspect of home information under the jurisdiction of the department concerned. They say that only ministerial rivalries were involved, but, taken together, these decisions indicated that there was going to be no general unleashing of propaganda forces as we have had it at other times; and that whatever there was to be, was going to be under the strictest ideological control. Let's face it. Here we have a clear characteristic of the period. It can, of course, be seen even more plainly, not to say blatantly, in countries like Canada and the United States, where the arts of public expression – not to say the sensibility to liberal values – are still in the primitive stages of development. Our good old liberal attitude to documentary, and the liberal tradition of personal freedom which went with it, have been declared, in terms often arrogant and illiterate, to be a public danger; and not even the normal decencies due to tried public servants and artists have been observed. But it is the fact, however put and however personally it may apply, that matters. In these days, political issues are such that the personal freedom so many innocently seek cannot readily be expected where government funds apply and inevitable propagandist effects on mass audiences are involved. The very warmth and commanding physical power which are the pride of the documentary idea are its chiefest limitation today, save where documentary is engaged in patent pursuit of orthodox policies.

Now, in almost all the criticism of the documentary position today it is implied that the patent pursuit of orthodox policies does not allow of such warmth and such commanding physical power. It is implied that freedom beyond the orthodox political policy is necessary. This can only mean one or other of two things. The first, the 'innocent' meaning, is that the search for 'flesh and blood' has no political significance – and that we shall be content with the birds and the bees and the cigarette trees of lyricism and drama, with absolutely no root in, or reference to, ultimate political satisfactions. If so, there is certainly a successful case to be made for it; for the imaginative possession of, say, the English spring is as important to national morale and the willing acceptance of government – any government – as Britain's brilliant Health Act itself. But if there is a less 'innocent' meaning in the attack, and what we are really saying is that we want again to be radical beyond our time, then I think a sense of political humour ought to be brought into exercise.

If it may console those who presently wonder how to be left of our present political centre, at political centre's expense, let me admit that for a short period I missed the point. I thought too much in the immediate post-war period of the analogy of the 1919 post-war period. I thought there would be a lull before the new storm, of some ten years or thereabouts. I thought that the wartime discovery of social fronts and the conjoining of the Roosevelt liberal force with that of British Conservative socialism would, for a period, command the political scene in the western world and its related territories: that in the home field it would bring new reforms to the southern States as to the East

End of London; and, in the foreign field, to the sovereign poverties of Latin America as to the unsovereign poverties of Africa and the East. It was, of course, not on the cards, whether in the name of Chisholm of WHO, or of FAO, Huxley of Unesco, or myself. As the *Chicago Tribune,* the State Department, Edgar Hoover and Senator Bill Benton with his World Radio Network quickly announced, the war was on before the peace was started. No one should mistake, therefore, where documentary, costing what it does, gets off. It gets off where events and their interpretation by the forces in power allow it to get off at. The rest, however you slice it, is not art but politics. But who, for that matter, will say that the prospect is not as wonderful as ever it was in the whole history of mankind?

For those who are not immediately or professionally concerned with the political task as such, I have already noted certain promising fronts on which, within stated limitations, a man may richly work. The work to be done for the undeveloped peoples is enormous, whether it be in teaching new techniques and social patterns, or in reflecting the great and wonderful force they represent in our contemporary world. I have noted that the battle for lyricism can be fought and won, even in such preoccupied areas as present-day Whitehall, if the young men will give their hearts to it; for this is so much within the logic of the present phase of politics that if the socialist ministers do not encourage it, be sure the Conservative ones most promptly will. Likewise, I have suggested that there is nothing in the present situation to prevent all sorts of approaches to the sponsorship of 'flesh and blood', so long as it is the flesh and blood of orthodox political policy. There are forces within the more powerful western regimes who would give much for a school of documentary which will preach the British way of life, the American way of life, etc., in the strategic areas of the world and bring alive western 'democratic' principles to those exposed to other-than-western 'democratic' principles. There is, so to speak, still money in Magna Carta if you want it that way. *Chacun à son gout.* We have, as I write, the interesting spectacle of Canada, from the environs of Duplessis and medieval pre-revolutionary Quebec, planning a programme which will teach the European heirs of the revolutions of '79 and '48 what their great-great and great-great-great-grandfathers were fighting about. God rest the soul of Mackenzie King! Similarly, anyone can be as lyrical and human as he likes on a theme which, like the Rhine, might have its effect on eastern European loyalties. For ECA, or OEEC, will be there at his elbow; and to tell the truth, to this moment, they have been most imaginatively at various elbows, seeing precisely, as professional propagandists should, where identities of interest can be established between frustrated liberals and their American terms of reference. On a bet, anyone with a care for WHO, or FAO, or Unesco will find a friend in ECA, though the terms of the contract will also be precise. So it goes, as it must; but so too it goes where other and different political ortho-doxies are involved.

For the purpose of this analysis I am, therefore, in the position to register a double prospect of comfort, with Marshal Tito, King Farouk and Dr Malan not by any means to be disregarded as potential, most generous, sponsors of all adventures into their particular areas of 'flesh and blood'. If, as an old radical, stil very conservative in my memory of what the Clydeside taught, I note all these courses and choose other-wise, it is because of my belief that there is yet another true dramatic implication in the phase through which we are passing. The Clydeside cult was the most humanist in the early socialist movement. This was its deep political weakness, as Lenin himself pointed out, and men like James Maxton came practically to demonstrate. But while recognising this, as one must, the overriding humanist factor did not thereby lose its ultimate validity. It has seemed to me, on the other hand, to assume more and more validity as the harder forces of political organisation have taken control of the thoughts we had and the sympathies we urged. For myself, I shall only say that what I may have given to documentary – with the working man on the screen and all that – was simply what I owed to my masters, Keir Hardy, Bob Smillie, and John Wheatley; and no one will understand me better in this than the Rt Hon. Walter Elliot who calls himself a Tory. But still larger forces have, over the generation, been following the line of remaining ever close to the people and, in the very midst of socialist success, expressing their disquiet lest the contact be lost. Bernard Shaw from his earliest period and H. G. Wells in his later disappointed period were peculiarly aware that the pro-gressive order they so greatly urged had its other and counter-half in the rich and variant force of human beings themselves. That is why G.B.S. was so quick to qualify his own arguments and even demolish them as he called up his images of the life-force or produced his Doolittles and Undershafts as token of continuing reality. That too is why our social-democratic generation had almost of necessity to pro-duce G. K. Chesterton and D. H. Lawrence and declare, sometimes with passion, that there could be no unity without difference and no progressive ordering of society without creating a complementary hunger for variety. One sees now a strange, almost perverse, dislike in high quarters for the celebration of regional vitalities, and for anything that savours of satiric reference to the new and wondrous forms of the socialist state. You can trace it all the way from ministers and their PEP boys to the BBC. This is to be expected of socialism-in-early-power; for its first efforts were bound to put restraints on the hopes of the working people who brought it to power; and it could not do other than concentrate first on the centralised plan. But for these very reasons, the perversion of ultimate progress can be but momentary and one is not the less aware of this in the light of socialist experience elsewhere. From this I deduce that we shall be finding the people again in the regional variation, in satire of the very forms which are presently our pride, and in description of the living reaction to the changing social patterns everywhere. Our social-democratic ministers may not directly finance it yet, at least not in the name of public information, and that is just too bad, of course, for the Crown Film Unit and such.

But, on the other hand, if the coincident hunger for variation, or the *élan vital*, or whatever you like to call it, emerges with the logical necessity that I have suggested, it must appear in terms of theatre demand. If so, it cannot fail to interest the economists of the film industry and the Boards of Trade who stand now, more and more deeply, behind them. So, with any luck, you may play the swings as well as the roundabouts. I look on the happy success of the Italian films recently, the miraculous return of Charlot and the prospering fortunes of my old friend Joe Burstyn in the 'art' theatres of the United States, and I think I see a light. Dare I say it? In spite of all Hollywood and State Department evidence to the contrary, it may be that there is also a gal in Kalamazoo.

With which, let me invite you one and all to look upon the record and make your own estimate of where so great and present a medium is now to go.

ART AND REVOLUTION (1966)

Now this business of revolution in the arts is, as you know, a large subject which can be approached from many angles; but I will put to you first a simple proposition which I think will take you quite a way – not all the way but quite a way. The proposition it this – and I merely put it to you as a primary exercise: that *while you may consider Russia as the great homeland of political revolutionaries in our time, you may well consider America as the great homeland of aesthetic revolutionaries in our time*. And it's an odd thing: you may not breed all the revolutionaries yourselves but most of them, wherever they come from, tend to finish up under your protection.

If this is true, or even half true, I think it would be interesting to wonder why. As some of you may know, I have spent some years of my working life in North America and as a foreigner I have certainly been very much influenced by it. I think therefore it would be very proper to our argument if I told you something of the America which imposed its image on me and on my work as I first came face to face with it in 1924.

I had a perfectly good degree in philosophy at the time and a perfectly good fellowship; but against all academic advices I elected for the maelstrom of Chicago. Well, first of all, there were the attractions of people like Sandburg and Vachel Lindsay and Sherwood Anderson. Here too was where Upton Sinclair had roared his head off and the Shame of the Cities was supposed to most manifest.

I am afraid I approached the Shame of the Cities with no great moral fervour but rather with a sense of dramatic anticipation; and I certainly wanted a sight of the yellow press at its yellowest. There was too, of course, the great giant figure of Frank Lloyd Wright in the mid-western background. In a sense he meant more to me than anyone, and still in that same sense does.

But what decided me was another kind of reality and in fact the kind of reality from which, as I shall maintain in this talk, aesthetic form finally derives. It was the long immigrant length of Halstead Street. Here was the melting pot. Here was where the people of many lands were made over into Americans in three generations. Here if anywhere was my generation in the modern world on the progressive boil and I wanted to know. In fact I not only elected for Chicago but elected to come as I thought an earnest student of the real America should. I came in a bootlegger charged with the solemn duty of delivering thirty thousand cases of Scotch whisky to these eager all-absorbing shores. 'Give us your poor', you asked on the Statue of Liberty. I brought you the whisky.

This Chicago of 1924 or 1925 or 1926 was certainly an exciting place for a young man to be around. The gang wars were only one aspect of the growing pain of a fast-growing immigrant town. It was the sort of thing you might expect in a city where the foreign origins and loyalties were not yet resolved. The first generation of immigrants was caught up often in foreign-speaking households with their own European loyalties and the new community had its very different loyalties. As a result the new generation often grew up in the streets without real benefit of either.

Yet the desperate effort to become American had its own crude influence on the approach to the arts. I am thinking of the mental habit which developed of thinking old things bad, and new things necessarily good. In the circle I knew best, the word 'modern' had a sanctity which it never had in the Europe I had left. One year when Big Bill Thompson had a city exposition he was reminded that he had better do something about the arts. OK said Big Bill, but none of your old stuff, nothing but new, nothing but the modern for this, the greatest of all possible cities of the future. And modern it was; under the direct influence and auspices of a mayor who, to say the least, didn't know Picasso from a hole in the ground.

I'm sure that much of the American interest in modern aesthetic movements and America's creation of them derives from this American desire to be forward looking at all costs; but there were other aspects of the life of Chicago which even more directly dictated drastic approaches to the arts.

I myself came out of Chicago with a theory about film-making which has in its day been regarded as a novel and even dynamic contribution to cinematic theory. I want to take you back for a moment to Halstead Street and the problem of making over the immigrants from the European way of life to the American way of life. My natural interest in the yellow press didn't turn out to be altogether useless because I quickly came to the conclusion that the yellow press, for all its sensationalism, was the most important factor in this revolutionary educational exercise. It was the only English press the immigrants read because it was in fact the only one they could read, with its simple headline stories and its pictures. What fascinated me as a European was the way the Hearst press and its imitators on every level of journalism had turned into a 'story' what we in Europe called 'report'. They had in fact made the story, that is to say a dramatic form, the basis of their means of communication.

This seemed to me a highly logical way of approaching the problem of mass communication. What was most significant was that the story line was a peculiarly American story line. The reportorial headline of Europe was out. The contemplative headline was as dead as the dodo. The active verb had become the hallmark of every story worth while. Something had to do something to something else. Somebody had to do something to someone else. In fact the world the newspapers reflected was a world on the move, a world going places.

All I did in my theory of the documentary film was to transfer that concept to film-making and declare that in the actual world of our observation there was always a dramatic form to be found if you would only look for it enough. Something was doing something to something else, somebody was doing something to someone else. I saw in it an instrument not only of education and illumination in our highly modern world but as an instrument highly necessary to a democratic society.

Of course I saw it not only as a cinematic way of revealing the *dramatic* nature of the actual but also as capable of revealing the *poetry* of the actual. And this I could not help noting because already in America in the pioneer work of Flaherty you had shown the way to the combination of the dramatic and the poetic in describing the actual lives of the peoples of the Arctic and Polynesia. What Chicago and the journalistic approaches of America gave was the vital thought that there, tucked away potentially in the cinema, was a medium of illumination and persuasion to be put in the hands of democratic forces everywhere.

Well, we have seen how the early Hearst example has developed dramatically and visually to produce the powerful magazines of the world. And the documentary version of it, allied more specifically to educational ends and public purposes, has had its own successes all over the world and its own influence not only on the cinema but not least on television. But remember the origin because it is from such real origins always that innovations in art derive.

There were other democratic forces at work in the Chicago I speak of and other fresh contributions to the arts of expression. I was not long there when I first heard a young man called Louis Armstrong blow his horn. In fact we were in the early pioneer days of Chicago jazz. Much came from that as you know. I was quite sure then that it would inevitably contribute from its fresh and different springs of inspiration to the main stream of music, just as the folk songs of Europe had contributed to the classical music of Beethoven and Brahms and Bartók and Sibelius. Some of the musicians among you must tell us why it hasn't – but certainly jazz represented a movement in the arts which has affected people everywhere.

Here again the origins were very real ones to which you Americans can readily give a habitation and a place. But when you talk of the Negro's racial memories, the Negro's peculiar attachment to religious feelings, the Negro's reason for sadness and sorrow and consequent power to express the melancholy of a people, you must think too that it was the triumphant beat and the triumphant blast of the horn which made jazz all-American and one of the great images of the all-American in the world today. In that matter, it may be that the Negro American has been as sensitive to the positive aspect of the American vision as any other of America's constituent citizens.

At this point I should mention a basic source of change in the arts. *Art changes as society changes, as new economic forces and widening horizons establish new habits of thought and new values among men; and as these, in turn, suggest new dramatic patterns and images of beauty.* This I shall have to return to as one of the fundamental laws governing aesthetics; but here let me speak of a man I met in Chicago who taught me much. He was Rudolph Weisenborn the painter. I spent a lot of time with him and much of that time we spent just wandering round the city looking and looking at its sprawling growth, sprawling outward and sprawling upward, building and boiling. I never knew a man so dedicated to his home town; but not as William Alan White was in the case of Emporia, Kansas, because of the worthiness of its citizens and their devotion to the ultimate cultural decencies. Weisenborn was excited by the thing in itself: the image of action everywhere, the visual dynamics that went with this city on the build; images many of them that had never been seen or seeable before the vast volumes of the buildings and the bridges and the overhead railroads and the swinging curves that connected them. And above all there were the extraordinary effects of light on the new materials the builders and engineers disposed of. An asphalt surface could look brighter than the bright of the sky above. The concrete and the glass and the aluminium and the steel and the synthetic materials the architects were now using were catching the light in a new way as indeed by all the laws of nature they had to. You were a world away from the light on satins and silks and velvets and all the substance of ancient interiors. You were a world away from the natural surfaces of nature itself.

There was another powerful shift in our visual attitudes. We were no

longer seeing a prairie stretching away to the horizon; we were no
longer seeing a man against the sky. Our world of space was no longer
that kind of space at all. Wherever we were, we were seeing up and
seeing down; we were at the *centre* of seeing. This was in simple fact
what our man-built metropolitan world necessarily imposed on us. At
that time the cinema was growing up and some of us, when we put
our minds to it, immediately realised that the eye level of the camera
could be anywhere at all, that it was not necessarily tied to the human
eye level of a man moving around on his feet in space. We pioneers of
movie criticism were supposed to be very bright when we announced
the new visual logic of the Kino eye. But there we were in Chicago
actually seeing with Kino eye simply because the shapes and sizes of
our modern city imposed the Kino eye upon us.

By that illustration I am suggesting to you that our sense of relationship with the world of modern art can come to us as quite a natural
phenomenon, as an even inevitable result of the new world we have
built to live in and actually observe. I am suggesting to you that what
some people think of as *abstract* art may be in fact the most *naturalistic*
and the most *realistic* description of what we see, consciously or
unconsciously, as we move about in our metropolitan world. And so
constant must be the impact that this new way of looking, this new
way of seeing every angle and in terms of a dynamic whole, is in fact
becoming a natural and necessary habit of vision; so that when we
come to landscape we must see it likewise. And again I suggest for
your thought that there is no country in which this new way of seeing
can be so natively and naturally come by as America. If this rule is
valid, the same shift in the habit of vision will affect your appreciation
in all the arts of expression.

Now I am afraid I must return to that fundamental principle which
governs all remarkable changes in art. Have you ever stopped to consider why perspective came into painting with the Bellini in Venice? Or
why the introduction of real characters came into painting, and into
drama too, in countries like Holland and England? I think it was your
American Mumford who first noted that perspective came into Venice
because Venice was the first great port of our expanding world, a port
where the habit of thought was in terms of navigation and the mastery
of space. Just think of it; they had had to understand perspective to
make their sea-going charts.

Then again with the growth of commerce the formal hierarchy of values of the Middle Ages had broken down. The initiative of the individual assumed a new importance; and a new leadership, with different habits of thought, came in every sense into the public picture. It was a world of real characters instead of formal ones. That was when the burghers of the ancient and royal town of Reading hanged the Abbot of Reading on the doorstep of his own abbey. It was as significant an execution as the execution of Charles I and Louis XVI later on. It was an American, Frank Lloyd Wright, who most loudly questioned the importance of the renaissance of Greek and Roman values in the fifteenth and sixteenth centuries. Consider this simple possibility, that the revolution came wherever the ships and the shipman were, wherever the horizons were in fact widening and the individual seaman or merchant had become master of his fate. You will find an odd comment on this in another American writer, James Branch Cabbell. He once wrote an essay called *Beyond Life* in which he viewed with horror the appearance of individual characters in the drama and, if I remember, suggested that Marlowe was the big one and that the British theatre went to pieces with Shakespeare.

I very much recommend to you this controversy about the true nature of the aesthetic revolution associated with the Renaissance. You may think as I do that the revolution came from the very real changes represented by the ships and the new horizons and the new men and the new habits of thought that came with them. In that case you will have to look on the neo-classical architecture as merely a fashionable exercise in status symbols on the part of the *nouveaux riches* of the time. You will remember Voblen and the principle of conspicuous waste. If you are wise, however, you will also quietly take a reservation on the thought that the classical architecture was in a sense symbolic and expressive of the new inclination towards the ordered and the rational in the management of society.

I myself find it pleasant to think that your own neo-classical phase with its colonial splendours had less to do with the reality of a frontier country than it had anywhere in Europe, and I am not surprised that that old dyed-in-the-wool American Frank Lloyd Wright exploded at the static and totally inappropriate presence of the neo-classical in your dynamic midst. Sentimentally you may regret such a conclusion, even as I do, because like all the students of all the older universities in Europe I was soaked in the Renaissance, and taught blindly to respect it. I am bound, however, by any understanding I may have of aesthetic, to drive you in a different direction for the revolutionary art of that period and to direct your attention rather to the inner nature of the Elizabethan drama and of the carvings and paintings associated with Holland and Germany and in fact all the countries of the Hanseatic League.

When you think of your colonial arts you may also conclude that a political revolution does not necessarily lead to an aesthetic one. You may well have a political revolution, you may well destroy an old political regime, without changing the habits of thought that existed before the revolution. In the case of America, the revolution was very late in the day. It was of course the same mercantile revolution which had taken place in England in the seventeenth century, and in France in the eighteenth; and the new habit of thought, and all the new arts that went with it, were already well established everywhere when the Americans came into the battle.

What you can say is that the changing habit of thought deriving from new economic and social dispositions, and the arts which express them, are more likely to create political revolutions than vice versa. You have an excellent illustration in the eighteenth century in France. The divine right of kings had been long challenged by the growing powers of the merchants who were footing the royal bills. The rationalisation of their claim to civic position expressed itself brilliantly in the individualistic philosophy of men like Voltaire and Rousseau and in the splendid literary works of their circle. This in turn with its declaration of the rights of man conquered men's minds and made the French Revolution the historical landmark it was.

Here in America you of course took over the rights of man and wrote them into your constitution, but in so doing you took over certain implications within the rights of man which were not altogether evident in the eighteenth century. Dear old Jean-Jacques Rousseau had carried the theory to extremes. Forgetting all about the merchants who had started the whole business, he pictured the absolute worth of the individual whether he was a merchant or not. The eighteenth-century theorists had considered the individual as a rational being only. Rousseau thought of him as an emotional being too, not to be measured for his reason only but for himself. In fact by the time the eighteenth-century masters had done they had started another and very real revolution in the arts. They had started the romantic movement, the return to nature. A man was a man for all that whatever his origin or status. Of course much in the way of poetry and painting came from that, and you have only to think of Burns in my own country and Wordsworth and Byron in England and the flood of romanticists that came after them.

I don't think these more romantic implications of the French revolutionary theory got very far as a political revolutionary force in Europe. It came unstuck with the revolutions of 1848 and has been unstuck to this day, not least under Communism. The doctrine that a man's a man for all that is held to be an anarchic and dangerous doctrine, as it may well be. It threatens the disciplines of the community. But it was certainly tailor-made for a young and growing country which more specifically depended, on every frontier, on a man being a man for all that, a country which more specifically had to believe that a man was a man for all that, as it invited the peoples of all orders to its all-embracing shores. In fact while the romantic movement found its first poets in Europe, it belongs to you in America far more deeply, because you alone were in a position to find an economic reality for it.

But as you pursue the influence of the romantic movement on your arts all through the nineteenth century, you must find, even as Europe did, that its ideals proved also to be impractical. One of these days you younger students of political philosophy will come to a dissertation by Lenin called 'Left-Wing Communism an Infantile Disorder'. Stop and ponder; because he is really talking of the very romantic doctrine which for a whole century informed your lives and inspired your arts. And when in the classrooms you consider Jean-Jacques Rousseau or are invited to celebrate with whisky and haggis the glory of Burns, you will doubtless remember that the romantic songs of the itinerant workers of America came to be songs of disillusionment. The invitation to the bees and the cigarette trees and the lemonade springs where the blue-bird sings by the Great Candy Rock Mountains is in fact the song of a social castaway. And when you note the poetic strain in the last address of Vanzetti you will doubtless note that it is the same identical poetic strain of that other prisoner of society, Silvio Pallico, long years before.

The romantic movement did, however, do something very important for the American arts. It started you looking at your country with American eyes and not with European ones. I personally think well of Longfellow, if only because he stood his American ground and asserted the positive existence of the forest primeval and the murmuring pines and the hemlock, and the dark cypresses of the Mediterranean be damned. But of course that's a story you know far better than I do.

What I think interests the European most is not the delighted discovery of your frontiers in, say, Mark Twain, but the fate of all his possessing idealism which swept over American expression in the nineteenth century. It seemed that Hegel, with his upward and onward pursuit of the absolute, had a whole nation at his feet: with Emerson of course the all too certain voice of the prophet at one end, and Walt Whitman the all too certain voice of the poet at the other, demonstrating that here in America at last it was going to be for the best of all possible worlds.

Here again of course the special character of your arts was determined by the reality. You had a wide, wide world for your domain with every seeming potential of wealth and welfare. You were drawing from all the world men who were putting poverty and frustration and even slavery behind them and reaching for a new heaven and a new earth. Give us your poor, you spoke grandly on the Statue of Liberty. Your literature, your poetry and your painting duly reflected that faith and were duly splendid in rhetoric. For us outsiders Winslow Homer carried the same sort of wallop as Whitman.

But of course, as ever in the history of art, new realities were waiting for you round the corner. I am not thinking of the individual scepticism about the glorious cavalcade of American progress which you get I think in Thoreau on one line of thought and Edgar Allan Poe on another. I am thinking of the more general basic disillusionment that came with the discovery of evil and the muckrakers. At the least, Captain Ahab might go down heroically with his ship and even then if you remember he nailed his flag to the mast as it went under. But the great white whale, the embodiment of evil, had beaten him and that in a sense was your great moment of national truth.

I have seen it repeated over and over again that the significance of Moby-Dick was first noted in Europe: and that would be no wonder because the power of evil is something we traditionally know about. Naturally and natively we allow for the permanence of tragedy. Even Trotsky, you may remember, found that he had to break all the Marxist rules and allow for the permanence of tragedy. For Europeans certainly it is a remarkable phenomenon in the history of your arts that you alone of all peoples actually went through the process of rediscovering the permanence of tragedy as though it were a new revelation. It accounts possibly for the sometimes violence of your approach to the tragic in literature; it accounts certainly for some of the sense of disillusionment and even bitter and brutal disillusionment which has to some extent informed your arts in general. And when I say that there is something in you so deeply rooted in romanticism that you do not really accept the permanence of tragedy even now – that in fact you *refuse* in your hearts to accept it – it explains a great deal in your arts. It certainly explains Hemingway.

Other countries in our own times have certainly had more immediate reason for despair and you have only to think of Germany after the First World War. There, as you now see in France, the sense of defeat drove the artist in on himself, in on his own mind, in on his own fancies; and indeed much of the art that came out of both Germany then, and is coming out of France now, may reflect not the ancient and basic aesthetic tradition which is to seek a harmony in the world of your observation but rather the opposite: a drive to express in disharmony one's conviction of disharmony as an absolute fact of one's observation. This is a danger to be watched at all times; the art of the negative is going nowhere.

As I keep reminding you, the changes in the reality dictate the changes in the arts. What I think we have most surely to do as observers of the arts is to realise the great shapes of change in the reality which drive the arts historically forward. Lack of personal faith in human progress cannot possibly be one of them. The artist, however sensitive and however hurt, cannot contract out of his aesthetic duty to life itself, which is a duty to the positive future of the world he lives in, for all its immediate disappointments. The most bitter of all satirists, Jonathan Swift, still kept swinging to the end to demonstrate that in satire hate is forever a love–hate, with the love even more manifest in the end than the hatred.

Now I will suggest to you what I think are the great basic changes in our modern reality which have most affected the modern arts. First I will remind you that the march of science and the impact of scientific thought and scientific images have been one of the most powerful facts of life in the last century. The new images which the architecture of Chicago imposed on me, as I noted, were after all only made possible because of certain scientific developments. Think too that the study of light which became a passion with the impressionists arose from the new scientific understanding of the nature of light. Think too that post-impressionism and cubism after that and many of the experiments associated with the Bauhaus were a reflection of the new world of shapes which science was revealing to us or making possible for us. It is my own habit to see films shot on every possible frontier of human observation and that of course includes the world of physics, the world of biology and the worlds of scientific enquiry in general. The shapes that are now common to my observation are bewildering in their variety. And they must mean an intensive visual enrichment for every man with any appreciation of shapes. I don't think you will find it difficult to see the impact of that rich world of observation on both our architecture and our painting.

I would go on to say that the common appreciation today of the world as a changing world, a dynamic world, is quite a new kind of common appreciation. You only have to think of a relatively static society like Athens to realise how different the impact of our own world must be on human thought. And this in turn must mean that, as we see action as ever more important in the world we live in, our images and our designs must inevitably attempt to reflect our appreciation of action.

Here I would refer you to yet another of the basic changes in our era. It is a change in ourselves. I have talked of how we are bombarded with the new images of the new worlds which our scientific discoveries have created; but I can't think of any atom bombardment greater than this constant bombardment of our minds with the actualities of our widening horizons; and the fact that we have not altogether been blinded by our own sciences demonstrates a remarkable resilience of the human spirit, and not least the resilience of the common man who is less equipped to cope with what is, for the best of us, philosophers and artists alike, a bewildering spectacle. But this same development has created a new world for us as social beings. We are no longer the citizens of a feudal village or a walled city. Our immediate community is tied inalienably to a wider community and in the last resort, as Wendell Wilkie said, we are citizens of one world. This again must have its effect on our aesthetic perception just as it has a profound effect on our lives. Again our ever widening habits of thought must affect our valuations and therefore our sense of appreciation.

First of all there are negative reactions. The new world can be felt as so large and so complex that it seems to overwhelm our capacity to find the harmonies within it which the human spirit forever seeks and must seek. One tendency, as I said before, may be to see only the disorder. There must be a tendency to feel a certain hopelessness of finding order within that seeming disorder. You will therefore expect some pessimism and even some despair in our present aesthetic expression in general. I refer you to Beckett's *Waiting for Godot* as a remarkable account of this modern dilemma. Waiting for Godot we are, all of us; but what of course is hopeful in the situation is that in merely believing in Godot you find him.

There is even an element of mental breakdown in the individual to be taken account of. Brought up in old-time individualistic expectations we have come face to face with the fact that we are expected to be organisation men, subject as individuals to responsibilities determined by corporate ends and not individualistic ones. The very presence of these psychological problems must again affect the arts. I don't think I am wrong in seeing a certain relationship between the modern psychological dilemma and, say, some of your own American experiments in ballet and music and comedy. I don't wonder that the words 'beat' and 'sour' now belong to the aesthetic vocabulary. They are the marks of much that is personally unresolved in our experience as citizens. And why do we like it sour? Because it is a true reflection of a very deep reality indeed, even if it is only a temporary one.

Mind you, there is much to occupy and console us in this aesthetic Odyssey of ours. The seasons will still follow their ancient order. The dew will still be pearly early in the morning. Love will still be hopeful or hopeless as the case may be and still in one way or another seem ultimate to someone. There will in fact be the lyrical absolute to take hold of whether it comes as Dr Seldes's Krazy Kat and the feather that Jeeza Weeza is so foolish with, or with Mann on flute, or for that matter with Shelley's skylark, which I am sure is still up singing.

Fashions of expression will change as they must do but the arts must continue to be, rooted finally in the traditional absolutes of human destiny. Macbeth will still be Macbeth even when he turns up as a First Secretary of the Party in Moscow or for that matter as an ambitious baron of General Motors. One can still see Hamlet dithering for a long time to come, and not the less so when, as now, there is much to dither about. Nor can I see Bach and all he represents in music beaten out of his place in our minds, and for the simple reason that the will to order is an absolute of the human spirit at all times. I personally, excited as I am about all the changes in the arts, both positive and negative, intrigued as I am by the changing habits of thought which cause them, do not feel under any particular duty to deny the majesty of

Michelangelo's images of human splendour. Nor do I find the 19th Psalm out of date for all the discoveries of the scientists. The Heavens declare the glory of God, it says. One might conceivably think that the scientists have simply given us more to declare glorious.

Perhaps we don't yet match the arts of other times when they arrived at their particular peaks of expression. That would be too much to ask. But there is much we have in our midst that comes out of the same spiritual force, the same aesthetic drive which informed the master poets and master dramatists and master painters and master architects of history. I for one, for example, would not trade the blossoming architecture of America for any other architecture I know – or trade our modern painting for any other painting I know. That is where we live and have our being. The arts of older times we can admire, but it is in these even now unfinished and incomplete arts of our own time that we must draw our strength as present and living beings. So I say to you finally with Sir Christopher Wren – *Circumspice Circumspice* – look around you, look around you.

ANSWERS TO A CAMBRIDGE QUESTIONNAIRE (1967)

Q. 1 As a director and producer do you see yourself as an educator an artist or a philosopher?

This will be a collection of bits and pieces. I shall go on as your questions lead and doubtless will repeat myself and contradict myself. But no matter.

Rather than answer your questions in personal terms I think it would be more useful to remind you of (1) the nature of the documentary idea; (2) the development of the documentary idea on various levels (e.g. (a) reportage, (b) reportage in depth, (c) dramatisation of the actually observed, (d) poetic interpretation of the actually observed, etc.); (3) the development of the documentary idea in its *uses* – (a) in the theatre for its ancillary entertainment values, (b) by governments in the presentation of the nation's image to itself and others, i.e. propaganda in the larger long-term interpretation, (c) by governments for its more immediate instructional and propagandist uses (as in many emergent countries today), (d) by commercial and industrial organisations for (i) local instructional purposes (including, in some areas, instruction in nutrition, health, etc.), (ii) the improvement of its public image in depth (i.e. the larger public significance of its operations) (Shell is a good example in both categories).

Even this analysis does not give anything like a complete picture of the many various developments of the documentary use of film. You have to take note of that development against the many and various political and economic backgrounds of the scores of countries (socialist and non-socialist) who, largely from the example set originally by the UK and Canada, have developed the documentary film as a deliberate instrument of public policy.

Above all, you should be guided by the inalienable fact that film is a relatively expensive medium, and even at the single-minded amateur level. Contrast the position of the free poet, free painter, free writer, with the would-be free film-maker, from an economic point of view. He must depend largely on personal wealth or access to personal wealth. For the most part, and you must take it as an invariable rule, he has to come to terms with the economic and political realities from which access to the means of production and distribution derives. In some cases (France and French Canada provide amusing examples) he will make his deal with the political and economic realities, then proceed to double-cross them in the name of freedom of expression, etc. But he will not get away with it often.

On the other hand, he can, in all fidelity to his public undertaking, emerge with a film far beyond the expectations of his sponsors in the matter of aesthetic quality. He may even, in certain ideal personal relationships with his sponsors, establish an aesthetic expectation of his public work, and further establish the long-term advantage of it. This is what happened to the British documentary movement in the thirties and at the Crown Film Unit during the war. The National Film Board of Canada is probably the best example because its relationship in depth with its public contract (including aesthetic depth) has lasted longer than anywhere else and is in very good health today.

Holland is a good example of this higher sponsorship, partly due to the personal powers of persuasion of individuals like Haanstra, but partly also to a correct reading, by both the Dutch Government and the larger industrial sponsors, of the English example.

In all the socialist countries, public sponsorship is permissive of aesthetic achievement – but there are many, many variants – from the USSR at the one end of the scale to Yugoslavia at the other – dependent on other factors than the powers of personal persuasion on the part of

the documentary film-makers and the personal imagination of the
responsible public officers: e.g. national or sectional emotions over-
coming the doctrinaire party line in Poland, Czechoslovakia, Hungary,
Romania and Yugoslavia, with interesting new signs from the outlying
studios of the USSR.

You may conclude: (1) that access to the means of production and
distribution being paramount, the political and economic factor in
documentary development has been the key to its world-wide development, and that it was this basic assumption which made the United
Kingdom the paternal source of the whole process; (2) that the many
various forms of documentary construction and use will inevitably
emerge; (3) that even within the limits so set, an aesthetic result of the
largest quality is possible; (4) that what emerges in quality, especially
in the more obvious aesthetic categories, will depend on: (a) the powers
of persuasion of the documentary producer *vis-à-vis* the political and
economic reality, (b) the imagination of the ministers and public officers
who provide the authority and, as a last resort, the defence for experiment and adventure, (c) ideally a personal relationship on the highest
level between (a) and (b).

From all that you may get some sort of an answer to your Question
1. I could say shortly: (1) I have been associated with some large exer-
cises in national and international education (in the widest sense of the
word). (2) I have been associated with making many good films. (3) My
basic academic origin was in political philosophy but I would rather
note that I have been a highly practical operator in the field, in the
sense that the original analysis of the documentary potential was
largely mine, and its management in the original key situation was
my responsibility. A point worth noting is that at all times I was both
the producer-in-charge and the public officer with the necessary government authority – worth noting because the development in some
places of a gulf between the public authority and the production
process has diminished the quality of the 'movement'.

I shall do that last piece over again because of a new question
suggested. Consider the development of a 'movement' like documentary, and you had better call it a 'movement' or a 'drive' or something
because it was a considered effort to mobilise an economic place for
the serious film-maker within the politico-economic framework (first
in the capitalist–socialist framework of the West, thereafter in the
more self-conscious socialist countries). To make it work involved (a) a

theoretical analysis of the possibility, (b) a promotion of the idea, (c) an involvement with the politico-economic power and a certain participation in its management, (d) a production and distribution process and organisation of the machinery therefor.

(a) means that you are an analyst of some sort of the political condition and of the relations of the artist with the community and of the confusions and arguments that must arise on that score in (i) fast-moving revolutionary periods like, say, the eighteenth century, or the nineteenth century of industrial Britain, (ii) the contemporary period of mass management and mass communication and absentee landlordism in the biggest way. (b) and (c) above mean that you will have to be a bit of a propagandist for the idea *vis-à-vis* the persuaders (e.g. in my case, the *London Times* and influential individual supporters like H. G. Wells); *vis-à-vis* the powers that be (e.g. in my case, ministers like Elliot and Mackenzie King), and *vis-à-vis* civil servants and accountants-general not least. This in turn makes you incidentally something of a teacher or even a preacher: certainly a fellow traveller in the national and international business of communication: certainly also a bit of a politico.

Consequent success on these levels might leave you *tout simple* a propagandist for the powers that be. But watch. In the process of promotion you have built up an idea because it has public worth, and public value for the powers that be. In the documentary story this hinged basically on its dramatic educational potential in the field of communication. You will not have said much about the aesthetic potential, not to mention any personal aesthetic ambition you may have. It is not of primary concern to the powers that be. This you will only reveal to individuals who natively appreciate the aesthetic factor in mass communications and in public management and have a personal concern for the personal contribution which the aesthetic factor supplies. But when you talk politically of '*bringing* England *alive* to herself in the modern world', 'filling the Canadian mind with such images as will give its citizens a more vital appreciation of Canada's individuality as a nation and so *condition* their mind to a greater will for the future' – you have involved yourself not only in the propagandist implication of the word 'condition', but also in the aesthetic implication of the phrase 'bringing alive'.

In other words, I cannot answer Question 1 as you put it in your subdivisions. Your subdivisions are all part of the same thing so far as I am concerned. One thing you may find interesting is this. Except under the special circumstances I have noted, you do carry a *secret* intention (the aesthetic one). You will find an excellent presentation of this in Trilling's essay on Izaac Babel. That 'secret' intention cannot always be revealed, but there will be much sensing of the fact that you carry it. So you will always be subject to a certain mistrust and even a certain inarticulate opposition at many points of your bureaucratic journey. After all, you *are*, from many a point of view, taking the wooden horse of aesthetic into Troy. The story of the documentary movement is, in part, the story of how, not without a scar or two, we got by. Maybe you win more or less for keeps, as in the case of the National Film Board of Canada. Maybe you lose, though never altogether, to the bureaucrats and the other boys behind the woodwork (e.g. the Crown Film Unit and the present Central Office of Information in the UK).

The fact is that there are many real sources of opposition to the idea of art (activist) in the public service: and they will only be overcome where you establish a most manifest need, and secure a measure of imaginative indulgence on the part of the powers that be.

Ordinarily one must expect opposition from the following sources: (1) the genuine old-fashioned disbelief in a government's indulgence in an instrument of propaganda (this is now altering greatly in the general acceptance of the idea of ministries of 'information'); (2) political fears on the part of opposition parties, at the initiatory stage, that the government party is giving itself an advantage; (3) jealousy between ministers as to who will control the power; sensitiveness to the danger of ministers using the new power for their own political ends; (4) the opposition of routine bureaucracy to any operation which is interpretative and involves a 'quality' judgement; (5) fear that the artist will occasionally be too adventurous for easy defence in Parliament; (6) a genuine attachment to the 'quietist' approach to culture and a positive dislike of the idea of art-in-action.

These sources of opposition – which one can accept patiently or not as the case may be – have been demonstrated in most countries, but vary according, as indicated, to the feeling of manifest need and indulgence to the aesthetic factor in high quarters. Obviously the sense of manifest need must be established more firmly than can be done by individuals, however powerful in their persuasion. The manifest need of art (activist) in the management of society must I think be given a deeper base in academic teaching of the highest order. In other words, the future of art (activist) in modern society will come, not from the artists, but from the academicians. This means that the teaching of political science, etc., must be brought up to date to cover the relationship of culture in its new powers and formations with the nature of the modern state in its new powers and formations.

Q. 2 Should a documentary record its subject with the greatest possible verisimilitude in the belief that the subject is the meaning, or is it a case of the true interpretation?

Q. 3 You mention the importance of Lévi-Strauss for people thinking about films today; could you say just what this importance is?

In any creative treatment on any level of penetration of the given phenomena, you seek the noumenal which is variously described by the philosophers. 'Meaning' is the least evocative word; the 'thing-in-itself' does more for you; *'sub specie aeternitatis'* does a lot; but 'reality' is the basic word you arrive at, as it was at the beginning. So observation in depth will always lead you to some significance or some 'meaning' in the subject. You will always be referring somewhere along the line to a larger context of social significance or to dramatic or poetic or other forms which make the subject more deeply communicable to others (who are likewise concerned in finding the meaning or more ultimate shapes for their own observation and experience).

I know there is a good deal of concentration just now on observation as such ('cinéma vérité', the 'non-film', the 'non-novel', etc.) One understands it as representing a revolt against the established shapes of social observation and aesthetic forms established. But it is, *a priori*, a cul-de-sac, and even the imagination of Freud does not provide a very solid foundation. As Ivan Karamazov's Grand Inquisitor demonstrated, the cult of the person has always been wide open to authoritarian take-over, and in its crudest forms. This is not accidental. Consider the comment by Lévi-Strauss in his essay on Sartre ('History and Dialectic'):

> A Cogito which strives to be ingenuous and raw, retreats into individualism and empiricism and is lost in the blind alleys of social psychology. For it is striking that the situations which Sartre uses as a starting point for extracting the formal conditions of social reality – strikes, boxing matches, football matches, bus-stop

queues – are all secondary incidentals of life in society; and they cannot therefore serve to disclose its foundations.

Another consideration. Technical adjuncts to observation carry their dangers. It is noticeable that an otherwise simple character with a pair of binoculars can become a pretty conceited fellow. The more so when you add to your otherwise simple fellow the multiple adjuncts of a movie camera. He can now see every which way, up and down, and all around, and near and far, and slower and faster, etc., etc.; and no wonder the wonders of the possibilities on the mere observational level were celebrated early by Vertov in his Kino Eye. But all this does not necessarily take us far in the field of comprehension.

When I first got interested in these visual possibilities of the movie camera (around 1919) a friendly professor said: Be sure you are not pursuing the shadow instead of the substance. I thought it a pretty jest about the cinema in general, but I don't laugh at it any more. The fact is that the multiple visual aids given by the movie camera have turned out (in simple fellows) to be not an aid but an actual barrier to comprehension. The pursuit of the cinema-of-the-subject as a cultural pursuit is too easy; providing as it does the illusion that by seeing a lot interestingly, you see much. I sometimes wonder that students at great universities give it so much consideration; so much more than they give to say architecture, painting and sculpture – which have to stand up and for a long time.

So an interest in the nature of comprehension is for me fundamental to all interest in the creative process. Philosophy is obviously vital in one or other or all of its disciplines (pure, political, social, aesthetic, etc.). So too is history in all its disciplines (political, constitutional, scientific, social, etc.). (The trouble with historical discipline is that it is damnably tied to a particular sense of time.) When anthropology becomes a study in the nature of comprehension in the 'savage mind' (as in Lévi-Strauss) it becomes enormously interesting to anyone concerned with the extension of observation into comprehension because it is, in 'the savage mind', notably based on direct observation (of sky and land and water, of the seasons, of meteorological phenomena, flora, fauna, etc.). If, in fact, the deepening of the art of observation in the cinema involves many perspectives of comprehension, you would have to consider, with the social, the historical and the psychological, the perspectives suggested by that very same 'savage mind' which is, equally, in all of us. Among other things it might add to the art of the cinema a sense of 'in time' or, if you like, 'timelessness', which is sorely lacking in its present concentration on observation for observation's sake.

Having said this I will now cheerfully appear to contradict myself. I am all for subject enjoyment. Some of us get a unique kick out of what we think of as 'movie' – movie-as-such. We say: that's movie – and we mean just that. We also have a notion that we are in the same sort of minority of appreciation as those who have their immediate recognition of architecture, painting or sculpture as such.

I here remind you of Kant's odd aesthetic category involving 'purposiveness without purpose'. Oliver Wendell Holmes has the interesting phrase: 'lazing busily'. The French have their conception of *'bricolage'*. There are contexts in which the 'inconsequential' is enjoyed or admired. This 'purposiveness without purpose' gives you, among other things, the pleasures associated with games, carpet designs and the abstract arts of various sorts, as well as the immediacy of enjoyment involved in standing and staring and spitting over a bridge. Maybe you spoil the experience or lack a sense of humour or something when you get to considering perspectives or meaning for, say, the fact that infants and animals are liable to 'steal a picture'.

Personally, I never accepted the 'purposiveness without purpose' judgement as categorically different from the 'teleological' judgement, but never wanted to make much of it. If pressed, as I don't want to be, I would have a shot at putting the whole lot in some perspective or other of comprehension, including the most abstract of the abstract arts. Why, for example, their differences of focus?

Q 4 Is there any director working at the moment whose work you particularly admire, and if so, why?

Many, but tho only ones I would be primarily interested in are the men who have broken through to economic viability in progressive modern terms and are sharing opportunity with others and particularly with younger people. It is difficult to put names to them at this time of great fluidity. Many individuals have broken through on their own personal account. I leave them out of the argument. I obviously do not share the interest in individual work which one comes across in film societies and other 'in' circles. Most of the once-good things look a bit amateur today, and certainly not as significant as once was claimed. One thinks more of Sennett, though you can't exactly nail down anything he did. One thinks more of the 'wave' that was Chaplin and Laurel and Hardy than of individual pictures. One thinks more of the wave that was Eisenstein and Pudovkin than of all perfect classics. No, today the significance I'd expect would be in nailing down the people who are responsible for the different waves of film-making. For names I would think personally of Joris Ivans and his influence on the young filmmakers of the socialist countries, of Tom Daly in Canada and his influence over the many films at the NFB, of Arthur Elton's influence on the scientific-educational front, of Anstey's patronage of young filmmakers, of Bert Haanstra and his influence in Holland and Storck's influence in Belgium. I wish I could name the individuals who have swung things in Czechoslovakia and Yugoslavia, for many good things are growing there because of one persuader or another. We know the important work that Bossak and Toeplitz have done for Poland. As you see, I am not interested in single films as such, only as they contribute to the larger thesis – and individuals likewise. Film cannot of its nature be a purely personal art, except, as it were, miniature and on one's own money. A few have managed it but they are not significant. The nature of the cinema demands collaboration and collusion with others and with many variant purposes; and its significance derives from those who can operate and command purposively and aesthetically within those conditions. Ask yourself who is *actually* the most commanding producer in the United Kingdom. Well, on first principles he is bound to be at the BBC, whence the biggest and best creative visual flow derives, and one must assume that he is Wheldon.

Q. 5 Do you think that images on the screen have a psychological force that words spoken or written do not have?

No, except in the fact that film has an automatic audience of millions on screen or television. Nevertheless there is such a thing as 'movie' *sui generis*, much beloved by some, including myself. But I am not sure by how many, though I have had some odd experience of appreciation of movie *sui generis* amongst my own TV millions. I have done much, for example, to spread the observation of abstract films and find I have built up an audience for them in the most unexpected quarters. Here is an unknown territory for enquiry.

Q. 6 Can a fictional film compete in depth and profundity with a novel, or should it be aiming for a completely different effect?

I wouldn't think any film you and I have ever seen could compete in depth with say Tolstoy, Dostoevsky, Balzac, etc. Film for the most part is addressing millions and at the same time. Its economics prevent the same consideration of depth. Perhaps the technical complexity of its manufacture also does.

Q. 7 Does the fact that an audience cannot 're-read' a part of a film which they have not understood limit the film-maker to the simple and obvious?

Yes. But some take a long chance (e.g. Basil Wright in *Song of Ceylon*) and have been justified in the event.

Q. 8 Your work in films has been mainly documentary, and production and organisation, with little attention to fictional films. Is this a matter of talent or conviction?

The answer derives from my premises. Who, in his senses, *except in the socialist countries*, could pretend to share in, and manage to further public ends, the economic costs and hazards of fictional film production? I have been associated with the production of a score of fictional films, but only under the guise of providing employment and experience for young directors and actors, etc., and under the protectorate of the Board of Trade under Harold Wilson. The BBC achievement in this field is worth keeping an eye on, but its funds are limited. With the fictional film, I trust only where public trust is associated with it. The future for fictional films in the UK, so far as I am personally interested, is with television under public authority of one sort or another, or, alternatively, with the development of the National Film Finance Corporation in its public responsibility.

Q. 9 Documentary today seems to lack some of the energy and idealism of the 1930s. Whose fault is it?

You must be provincially referring to the United Kingdom, because documentary flourishes greatly in some countries overseas, and with similar ideals. The fault in the UK is partly in the changing, more inward-looking context of national politics. But don't forget that the BBC has taken over much of documentary's original work, and is doing excellently by it, and *will do better when it transcends its present reportage complex*. The real documentary centre in Britain today is at the BBC. That is where it is to be judged and, if necessary, criticised: and called to, and financed for, larger horizons.

Q. 10 You have been an advocate of a dramatic process of education, using films and other methods of propaganda to teach people 'citizenship'. Has this been done?

Yes and all over the world and spectacularly so and not least in the emergent countries. See also the above reference to the BBC.

Q. 11 In spite of your efforts Britain seems to be less conscious of a purpose or a destiny than ever. Do you think this is true and what can one do about it?

This is too big a question. Britain has hard economic changes to make and tends to be inward-looking at this period: (economically-in-the-short-run-preoccupied). But I doubt if its 'destiny' is any less manifest than, say, that of France or Germany. America is all mixed up about its 'destiny' and much of its imaginative creative work is not too obviously involved in the pursuit of national ends and making them manifest. But consider: creative effort in defiance of popularly declared national ends may in the long run reflect the labour pains of discovering a more real national 'destiny'. In fact America must be for us (in English) the most exciting field for the study of the aesthetic–community relationship and it is a big and difficult field of 'destiny' to get into focus. The more so with the USSR and China.

Ironically, the countries most clearly sure of 'destiny' are often too poor to give a creative form to it (e.g. Egypt). Others are too hamstrung by entangling alliance to give them a clear individual character (e.g. Canada in one sense, Poland in another). On the other hand, I look to all three for a progressively good flow of pictures, because the artist is – in spite of all – being positively treated as an ally by the powers that be, and a relatively free ally.

But I return to my notion that the 'destiny' of Britain is not less manifest than that of France and Germany. Washing buildings doesn't matter very much, nor calling up echoes of the grandeurs of the past.

Remember among other things that national 'destinies' are out of fashion – and after Buchenwald have every reason to be.

Set against this the recent invitation by the American J. K. Galbraith to the British Government 'to think strategically instead of tactically . . . to accept the full implications of the goals the government sets itself . . . *and to do this publicly and with fanfare'*. In that latter context there would be creative opportunity enough for the documentary film to be busy about 'destiny'. In fact I cannot think of the British Government considering what Galbraith proposes without remembering that the documentary film was from the very beginning dedicated – *and by the British Government itself* – to this very same analysis and this very same end.

When we see the documentary men doing a Lazarus outside the gates, as they now are in England, it simply means that they have got into servile ways and forgotten what it originally was all about.

I REMEMBER, I REMEMBER (1970)

At that time I was involved with some other theorists at the University of Chicago. We were working out ways and means by which the peoples of the new world would get to know about the world they lived in. Remember it was in the twenties. They were called the roaring twenties. Everything was growing and at a great pace. Some were thinking what the newspapers should do in this new world and that was when *Time* magazine was born. Some were thinking what the radio and what television still to come would do for the modern scene. As for me I got my sights on the motion picture and all that brave territory Hollywood was occupying. We have the comedies, we have the westerns, we have the newsreels, but they were nothing much. There was the real world, almost totally neglected. You could say that they were pursuing the shadow instead of the substance. The film camera could go everywhere and see everything. Every which way and round about. It was a window on the whole wide world, but the shutters were up.

So I started to write about this window on the world. It was clear that Hollywood wasn't interested, but I thought that governments certainly should be, that people everywhere needed to know about the modern world if they were to be citizens of the modern world, and that was very much the business of governments. It sounds very obvious today, and in fact it happened as I thought it would. Governments listened and in particular my own British Government listened, and national organisations and the forces of education everywhere listened. In fact the documentary film took hold everywhere. This window on the real world was for modern education a real godsend. It was needed.

I'm saying this because I have been so closely associated with the documentary film in many countries, and with the serious uses of the documentary film, that something gets forgotten, something that is very dear to me. I just don't think I would have got very far or enjoyed myself so much if, in the first place, I hadn't loved the magic of the movies. . . . Certainly the film can tell you importantly about important things but the really wonderful thing is that the motion picture can see beautiful things. And the camera doesn't just give you a new language. It gives you a new poetry. I have known film-makers all over the world, some of them very serious and very important gentlemen indeed, but the real brotherhood is between the people who see the beautiful things, the people who see the shapes and the movements, the faces and the people, in the new poetry which the eyes of the motion picture can give us.

So please don't expect anything very pompous about this collection of film pieces. Nothing serious, nothing far afield, just about the sights and the sounds and the shapes of the world where I grew up. I don't suppose it's very surprising but the first film I ever made was about the sea. I'd been to America, I'd written all sorts of grandiose things about the future of the documentary film. I was telling governments that they should do this and that, but when the British Government said: all right so show us a picture, well, all I could think of was right back home where I started. I made a film about the sea and about fishermen, the morning, the day and the night of the sea, and the fishermen against the sky. It was called *Drifters* and it made a startling impression at the time. It was something altogether new to be looking at ordinary things as if they were extraordinary, and I recommend that formula to you one and all, to look at ordinary things as if they were extraordinary things. In *Drifters* all the shapes, and the very simplest and most ordinary shapes, slung together joyously in what I hope is still a kind of visual poetry . . . here is another little sequence about the sea. I include it for personal reasons, but also to show you how utterly simple film-making can be. I was caught in a gale once, in a trawler out in one of the local fishing harbours, Granton. It was called the *Isabella Greig*. I had a camera with me and, just because it was heavy weather, and I had been a sailor and can stand up in heavy weather, I shot for a couple of days. The noises, such as they are, were added in an afternoon. So it's altogether an indication of what almost anybody can do with simple resources.

These fishermen in *Drifters*, these fishermen and their nets, represented the real beginnings of the documentary film movement as a movement. Soon many countries were getting into the act of showing the real world to their peoples and making them proud of what was going on. Others before me, for example Bob Flaherty in America, had made pictures of real life – but mostly about faraway peoples. Very beautiful Flaherty was. What was really revolutionary in our stuff was this business of making films about ordinary everyday people, and making them look dramatic. And we were, I think I can say, good editors. We could put the bits and pieces of observation together and make them swing. It was not just a new language in which we could describe our own lives and surroundings; – it was a language in which we could sing. Anyway the British Government got excited about the public reaction when we actually had audiences in the West End of London cheering their own British workmen – I'm sure for the first time in their lives.

I collected a lot of artists around me, among them Flaherty himself, Cavalcanti, Wright, Elton, Legg, Anstey, Rotha, Jennings, Taylor, Watt – a host of them: with Auden for poet and Britten for composer. Believe it or not they were all together in one small studio in London in the thirties, great and good names today all of them. We made a lot of films together, but as often as I could, I would swing the locations to the places I knew best, so that is why I can collect now these pieces from my Scottish homeland.

I had grown up close to the sea, but I had also grown up close to the great Carron ironworks, famous from the earlier days of the industrial revolution. We stood at night on the local hill to watch the glare from the furnaces. So I took very easily and very cheerfully to the steam and the steel of the modern world, and I still do, and with aluminium added. I like the big shapes. I like the extremes in black and white and the great arrays of greys in between. Then there were the pitheads and the miners. I grew up with them too. They were my neighbours. It was an industrial world, a world that I tried to celebrate in a film called *Industrial Britain*. It was shot mostly by Flaherty and he had the most wonderful eyes I ever knew in a man. Certainly, if you see quiet patterns they are from Flaherty. If they are violent, they are most likely from me.

If it is all very poetic as in the film *Coal Face*, be sure Auden is on the words, Britten is on the sound, and Basil Wright is on the camera. That was a sweet combination.

You may think today that was quite a revolution in sound for 1934. The odd thing is that we never went very much further. We got involved in campaigns for social welfare, and then in the propaganda of the war, and, in a way, the experimental days of sound cinema stopped around 1936. I wish some of you would take over again. We were just beginning. The trouble with that last mining film was that Auden's lovely lyric didn't come through the complex collection of noises. It's the lyric that begins 'O lurcher loving collier black as night, follow your love across the smokeless hill.' Anyway, in the next film, *Night Mail*, we decided to make the poetry simpler and speak it to the beat of the train. I expect some of you Americans will recognise the real origins of the idea. You get it in Vachell Lindsay's poem on the congo: 'Fat black bucks in a wind barrel room – barrel house kings with feet unstable'. You get it again in Carl Sandburg's 'Slabs of the Sun-Burnt West': 'Into the night, into the blanket of night, overland goes the overland passenger train.'

What happened with *Night Mail* was that the Post Office in London wanted a film to celebrate the mail train journey from London to Glasgow. I on my part wanted a film dedicated poetically to the crossing of the Scottish border. So our ends were identical and I had all the talents around me. 'Here is the night mail crossing the border, bringing the cheque and the postal order.' The words by Auden, the music by Britten, Cavalcanti on sound.

The city the night mail fetches up in was, of course, the city of Glasgow. Glasgow was thirty miles down the road from me but I went to school there, and it's the sort of city that some people don't think beautiful but almost everyone discovers to be great. Just because of these shapes which have haunted me all my life, I have always found Glasgow beautiful too, and there came a day when there was a chance to say so – and we brought Hillary Harris over from New York, to make a film about this city that had the big shapes and the big sizes. It was called *Seawards the Great Ships*. I have cut out all the words. Only the shapes and the sounds and the music remains. You may come to think that films can be very good that way.

Now you may think that I have taken you a long way from the usual sort of documentary film – and I hope I have. Most people, when they think of documentary film, think of public reports, and social problems and worthwhile education and all that sort of thing. For me it's something more magical. It is a visual art which can convey a sense of beauty about the ordinary world, the world on your doorstep. You could say that all things are beautiful if you can only get them in the right order. The cinema is like painting. It can see the beautiful pattern in things, in fact, in the unlikeliest places. And when it is very very good, why it's the same wonderful world of observation as for Picasso himself.

Now I'm going to demonstrate this point with a very abstract piece of film observation. Don't be frightened by the word 'abstract'. Abstract just means order, just means pattern. Everything you put in order is put into a pattern, and we live by putting things into orders and patterns: in the school, the kitchen, the field and the factory, the streets and the highways, the railroad tracks, the car parks, the supermarkets, everywhere. Why, we live in patterns and by patterns. . . . Now, directly or indirectly, I have had something to do with all these pieces of film and I have not gone very far from where I began. I have of course made films outside Scotland and I have been a bit of an educator and a bit of a propagandist in other countries. But I have a very special feeling for the films which demonstrate the visual art of the documentary cinema. The documentary film I gave a push to forty years ago was a richer form of art than I ever dreamt of, and a hundred other talents than mine have proved it so.

Chapter 3

PAUL ROTHA (1907–84)

COMMENTARY

Although in his published writings Paul Rotha has always defended the documentary movement, he was always at least semi-independent of Grierson and the others, and only briefly employed by Grierson. Basil

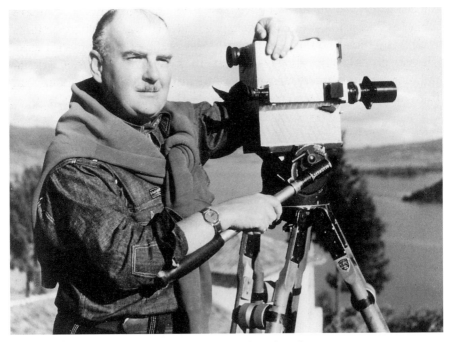

Figure 3.1 Portrait of Paul Rotha.
Source: BFI. Copyright could not be traced, but the publishers will be happy to make amendments in future editions of this book.

Wright has described his relationship with Grierson as one of 'contin-uous unarmed combat' (interview with Ian Aitken, 1987). Like Grierson, Rotha was a committed and strong-minded individual, unable to accept anything other than a leadership role. This led him to leave the documentary movement early, and engage in his own film production work, a move which enabled him to reach a critical perspective on the movement which escaped many of the other film-makers. Neverthe-less, this degree of independence, and freedom from Grierson's over-bearing presence, did not lead to a great film-making career. Some of the documentaries made in the thirties remain important, but, after that, few films of significance appeared. Rotha's strong, sometimes belligerent personality also seems to have left him somewhat isolated during the last years of his life. Orbanz (1977: 38), for example, depicts him as having few friends apart from Basil Wright, more or less ignored by the younger generation of documentary film-makers, and enwrapped in his memories.

In his 'Afterthought' (1972), Rotha makes a number of fairly strong criticisms of Grierson. He states that he did not share Grierson's 'almost blind allegiance' to the journalistic film, and describes the films which Grierson produced at the NFB as 'ephemeral', 'let off with mis-sile speed', and having no lasting qualities. He is also strongly critical of Grierson's decision to leave the GPO Film Unit in 1936, arguing that this was a major factor in the disintegration of the documentary move-ment. His opinion of Cavalcanti appears to be low: he is seen as a rather unreliable opportunist. Rotha also argues that the documentary movement was let down by the Labour movement both during the 1930s, and after 1945. He argues that Labour 'had no ear for such an approach to imaginative public service', and unlike the Communist movement, which supported film-making, did not commission films. Rotha sounds particularly bitter on this point.

In 'Films and the Labour Party' (1936), Rotha argues that propaganda is an essential part of society, and that film is 'a weapon that can model the minds of multitudes in any given direction'. He is not worried about this, but argues instead that, since ideology works to reproduce dominant interests within capitalist society, it is essential that the working class create its own instruments of propaganda. The bulk of the paper is taken up with an examination of how commercial cinema reproduces the status quo, and includes a complaint that Griffith's *Birth of a Nation*, a clearly racist film for Rotha, is still allowed to be shown. Rotha also argues that, given the conditions of the time, the makers of documentary film could only show the working class during the 1930s, but could not comment on its exploitation. That was 'beyond their power'.

AFTERTHOUGHT (1972)

Discouraging as they may be, the economic facts of documentary film production and distribution have to be faced. No matter its social, aesthetic, educational or other purposes, a documentary film costs a good deal of money to make, and sometimes to show. However the cinema medium is approached, the irrevocable fact is that, even allowing for technological improvements in equipment, it is an expensive medium, even for solo amateurs. The film-maker, whatever his choice of genre, must depend for his materials either on his own private source of finance, or on the finance of friends or family, which is rare. The great majority have had to square up to finding private investment which requires adequate return on outlay, or alternatively involvement by a state-run industry which may carry obligations of political propaganda, or at least some kind of public education.

In the mixed economy of the United Kingdom, the documentary film has in all but exceptional cases been dependent for its production finance on (a) government, at both national and local levels, (b) institutions or societies of some kind, and (c) industry, either private or nationally controlled. The distribution and exhibition sides of the three-tier commercial industry, as organised over many years now, do not permit the self-financed documentary film, even with quotas and funds, to make an adequate return on its production capital outlay.

A film-maker must establish a good working relationship with his sponsor. At times, a film can emerge with aesthetic qualities, and hence audience and critical appeal, beyond the expectation of the sponsor. *Song of Ceylon* and *Shipyard* are good examples; Haanstra's *Glass* and Lorentz's *The River* are others. These are the work of individuals who create a personal reputation with which a sponsor wants to be associated. In the 1930s, Strand Films secured contracts to make films with such bodies as Imperial Airways, the National Book Council and the National Council for Social Service because of the prior reputation of the producer they engaged to be in charge of production, and thus guarantee quality of product. Government departments, like the

Ministries of Labour and Agriculture, went to the department of the Post Office for advice about their projected film activities not because of the Post Office *per se* but because it employed Mr Grierson, whose reputation for a quality and style of film-making had become known way outside the bounds of Post Office reference. The fact that there was an official post known as Government Film Advisor did not change this fact; it seemed he mainly swept up the dust in official film vaults.

When some British-made documentary film, as was sometimes the case, won an award at an international film festival and gained critical praise outside its country of origin, it acquired a prestige that did not pass unnoticed at home. (*Song of Ceylon* and *The Face of Britain* were examples.) The sponsor of such a film could as easily have put his requirements on the order books of the makers of advertising and publicity films, but public relations men in the 1930s, like Beddington, Leslie and Snowden Gamble, saw in the documentary film a medium of far wider prestige and influence than the buying of space for advertising in newspapers or time on commercial radio.

At the same time, the need for sponsorship widened and the idea for documentary films had to be propagated and nurtured all through these years. Hence the reason for the formation in 1935 of the Associated Realist Film Producers group to undertake promotional and publicity work. Grierson never tired of writing that in the first place Whitehall did not ask to make documentary films; what few films government ministries made were put out to tender to a handful of commercial companies that made publicity pictures. Here perhaps the experience of the Government Film Advisor was sought in comparing submitted tenders for a contract so that the lowest could be chosen. The civil servants involved were satisfied with such results and, until Mr Grierson's arrival on the scene, all jogged along smoothly. No one, least of all the press, MPs and film critics, were aware that such films were even made. They were shrouded in peace and quiet.

Civil servants, for the most part, are not exactly renowned for their interest in creative matters, especially the Treasury when it comes to spending money, and public money at that. On the contrary, their background and training engender fear and mistrust of anything to do with 'art' or 'aesthetics'. That is why Grierson so often tried to dissociate the word 'art' from 'documentary', and substituted instead such words as 'information' and 'public service'. He analysed rightly that Whitehall would be less suspicious of 'public education' than of 'aesthetic purpose'. Tallents's (or was it really Grierson's?) happy phrase 'bringing alive' must have smoothed many a Civil Service qualm; it was a slogan capable of easy understanding, not the aesthetic jargon of the arts which was anathema to the bureaucrat mind. Grierson said it thus:

> The story of the documentary movement is, in part, the story of how, not without a scar or two, we got by. Maybe you win more or less for keeps, as in the later case of the National Film Board of Canada. Maybe you lose, though never altogether, to the bureau-crats and the other boys behind the woodwork. . . . The fact is that there are many real sources of opposition to the idea of art (activist) in the public service; and they will only be overcome where you establish a most manifest need, secure a measure of imaginative indulgence on the part of the powers that be. Hence always the emphasis in our writing at that time for documentary 'to fill a need', but I doubt if you had asked a civil servant, 'What need?', he could have answered.

It has been seen earlier that it was Sir Stephen Tallents within the government service (with Grierson at his elbow) who first persuaded government officers to embark on waters outside their previous sphere of public operation. The naive questions and some of the answers given before the Select Committee on Estimates in 1934 fully confirm this state of ignorance.

Separate in identity as were the documentary units (EMB, GPO, Shell, Strand and Realist), the unity of the groups, or movement as we liked to call ourselves, expressed itself in the main through its senior members. Only two or three of us, besides Grierson, were so involved; everyone else (including us) were at the full-time job of making films. Documentary progress was dependent on intense activity on three interrelated fronts, with a fourth to emerge later. First, in the field of finding and educating potential sponsors in the government and industrial sectors; second, propagating the documentary idea by as widespread journalism and lecturing as possible, and here our Fleet Street contacts seldom let us down; and third, obviously in making films as good as our circumstances and abilities and finance permitted.

The fourth front, which arose as the decade wore on, and which grew to be of increasing importance, was the field of distribution for our films when they had been made. Sponsors obviously wanted good films for their money, but they also wanted those films widely seen. Welcome as was the hard-to come-by and usually reluctant cinema release (*Drifters* via New Era, *Contact* via Wardour Films, *Cover to Cover* and *Night Mail* via ABFP) the slow but ever-widening access to the public by what came to be known as the non-theatrical market was more and more valuable and attractive to sponsors. The EMB and GPO film libraries had blazed the way. The gas and oil industries were to set up their own distribution libraries, in some cases making films (like *New Worlds for Old*) exclusively for such specialist release. As will be seen, this pioneer work by the big industrialists was to be of immense value to the nation during the war, when the Ministry of Information non-theatrical distribution was to achieve nationwide importance.

It should also be said here that we, as film-makers, had learned from Bob Flaherty that no film, however good, ever sold itself. He had gone out in the States and mobilised special audiences to go to their local movie-theatres to see his film *Moana*. We in Britain used the film society movement, spreading every year, as a showcase for our films and wherever feasible made an appearance and spoke about the film. No commercial distributor was interested in publicising documentary; we were and did.

Looking back at our documentary films of the 1930s, it is important to make a point about the aesthetic of film movement. No confusion of course should be made between this use of the word and its use to describe the ideas and purposes and work output of a group of film-makers with a common aim in Britain. Of the aesthetic of film movement, something of an analysis was made in 1935 in my book at that time, but a relook can perhaps be useful here. Several kinds of film movement are involved:

1. Movement of ideas or meaning conveyed by the contents of the film and its parts.
2. Movement of physical action being filmed in a shot or sequence.
3. Movement of camera (tracking, panning, etc.) and microphone in both visual and aural imagery; sound images can be either in harmony with the visual or in counterpoint.
4. Movement by editing, in which visual images taken by the camera and sounds recorded through the microphone are

placed in juxtaposition to interpret meaning, and to make possible intellectual and emotional response in the audience.
Transition can be made by placing shots one after another in
continuity of meaning and also of camera movement: the relationship of one shot to the next can be made by abrupt change
of viewpoint, or by a merging of one shot into the next (dissolve
or mix). The same process is possible with the sound images
(including speech and music).

Movement of physical action between shots can often be made to flow
by overlapping the same movement from one shot into the next, thus
using the element of filmic time and filmic space as distinct from
actual time and space as we know them in everyday life. The filmic
reproduction of what the camera observes and the microphone records
is usually made at the same rate of action as the human eye sees in
everyday life; but the film camera and microphone can record faster or
slower than the human eye and ear can see and hear.

These basic elements and/or principles of the film medium have not
changed basically over the years. As with other art media, especially
television, many kinds of tricks have been thought up to provoke new
audience sensations but they are ephemeral and as soon forgotten as
invented.

A good deal has been written about the symphonics of film movement and need not be restated. What needs to be remembered is that
visual symphonic movement, so satisfying to create and so visually
exciting to the eye, can obscure the meaning inherent in what is on
the screen and produce a superficial effect that masks or even ignores
purpose. (The classic example of this danger is in Ruttmann's *Berlin:
Symphony of a City*). The film medium offers so many slick and spuri-
ous varieties of creating effects on the audience, effects which are not
to be found in the other art media until television, that the film-maker
needs to use the utmost discretion in his approach to the medium. The
cheap, phoney technical tricks used in television have done some
temporary harm to the film medium but it will not last. Contrary to all
the recent hot air expended on the need to jettison the known and
accepted fundamentals of filmic expression, I believe that a film-maker
of any integrity must learn his craft by experience and by study of what
has already been done by the great film-makers of the past, after which
he may or may not, according to his talent, be equipped to express his

own attitude towards the drama of life through his chosen medium. There is no quick way to learn film-making. It is a medium far more complex yet subtle, far more stimulating and evocative, in its appeal to a vast audience than any other before it. The film offers a fundamentally new creative medium of incredible powers to the author–artist, which is one reason for its magnetism today, especially to the young generation. Television has nothing in its own right comparable to offer, except prostitution.

Grierson has suggested that the aesthetic of movement disappeared from the British documentary film after about 1935 to be replaced by camera reportage, that is to say that the aesthetic qualities of *Song of Ceylon* and *Night Mail* were replaced by the journalistic reporting approach of *Workers and Jobs* and *Housing Problems*. This I find an over-simplication and untrue in that it overlooks the development of the handling of human beings in such films as *Today We Live, Bill Blewitt* and *North Sea*, all of which came later than Elton's films. Thirty years earlier Grierson had also written:

> I think the greatest [documentary] advance of all came with two little films which, except among the far-seeing, went almost unnoticed. One was called *Housing Problems* and the other *Workers and Jobs*. . . . They took the documentary film into the field of social problems, and keyed it to the task of describing not only industrial and commercial spectacle but social truth as well. These simple films went deeper than earlier films like *Drifters* and later films like *Night Mail* and *North Sea*. They showed the common man, not in the romance of his calling, but in the more complex and intimate drama of his citizenship. See *Industrial Britain, Night Mail, Shipyard* and *North Sea* alongside *Housing Problems*. There is a precious difference. *Housing Problems* is not so well made nor so brilliant in technical excitements, but something speaks within it that touches the conscience. These other films 'uplift'. *Housing Problems* 'transforms' and will not let you forget.

It is hard to see why Grierson overlooked the sequences dealing with unemployment in *Rising Tide* and *Shipyard*, both made prior to *Housing Problems*, and harder still to explain his ignorance of *Today We Live* and *Eastern Valley* which, three years before he was writing, went far to meet his request; they both had 'uplift' and 'transform' and certainly did not let you forget. They also had one undisputed advantage, which is why I think Grierson forgot them. They were films as well as social documents. Basil Wright quotes from a letter he had from Grierson in 1942 which is relevant in this context. Grierson wrote:

> Documentary was from the beginning – when we first separated our public purpose theories from those of Flaherty – an 'anti-aes-thetic' movement. We have all, I suppose, sacrificed some personal capacity in 'art' and the pleasant vanity that goes with it. What confuses the history is that we always had the good sense to use the aesthetes. We did so because we liked them and because we needed them. It was, paradoxically, with the first-rate aesthetic help of people like Flaherty and Cavalcanti – our 'fellow-travellers' so to speak – that we mastered the techniques necessary for our quite unaesthetic purpose.

In this afterthought, let me try and be clear about this. Films like *Housing Problems, Workers and Jobs* and *Enough to Eat?* had little to do with film technique other than that they used celluloid, camera and microphone. Their drama lay in the (almost) spontaneous behaviour of the real people chosen to appear. Their subjects – slum clearance, the working of a labour exchange and the nutritional weaknesses of the British people – were of immense social significance, but their failure to use, in fact their deliberate resistance against using, the basic aesthetic qualities of the film medium caused a good deal of criticism among film-makers, film critics and general audiences. When I was showing our films in the US, it was very often said, *Night Mail* and *Song of Ceylon* are very fine films, but *Housing Problems* and *Enough to Eat?*, these are just illustrated reports of interest only because they use real human beings. I, who have always believed that an audience must be emotionally involved before it will absorb arguments, let alone facts and opinions, found myself at the time – and I still do – critical of what I consider is unnecessary suppression of the basic elements of the film medium to evoke audience response. On the other hand, it should be noted that some people became emotionally involved in *Housing Problems*. Basil Wright reminds me, for example, that when reviewing his journalistic *Children at School*, Graham Greene praised it for intro-ducing poetry into an apparently non-poetic film.

I did not share Grierson's almost blind allegiance to the journalistic style in film, denying the creative use of direction, photography and constructive editing, but I can understand its magnetism for Grierson. In one way, *March of Time* was a very bad influence before the war on a part of British documentary. Grierson, and others influenced by him, fell under its spell. Its string of images, usually thrown together with unrelated editing, its strident, staccato, one-level voice delivery, these made a powerful impact all right but it was an impact quickly to become dulled. To many in the audience, the words of its sound-track penetrated one ear and left the other with nothing behind. Its attack stunned the mind but did not make it think. What was seen and said was all too soon forgotten. No single issue had the long-term quality of a *North Sea* or a *Song of Ceylon*. This technique reached its pitch for me in an NFB film called *The War on Men's Minds*, an attempt to analyse propaganda methods during the war. I made a point of seeing it several times, each with a different audience of moderately intelligent persons. Not one afterwards could say what the film was about or what it was meant to impart. It can be said that *Today We Live* showed *March of Time* influence; that is true, but only in the prologue which was less than one quarter of the total picture.

Grierson has complained that the aesthetic of movement, the persuasion by dialectic argument, largely disappeared from British documentary in the mid-1930s. If this is true, which I doubt, then it was mainly due to his insistence on suppressing aesthetic values in favour of factual reporting. His argument that drama lay in the unvarnished facts themselves brought one stream of documentary to a dead and rather boring end. Exactly the same thing has happened in television; that is why all too much of it is so dull.

Not all of the documentary group accepted this diktat, however; for example, Watt, Jennings, Holmes, Shaw and I suppose myself. And it is the films of these people that survive today, not as a back-number department of facts and interviews but as living works of dramatic human appeal. This experience emerged clearly when I resaw many documentaries while making the research for this present survey. This was to be even more true in the oncoming war films, when pictures like *Fires Were Started*, *Western Approaches* and *The Harvest Shall Come* were to achieve as permanent a value as cinema can offer, whereas the journalistic output of the National Film Board of Canada, important indeed as urgent and immediate wartime propaganda and information, has no lasting qualities. That such a film as *Fires Were Started*, made before Jennings became too 'poetic', combined an important morale message to the British people with a full use of the cinema's technical and aesthetic assets is for my money more valuable in the history of the cinema than any number of the ephemeral NFB wartime films let off with missile speed and precision under Grierson's dynamic guidance. On the other hand, as Basil Wright has pointed out, the films by Jennings took a long time to produce and when they appeared 'they were celebrating past rather than present heroism', whereas the Sten-gun output of the NFB served an immediate short-term purpose.

And yet, for all his concern with spot-recording, Grierson still kept a nostalgia for the aesthetics of experimental sound images that began in the 1930s, partly under Cavalcanti's influence and supplemented by the ideas of Britten, Leigh and Auden, and waned when the so-called factual reporting approach loomed large. He suggested that the complex use of sound stemmed from *Granton Trawler* and *Song of Ceylon* through *Coal Face* to *Night Mail*, where it suddenly stopped. (Again this is not historically accurate.) This use of sound images represented noise at various levels of organisation and in various combinations of natural noises and orchestrated with musical effects, rhetoric recita-tion, poetic recitation as well as monologue and narration. Again in fairness it must be put on record that the sound-tracks of *Shipyard* and *Face of Britain* also contained many of these sound elements including fabricated, impressionist and synthetic sound and the use of the dis-embodied voice as monologue. 'But', maintained Grierson:

> this experiment ended when those who contributed to it were reaching out for direct reporting by dialogue in the search for social reality. When documentary went missionary, the greatest single drive in audio-visual aesthetic (*per se*) stopped and has not been resumed since.

Grierson also had much to say about the self-indulgence of the auteur concept in film-making and dismissed it as being 'romantic and old-fashioned'. He enunciated:

> I am not interested in single film as such, only as they contribute to the larger thesis – and individuals likewise. Film cannot of its nature be a purely personal art, except, as it were, miniature and on one's own money. A few have managed it but they are not significant.

The nature of the cinema demands collaboration and collusion with others with many variant purposes; and its significance derives from those who can operate and command purposively within these conditions.

Generally speaking it is true that the:

medium demands a lot of collaboration and collusion with others. It also demands cooperation and patience and persistence, one with another, not to mention as multifold and various and rich a collection of talents as the project demands and the wit of catalyst/ producer dictates.

But now Grierson is shifting the auteur status from director to producer, an argument that by no means holds true. Take *Song of Ceylon* as a good example. As its producer, Grierson contributed greatly in ideas to its final four-part shape; others, Walter Leigh, Lionel Wendt and Caval-canti, gave much to its sound-track, but it is quite impossible to deny – indeed who would wish to? – that it is a film by Basil Wright, and no other person. To anyone who has studied Wright's work, the shooting in Ceylon and the editing in London could be by no one else; they stem directly from the two short West Indian films, *Windmill in Barbados* and *Cargo from Jamaica*. The same cannot be applied to *Night Mail*. Here Harry Watt claims, and there is no reason to doubt him, that the great majority of the shooting was his. Most of the editing, on the other hand, was done by McNaughton and Wright. Grierson was the usual catalyst, Cavalcanti the alchemist of the sound-track aided by Britten and Auden as his accomplices, notably to get the damned train away from Crewe and hurl it across the border into Scotland. Thus on balance it was fair that Watt and Wright should share the main credit (although I have heard Grierson decry Watt's part in it), supported by the other contributors under Grierson's parasol; but the whole is not one man's film, as was *Song of Ceylon*.

This characteristic of the 'group' film that arose in the 1930s poses the relative merits of production by a group of creative talents, or by an individual working in close collaboration with a team of technicians. What must always be remembered, but is sometimes forgotten, is that the EMB and GPO Units needed a flow of overall good films and it was to meet this need that the group method was evolved. *Industrial Britain* was the first of such films and it truly grew out of necessity. As the good Bob brought back his footage, it was clear there was no film. His material, plus some additional shooting by Wright and Elton, was pulled into some kind of unity by Grierson and Anstey's editing. The series that included *Weather Forecast, Cable Ship* and *Six-Thirty Collection* was essentially the product of group working, although they were credited respectively to Evelyn Spice, Stuart Legg and Edgar Anstey. None of them had any individual characteristics of direction. Any of these three directors could have made any of the three films. Of BBC: *The Voice of Britain* Grierson said, 'The whole film went wrong at one point and we had to think up (and in 24 hours) separate sequences for various people to make; people who were not originally on the film.'

The other development of the individually made film, apart from *Song of Ceylon*, was represented, I suppose, by *Contact, Shipyard, Voice of the World, New Worlds for Old* and *The Fourth Estate*. They were produced in the main as lone-handed works, using hired facilities. The relationship between Bruce Woolfe and myself on the first two of the films could not in any remote way be likened to Grierson's relationship to the directors working at his unit. The personal style, or what Grierson called the 'impressionist' approach, may have risen from necessity. In no sense was it in competition with the Grierson group method; it was rather an alternative method of production using non-governmental sponsorship.

We have seen above that Grierson did not find himself interested in individuals *per se*. He says he had no interest in Joris Ivens except as Ivens influenced the Dutch documentary movement, or in Elton beyond his teaching at the Shell Film Unit. But, I almost hesitate to point out, if anyone influenced the Dutch it was Bert Haanstra, not Ivens who came earlier; nor, as Grierson also claims, did Henri Storck create a Belgian documentary group because there never was one. On the other hand, it is unlikely that the Shell Film Unit would have gained its rightful recognition without the influence of Elton, just as I am quite sure there would have been no British documentary movement as a whole without Mr Grierson, whether he would admit it or not. His argument is that the movement is bigger than its individual films, and to an extent he is right, but a movement is made up of individual films and the people who conceive and make them. The documentary movement in Britain in the 1930s can indeed be seen as a coherent relationship between peoples and policies and purposes, but these in turn cannot be analysed without regard to the individual qualities of the major films. *Night Mail* and *North Sea* cannot be divorced from the movement as a whole, nor the latter from the former, but that is what I find Grierson trying to do. He can, as he likes to do so often, talk about Mack Sennett's proletarian influence on Hollywood in the early years of comedy without naming a single film title, but the same can be said for few movements, including British documentary, in cinema history.

Critics at the time complained that the GPO films did not give, let alone comment on, the wage rates and working hours of Post Offlce employees in a film like *Night Mail*, or that *Future's in the Air* did not tell us the pay of aircrew or the extent of their leave periods. In view of their sponsors, how could they have done? If these films did not state these things, would it have been better that they should not have been made at all? In defence of documentary on this point, it should be remembered that the 'Voices of Commerce' sequence in *Song of Ceylon* carried implicit but nevertheless significant comment on the low industrial status of native labour in that island. *Today We Live* was outspoken about the ravages and injustices of mass unemployment and stated bluntly that the means-test dole was no substitute for real work. But note that it was a commercial propaganda board and a charitable society that, under documentary stimulus, found the money to make these films. It was the gas industry, admittedly with the long-term aim of selling gas where gas was most efficient, that made films about the need for slum clearance, about the need for a national nutrition policy, about the need for building new schools and the need to combat the menace of smoke pollution. These things happened in a Tory-governed country because a handful of public relations officers, prompted by a bunch of documentary film producers, had a social conscience that sought an outlet, and that outlet was not to be found in any part of the so-called left.

If the trade unions had commissioned films in a sensible way, the request of the critics given above might have been met. But in the 1930s the unions and the co-operatives, let alone the Labour Party, had an antiquated attitude to their public image. Lack of money was a threadbare alibi that became boring by its monotony. The wealthy co-operative movement squandered its money on having advertising pictures made by companies tainted by Conservative views. We have seen how a display of documentary films and projection apparatus arranged at the Labour Party annual conference in 1936 resulted only in funds being found to send on tour a play (not even a film!) about the Tolpuddle Martyrs. This rusty outlook was comparable with that of the British Council's use of beefeaters at the Tower and the Changing of the Guard as symbols of modern Britain. When, after the war, *Land of Promise*, perhaps the most socially progressive film to be made in Britain about the problems of planning and housing, was sponsored by the gas industry and offered free to the new Minister of Health in 1945, the film (which incidentally carried a certificate of merit from the Royal Institute of British Architects) was rejected because it was 'thought' that an actual rent-strike march in the East End shown in the film 'had been Communist inspired'.

As Grierson so often pointed out, it was the Conservative mind that first caught on to the inspiration of the documentary idea. Labour had no ear for such an imaginative approach to public service and public education. Labour did not even have an aesthetic approach, let alone a social one. What did a Tory minister hang on his wall at home? Maybe a false Stubbs or a Constable copy. And a trade union leader? Three china ducks in flight. At one of those abortive, dreary meetings of what was called the Labour Party Films Committee which Ritchie-Calder and I attended, I once asked out of politeness my companion at the table in Transport House who the chairman was and why he was chairman. 'Well, he plays the fiddle well at home', was the reply. It was a hopeless struggle.

We must have been naive to have thought that when the Labour Party actually became a more than sizeable government in 1945 it would implement an imaginative and purposeful national information service. Only one man in the Party (and I met most of them) had the instinct and wisdom to grasp that we could offer a service in the national good, but in effect it was outside his sphere of stewardship at that time. That man was Sir Stafford Cripps. Instead the need for national projection was split between the possessive vanities of Herbert Morrison and Ernest Bevin. The whole vital concept for a single National Film Board in Britain was jettisoned because of rivalry between these two politicians.

In a letter to *The Times* at a later date Grierson summed the whole matter up very well. He wrote,

The Labour Movement has had from the beginning a built-in distrust of information services other than its very own, and perhaps no wonder. I was a very near and interested observer of this phenomenon in the Clydeside days and when I helped to develop certain ideas about planned and national information services in a planned society, nothing ever surprised me more than to find a welcome for them, not where I expected, but among Conservative and Liberal Ministers. When this was put to Mr Herbert Morrison he said, 'It was double-talk' but was told that 'Mr Walter Elliot would understand it immediately.' Certainly when it fell to that Labour Government to liquidate the Ministry of Information it did so all too cheerfully and without a thought for what we might be losing.

This letter provoked no replies. Labour leaders failed even to defend their own effete attitude. But these are matters about which I shall expand in due course.

Even before the outbreak of war in September 1939, there were signs of unrest in the British documentary movement. The slightly uneasy relations between the GPO Unit and Film Centre could be felt across the Square, the disunity of Strand (which in 1935 had begun with such bright fervour), the decline of the Associated Realist Film Producers (set up with banners aloft in the same year), all were indications of disquiet. To me the last event was the saddest. When Film Centre took over ARFP's promotional and consultancy work (again we should remember that it was Grierson in the first place who suggested setting it up), the group changed the word 'Associated' in its title to 'Association' and opened its membership, which had been confined to only some of the senior people, to more than forty technicians and distribution officers. It was to lead to internecine dissension. The war claimed the group for an early casualty.

In this afterthought, I think that one major reason for this documentary disruption was Grierson's leaving the GPO Unit; another was that his absences abroad, in 1938 and 1939 and thereafter, left the movement without a helmsman. To those of us who knew him as well as he allowed himself to be known, Grierson had many faults – he fermented frictions and split loyalties – but he was a dominant personality who created confidence, inspiration and allegiance. He had a sense of power and a respect for it in others. If, in a dialogue, which he usually swayed, a case was well made against him, he would be known to modify his views. He did not readily accept opposition, but at the same time found a regard for it. He certainly exercised a very considerable influence on those who worked both with him and around him. His changes of mind might exasperate some of those whom he employed (not least the harassed, successive editors of World Film News who had to wrestle with his disregard for date-lines and printer's costs). He was ruthless in pursuit of his purpose, a purpose that was plainly declared, to accept (or reject), in his many articles and lectures. You might go along with that purpose but not always like the methods by which he sought to achieve it. He was known on occasion to double-deal but only, I swear, when he suspected that he himself was being double-dealt. 'There always has to be a bastard, as they say in Hollywood,' he once wrote, 'and there always has to be a catalyst, as we both very well know ourselves.'

Grierson had an expert sense of diplomatic strategy and manoeuvre which, clear enough to himself, could baffle some of those near him. In all, his influence and guidance over the policy and development of British documentary in the decade before the war was indisputable; in fact, except for those in a political position, few would refute it. In the whole history of the cinema, it is very rare to find a man of Grierson's talents who used them without reserve to pursue ends for fundamental good purpose. This kind of man does not easily survive in the poisonous nettlebed of the film industry. It was something of a miracle built from struggle that Grierson sustained his influence so long and made it so widespread. Many today should be the more grateful for his lack of self-gain.

Although he kept in transatlantic touch by articles, correspondence and an occasional fleeting visit, Grierson's absence was, as I have said, badly felt. No one could have filled his place, although at least one tried. But I have always had the thought that if he had stayed at the head of the GPO Unit, and his relations had continued to be as reasonable as could be expected with his Post Office masters and the Treasury officers, the British documentary movement would not have disintegrated, at least not so fast. No really satisfactory reason was ever to be known for his resignation. The main purpose given at the time, as we have seen, was the need for wider promotional activity outside the limits of a government unit, but such activity could well have been undertaken, and indeed had been begun at Grierson's own suggestion, by the ARFP group. The divergence of views between Grierson and Cavalcanti could have had something to do with it. After the former's leaving of the Unit and before the coming of war, there is the record that unhappily Cavalcanti became actively opposed to the Grierson social documentary policy. But I doubt very much that a man of Grierson's stature would have permitted such a fractious disagreement to deflect him if he had wished to stay at the Unit. Again, there may have been political and administrative problems arising between Grierson and the Civil Service mandarins to whom he was ultimately responsible; that is something about which he was always reticent and about which we shall not know now.

Or did Grierson foresee that the knife-edge equation between the government and industrial sponsorship in a capitalist system, on the one hand, and the socially progressive outlook of the majority of documentary film-makers, on the other, would inevitably come to an end? The idea of public relations and public service being interpreted in aesthetic terms by talented and honest craftsmen, like Wright and Watt, and later Holmes and Jennings, might not have lasted even without the war. The burial of *The Times* film showed that social satire, however subdued, could not be got away with under the guise of aesthetic appeal, at least not with such an intelligent and well-informed sponsor, who had to find the excuse of a 'peacetime' image being unfavourable in a 'wartime' situation to cover its confusion. And later, a great deal of pressure from high places on both sides of the Atlantic was brought to bear to stop *World of Plenty* and *The World is Rich*, both government commissions, from reaching the public screens.

Or yet again did Grierson look to Canada because he believed a liberal freedom for the documentary idea would be more capable of development by solid constitutional methods there than in a nationally governed Britain at war? If that had been the case, as I have heard argued, it is hard to explain why Grierson later relinquished his own creation at the National Film Board (unless he felt he had done his work there) or why he flirted with failure in New York (where he ran into the repercussions of the Canadian spy-trials, became frustrated in a constipated Unesco but where he did some basic groundwork which later showed results) and finally why he returned to England, first to wage a hopeless battle in a now Treasury-controlled Central Office of Information and, second, to an ill-conceived, experience-lacking project attempting a wedding between 'human' story films and the documentary approach, a wedding which Grierson had earlier himself decried. These are questions not easily solved in this investigation. Let the facts speak for themselves, so far as we know them, and let them suggest the answers.

So in spite of some remarkable output during the war years which had world-wide repercussions, and which will be dealt with in depth at a future date, the British documentary film movement ceased to continue as the unity it had been in the 1930s. The existence of a Federation of Documentary Film Units set up in good faith in 1945 did not last long. But I hasten to add that the war itself was not responsible for this break-up. The war was to cause chaos and confusion in the Ministry of Information until its Films Division was restaffed under pressure, and provided with a policy for its future work by the documentary people. But the Ministry itself had neither the power nor the ability nor even the wish to reunite a movement of film-makers so that its initial integrity of purpose could be rediscovered. I doubt very much if the successive Ministers Reith, Duff Cooper and Bracken – or their aides – Sir Walter Monckton and Harold Nicolson – even knew about the potential national value for projection of the British documentary movement. When I talked with Harold Nicolson, Parliamentary Secretary at the Ministry, in the summer of 1940, he knew nothing whatsoever about documentary's existence.

The purpose of the documentary idea so clearly defined in the 1930s became lost during the war among the self-centred production units dependent economically for the making of films on the Ministry's hand-outs. There was no real common policy except that their films, good though some of them were technically, were alleged to be what was called in the 'national interest'. For a time *Documentary Newsletter* tried to maintain a central policy and it was a useful vehicle for printing the articles that Grierson sent from Canada, but in time it lost its nerve and became more of a house magazine than anything else. Grierson's strategic diplomacy and political know-how were absorbed in drafting a Bill out of which would come the National Film Board, and between the Bill and the Board were his visits to Australia and New Zealand for the Imperial Relations Trust. It was during that time that war broke out. Invited back to Canada to head the Board, Grierson accepted for six months only. After that he decided to stay and in senior documentary opinion in England he did the right thing. In wartime Britain he would have been both shackled in his brilliant propaganda ideas and techniques, and driven mad, as were most of us, by the sheer incompetence and amateurishness of those at the top of official information and propaganda services.

As against the erosion of the movement in Britain, however, it must be remembered how in the years to come the documentary idea was, through its British exponents, to inspire growing points in many parts of the world – in Australia, India, Egypt, New Zealand and Malaysia among them. British documentary broke the boundaries of Soho Square (which it left empty), and opened up new horizons; but the first upsurge that was the ideological force behind the pioneer work of the 1930s will, I hope, be always remembered and not just in nostalgia, because it was sociologically and aesthetically unique in the cinema's scarcely eighty years of existence. In documentary, technical skill is all important but even more important and vital is social good purpose.

FILMS AND THE LABOUR PARTY (1936)

Films and the Labour Movement

Propaganda is the publicity of ideas. Quite simply, it is the task of preparing the mind of the ordinary citizen to accept a predetermined viewpoint. The motive may be political, social, or merely commercial. The whole process of our educational system is such that it may be called propagandist. Not only are selected facts and knowledge taught, but by such teaching a child's mind is shaped to a definite opinion. The aim of propaganda is to appeal to our sentiments and loyalties and to crystallise them into accepting a prescribed viewpoint which may often be against our real interests.

With the development of large-scale industry we see the concurrent growth of a vast machinery for making widely known the products of that industry. But it was the extraordinary conditions of the war that sharpened the weapons and methods of propaganda to a point unknown in previous history. The feverish 'patriotism' of that period was due specifically to the intensification of propaganda on a scale hitherto unimagined. Since then, two further immensely powerful instruments for mass persuasion have been perfected – radio and cinema. These weapons have played an incalculable part in the shaping of mass thought in the post-war world. Their significance in controlling and instructing the people in Russia, Germany and Italy today is too well known for comment. Propaganda is regarded as one of the most important instruments for the building or maintenance of a social system. It strikes closer to the heart of the ordinary citizen than any other weapon. Its application in Britain today may not be so obvious as in the authoritarian states because the economic conditions here have not as yet forced that section of the community in control of the productive forces to such necessity. Nevertheless, indirect though it may be, propaganda is as strong a force in England as it is in any other country.

The Power of the Film

Cinema, perhaps the most potent persuasive weapon of propaganda, has been developed in this country under the control of private enterprise. But, like all other instruments of propaganda, it has reflected and supported the political and social system under which its owners live by making profit. It is significant that the leaders of dictatorship, whether of the proletariat or of capital, appreciate more fully this function of cinema than we do.

Said Lenin: 'Among the instruments of art and education the cinema can, and must, have the greatest significance. It is a powerful weapon of scientific knowledge and propaganda.' Said Trotsky: 'The cinema is the most important of all the arts. It is the best instrument for propaganda.' Says Goebbels: 'As the film is one of the most modern and far-reaching mediums for influencing the masses, no Government can afford to neglect it.'

The cinema can exist only as a medium of expression in a society such as ours – that is, in an industrial age. Electricity, physics, chemistry and mechanics are the means whereby pictures and sounds may be combined and projected to give an illusion of real life.

The particular powers of the film to meet propagandist and cultural requirements are almost too obvious to specify. In brief, the film possesses:

1. An introduction to the public shared only by the radio.
2. Simple powers of explanation and portrayal; and a capacity for drawing conclusions which, if presented with a technique that takes full advantage of psychological values, is capable of persuasive qualities without equal.
3. The virtue of repeated mechanical performance to vast audiences, not once, but countless times, in many places, today,
4. tomorrow and, if the artistry is good enough, ten years hence. The power of mass suggestion; a power possessed only by the theatre, the church and the spectacle of tattoo.

Thus the film is a weapon that can model the minds of multitudes in any given direction, without those multitudes being aware of what is happening. It can create bias against which reason is useless. It can temporarily transcend the limitations of class and culture. It can persuade and be understood by the illiterate as well as by the educated, because it works through the combined medium of sight and sound, which is common to most people.

I will give you only one example, the showing of the Soviet film *Potemkin* at the Eton Film Society. Five hundred refined public school-boys, sons of our noble families and of our prosperous middle class, cheered loudly not only the refusal of the sailors to shoot their muti-neer brothers, but made the rafters of that ancient school hall ring with their applause when the red flag appeared at the end.

No surprise, then, that the cinema, like the press and radio, has been exploited by the capitalist class. No surprise, then, that the cinema, with its possibilities of substantial profit-making, has been used to propagate the interests of the class which controls its means of pro-duction. The cinema exists, we are told, as the entertainment of the masses, but the label 'entertainment' can be read in many ways. It is absurd to deny that most of the commercial story-films that are seen by 18 million people in this country every week are entertaining. They serve well the double purpose for which they are made: firstly, to make profit for their backers and, secondly, to make that vast audience forget or accept favourably the grim realities of the world in which they live and work mostly for the gain of others.

But behind this simple 'entertainment' motive lies the conscious or unconcious aim of propaganda. Perhaps it is true that the minds which order the policies of film production and exhibition are unaware of their social responsibilities. Perhaps, so long as the cinema trade continues on a satisfactory profit-making basis, the financiers and their executives are not worried about the effects of their product on the public. That is the charitable attitude for us to adopt. But we must never forget that it is to the advantage of a property-owning class to produce and perfect forms of propaganda for the protection of its interests. All institutions, whether political, sociological or religious, fundamentally reflect and assist in the maintenance of the predominating interests in control of the productive forces of their particular era.

Hence, it is clear that, under our present political and economic system, we cannot expect any commercially made story-film to deal impartially or truthfully with such subjects of vital contemporary interest as war and peace, unemployment, slum clearance, or the relation of the white man to the native. If this was attempted, even assuming that finance was available and the Censor asleep, it would lay open to criticism most of the fundamental principles upon which our society now stands and for which, I claim, the cinema acts, consciously or unconsciously, as a sort of deodorant.

Examples of such propaganda in films, that is propaganda to maintain the present basis of society, are so numerous that I need select only a few.

Almost every portrayal of working-class people in the story-film is either as creatures of fun, Cockney types or rustic half-wits, or as dishonest rogues, tramps and pickpockets. They are people who are so humbled and poor that they are shown as victims of their own inward weakness. If a poor person steals because he is hungry, be sure that he really is a rogue who can get a job if he wants one. Where serious attempts have been made to depict the common people, fishermen or slum dwellers, they are played by cultured actors who specialise in 'character parts', such as in *Turn of the Tide* or *Sing As We Go*.

Should a strike occur in a story-film set against an industrial background, the cause is usually due to a foreign agitator with beard, bag and bomb; to unscrupulous strike-breaking agents; or to the unrequited love of an ignorant miner who wins the strike and then shakes hands with the boss. Such was *Black Fury*.

The negro is either singing mammy songs, tap dancing, playing dice, or is quite satisfied with his life as a Pullman porter or cotton picker; or else he is a hanger-on in the gangster's underworld with razor and knuckle duster. Such were *Marie Galante*, *Trader Horn*, *Sanders of the River*, *Showboat*, and *Petrified Forest*. One of the greatest films historically and artistically, *The Birth of a Nation*, gave rise to the twentieth-century revival of the Klu Klux Klan. Today, in time of acute tension in racial feeling, that film is still being shown in the southern States of America, although it is twenty-three years old.

The rich are nearly always portrayed as hard-working men, but the nature of their business is obscure. Their offices are well appointed, their secretaries pretty and business is seldom transacted unless it involves a sensational Wall Street crash, thereby causing a convenient suicide. Such were *The Wolf on Wall Street*, *The Street of Chance* and *The Match King*. The poor in such pictures are usually shiftless, but become attractive ne'er-do-wells when they are forced by love to do something worthwhile. Most of them marry the boss's daughter. Love is, in fact, nearly always the solution to all problems. Even in that brilliant film *Mr Deeds Goes to Town*, the final implications were shirked in favour of a romantic ending.

Why is this theme of 'rape with virginity preserved' such a safe solution to the commercial story-film? Partly because it is an 'entertaining' subject but also because love is represented as a power of nature which has nothing to do with social conditions. It rises above them, as in *Seventh Heaven* and *Broken Blossoms*. This, we know, is a lie. But it is to the interest of the film as another prop of the economic and social status quo that love should be shown as superior to all class conditions. In reality, there are strong contradictions in the social situation. In cinema, love is paramount – or should I say, United Artists?

In films of so-called history, of which there has recently been a plague, like *The Scarlet Pimpernel*, *Catherine the Great* and *The Scarlet Empress*, the mob is the villain, drunken and dissolute, constantly occupied with beheading the upper class without trial or justice. And the screen performance of Soviet Russia in the American film is amateur. Bearded moujiks, howling mobs, plotting Bolsheviks, or 'Bolshies' as they are affectionately known to all experienced casting-managers, populate every film. The old imperial court is the movie's safest setting for wild parties and drunken orgies, but its princelings and counts always come clean in the end through the love of a pure peasant girl. Such were *We Live Again* and *The Dancer from Moscow*.

More recently, there are the 'bluff' films, films which look as if they deal with social problems but actually only deal with the effects and not the root causes of social injustice. They depict the conflict as between individual and individual unrelated to class and social conditions. Such were *The Mayor of Hell*, *I Am a Fugitive from a Chain Gang*, *Gabriel Over the White House* and *Modern Times*.

From its birth the film has been used to aid war. The American cinema was born in the Spanish–American War. Romania used films of its troops in the Balkan War to arouse world enthusiasm. Japan did the same during the Russo–Japanese War. In the last War, the American film companies formed a War Co-operative Council. In 1918 the cinema was said to have put 100 million dollars into the coffers of the American war chest.

Since then, many so-called pacifist films have been made. *The Big*

Parade, Journey's End, I Was a Spy, The Dawn Patrol and *Hell's Angels* are a few. That great film *All Quiet on the Western Front* was produced to the tune of £400,000 by the same man who, during the war, had made *The Kaiser, Beast of Berlin*. He was a German by birth.

In each of these films war is shown as a terrible and ghastly thing, but, despite that, a natural catastrophe. 'Men must fight' is the basis of the theme. 'It is imperative to enlist if your country needs you.' War is inevitable, like an earthquake. No responsibility is shown. Where an attempt is made to allocate the blame, we find many sorts of reasons but never the correct one of the competitive struggle for world markets. Lately, we have armament makers shown as villains, as in *The Man Who Lost his Head*, but we know that they no more cause war than submachine guns cause Chicago gang fights. By their fatalistic attitude, their mock pacifism, their physical excitement of battle scenes, their glorification of heroism and bravery, their comic interludes behind the lines, such films succeed in making war *entertainment*.

A recent analysis undertaken by James Forman for the Payne Trust of America showed that, in an investigation of 115 films, 33 per cent of the heroines, 34 per cent of the villains and 63 per cent of the villainesses were either wealthy or of the millionaire class. The poor amounted to 5 per cent only. The most popular occupation of the characters was described as 'independence'. 'Were the population of the United States,' writes Mr Forman, 'the population of the world itself, so arranged and distributed, there would be no farming, no manufacturing, almost no industry, no vital statistics (except murders), no economic problems, and no economics.'

As for newsreels, the amount of National Government and war propaganda is so noticeable that I need not stress the point. I would mention, however, the crude technical treatment given to Mr Attlee's newsreel appearance at the last general election in comparison with the sumptuous fittings of the fake set specially built to form an impressive background to the utterances of Mr Baldwin.

From these examples, which could be extended indefinitely, two things are clear. Firstly, no film dealing with any contemporary subject from a working-class point of view can be made under the existing conditions of commercial film production. Secondly, any socially or politically conscious worker in film production must be prepared either to accept the ideological terms outlined above or else to find other sources to provide the finance for film production. It was this second alternative that gave rise to the documentary film movement in Britain, a kind of film-making that has become of increasing importance.

Films of Fact

The documentary or realist film tries to take subjects of national importance and place them on the cinema screen without the use of fiction stories or glamorous actors. Its makers follow a policy which suggests that, by a common sharing out of everyday experience, a desire for a betterment of social conditions will arise. They believe in using cinema as a means of popular education. For their money to buy film stock and equipment, they have gone not to financial speculators but to educationalists and the publicity officers of our large public utility bodies and industrial firms. In the simple job of presenting facts as facts they believe that correct implications will inevitably be drawn. They have found in this everyday material of the streets, the factories, the fields and the foundries a certain freedom which has its true roots in public service. They have brought to the screen the dignity of human labour. They have believed that by dramatising the work of the coal miner and the riveter they are at least showing the complacent city dweller and suburban householder what the working class does for its living. To state wages, hours of work, victimisation and conditions of labour has been beyond their power.

Yet they have enabled workers to see not only their own work in perspective, but that of others. They have learnt also a mastery of their medium of sight and sound and brought to the screen a portrayal of the working man which does not stink of the commercial misinterpretation in the story-film. Their job has been to bring alive the everyday experiences of the common people within the limits of sponsorship and the idiosyncrasies of the Censor Board.

The increasing growth of the cinema audience outside the public theatres, in schools, lecture groups and private film societies, has broadened the distribution of such documentary films. The marketing of portable substandard projectors at comparatively low prices has made this possible.

That gas companies have made films of slum clearance and nutrition problems and that government departments have sponsored films of the life of their workers is one of the most significant successes of the documentary film movement. But such films cannot be regarded in themselves as an antidote to the propaganda of the story-film in the public cinemas. For that to be achieved, new sources of production and new places of exhibition are needed.

Need for working-class propaganda

But those in control of the productive forces in cinema have been quick to grasp the importance of propaganda. And, apart from cinema, a survey of the position reveals a capitalist monopoly of all propagandist channels. The radio, appealing to nearly seven million licence holders, implying some 75 per cent of the population, denies any outlet to policies other than those condoned by the political party in power. The combined circulations of the national newspapers (morning, evening and Sundays) is 96 million people per week. Of that figure, the working-class share is only 13 million. In short, I suggest that Labour's share of the propagandist weapons is totally inadequate for its needs. Not only this, but I suggest that Labour's plans for propaganda are immature in comparison with those of other political parties, which are already possessed of special film units. In its own interests, in the interests of the working class of Great Britain, I suggest that the situation is such that it is imperative for Labour to organise its propaganda without delay and to make use of the most modern and most effective instruments.

Since radio is a closed monopoly, and since you have already created your own newspapers, the film may be well selected as the most powerful and accessible instrument to hand. Used intelligently and imaginatively by people of experience, the film offers to the working-class movement an outlet for propaganda of every kind and a guarantee that its policies, ideals and plans will be projected before a large percentage of our population.

Chapter 4

ALBERTO CAVALCANTI (1897–1982)

COMMENTARY

For some time now it has been clear that Cavalcanti's contribution to both the documentary film movement in particular, and cinema in general, has been underestimated. Despite this no sustained critical account of his work has appeared in English. Few have seen his early French films, and little is known of his work after leaving Britain in 1950. The book which he published in Brazil in 1976, *Film e Realidade (Film and Reality)*, has never been translated into English.

Given the promise that he once showed, it seems unfortunate that Cavalcanti was unable fully to develop his career and realise his potential. Although a very different person from Grierson, he seems to have shared Grierson's proclivity for moving on rather too quickly to new situations, and making serious errors of judgement. Elizabeth Sussex's illuminating 'Cavalcanti in England' (1975), the first item here, touches on some of Cavalcanti's moments of bad judgement, such as his early decision to leave Ealing in 1950, despite Michael Balcon's entreaties that he stay. Cavalcanti's bitterness at the way he perceives himself to have been treated by other members of the documentary movement is also evident here. The extent to which Grierson, in particular, acted against Cavalcanti may never be known, but there is evidence to suggest that some harm was done. At one level it is difficult to believe that Grierson and Cavalcanti could ever have got on, given the differences in their personalities. Grierson was didactic, dogmatic, ascetic, homophobic and colonial in mentality. Cavalcanti, on the other hand, was a cultivated European intellectual with Third World sensibilities, something of a hedonist, and gay.

Figure 4.1 Portrait of Alberto Cavalcanti.
Source: BFI. Copyright could not be traced, but the publishers will be happy to
make amendments in future editions of this book.

Cavalcanti's 'The Evolution of Cinematography in France' (1936) reveals his influence from the Parisian avant-garde at the time. He talks about cinema's ability to create rhythm and movement, and create a 'semblance of the marvellous'. He also argues that the introduction of the sound film has produced a 'regressive phenomenon', and that the aesthetic systems of the silent cinema must seek to integrate sound in a creative and experimental way. In 'The British Contribution' (1952), Cavalcanti moves rather erratically between the French avant-garde of the twenties, the documentary movement, and the problems facing the contemporary Brazilian cinema. Amongst other things he argues that Grierson was merely an exceptional promoter, and that he had argued the documentary movement should be described as 'neo-realist' long before the emergence of Italian neo-realism.

CAVALCANTI IN ENGLAND (1975)
ELIZABETH SUSSEX

Alberto de Almeida Cavalcanti, a Brazilian who first made his mark in films with the French avant-garde in the 1920s, spent sixteen of his most creative years in England. He was a key figure first in John Grierson's GPO Film Unit and then in Michael Balcon's Ealing Films – the only two movements that have pioneered styles of film-making indigenous to Britain. What exactly was Cavalcanti's contribution to both these set-ups and consequently to British cinema, and has it been sufficiently recognised?

In recent years, evidence has emerged of a strong division of opinion between Grierson and Cavalcanti, but its true nature is still concealed behind what are represented as rather petty squabbles about things like credits. Was Cavalcanti's light being deliberately hidden under a bushel from the time he began to break new ground at the GPO and his name was allegedly omitted from the credit titles of his key experiment *Coal Face*? Did he make the contribution that really put British documentary on the map? Is he perhaps the most underestimated figure in British film history? This article, which is an attempt at reassessment, is based on recent conversations with Cavalcanti in his Paris flat and with Sir Michael Balcon at his home in Sussex. It also draws on the mass of interview material with Grierson and other members of his movement, collected for my book *The Rise and Fall of British Documentary* (University of California, 1975).

'I don't know very well how you can explain', said Cavalcanti. (He sat surrounded by surrealist objects both sacred and profane. Above his head hung a huge portrait of his mother. The family resemblance was striking.)

> I don't want to appear a nasty old man, and I don't want to appear as a man who is taking advantage, but I am puzzled and astonished by certain events that I learned in succession from time to time including this last winter, that made me sort of wonder and find that the disagreement was much deeper than I thought – because

as a matter of fact, being out of work, I wrote to Grierson in great innocence, which I wouldn't have done, to ask for a job when he was in TV in Scotland.

It seems that Cavalcanti, who has been lecturing at the Film Study Center in Cambridge, Massachusetts, over the last few years (at seventy-nine he says he cannot afford to retire), was told:

> partly by people from Chicago and mostly people in Canada that Grierson had a very strange behaviour towards me when he left the GPO. It had started in London when he was at Film Centre but I never paid any attention to it and never thought it was important. Knowing what happened when he went to Canada, I realised it was that he had a kind of bitter attitude, for instance films I had to do with were forbidden to the Canadian Film Board boys . . . All the films that I made at the GPO were forbidden, and that was very peculiar.

It appears to be true that Grierson banned screenings of early British documentaries to his Canadian team, and although his reasons for this are hard to comprehend they may have had nothing to do with Cavalcanti. All this was a very long time ago. When I met Grierson only a few years back he was full of enthusiasm about the early days and gave no indication of animosity towards Cavalcanti.

But Cavalcanti has also been upset by things like the discovery that his name is not included in the entry on British documentary in the Bordas *L'Encyclopédie du Cinéma*:

> It quotes all the names of everybody of the Grierson crowd and doesn't quote mine. I could very easily go to them and say 'Who is the person who gave you this information?' I think I have the right to do that, but I just did not care and said, 'Oh well, to hell with it. What I did, I did . . .'

The recurrent argument about credits is a very considerable puzzle. 'Everybody knows that the credits in the GPO film unit were full of fantasy, and of Grierson fantasy', says Cavalcanti, and Grierson himself said that he was quite sure some of them were still 'totally wrong'. 'The selflessness of some of the documentary people was a very remarkable thing', said Grierson.

They didn't put their names on pictures. People finally had to try to discover where the credits lay, and the poor old Film Institute has never quite discovered how the credits of documentary lie even today, because we kept on putting on the names of the young people, not the names of the people who were concerned. There were years when Cavalcanti's name never went on a picture. We weren't concerned with that aspect of things, with credits. It was only latterly that credits became important to the documentary people.

What credits in particular are wrong? 'My name is not on *Coal Face*', says Cavalcanti:

I cut the film completely myself, the whole conception of the sound. It was library film. Harry shot one sequence, and Jennings shot one sequence. We used some of the old Flaherty tests . . . I faked – I did lots of shooting in the studios to be able to cut the Flaherty material in, and I wasn't given a credit. I didn't complain. After all, it was a small film. It was an experiment for *Night Mail*. On *Night Mail* I have the Auden and Britten title for 'sound direction', which doesn't exist as a credit. Well I did much more than that because the whole cutting, the conception of the whole thing, is the result of *Coal Face*. But I didn't care about that at all. I had no credits for half of the stuff I did, so it's funny to accuse me of wanting credits. If I had insisted on being given what I made I would have many more, I assure you.

In 'Afterthought', wrote Paul Rotha in his recent *Documentary Diary* (where incidentally he implies that Cavalcanti had been complaining for many years that his name had been suppressed by Grierson from credit titles and publicity on GPO films):

I think Grierson had a valid point in this one-sided argument when he recalled that Cavalcanti had asked for his name to be left off such films as *Coal Face, Granton Trawler* and *Night Mail* when they were made because he felt that association with such avant-garde work might jeopardise his chances of employment in British feature film production at that time.

When did Grierson have this recollection? According to Rotha's foot-note, it was during an interview with him at Devizes on 17 June 1970.

The idea that he wanted his name left off for this reason infuriates Cavalcanti even more than the idea that he wanted it on:

> I wasn't named three-quarters of the time, and then they say I was trying to grab a position in the fiction industry. I stayed for seven years at a wage of misery – I had to begin with £7 a week – because I was tired of fictional films in France. I was doing them, and I was very successful with the comedies I was doing, and I didn't want to go on. I wanted to experiment in sound.

It is certainly very easy to find evidence which suggests that Cavalcanti's primarily aesthetic contribution to British documentary has always been a little underplayed by comparison with that of the social propagandists who took their lead directly from Grierson. Yet Cavalcanti's contribution is acknowledged to have been a large one. To understand it properly, I think we have to go back to the beginning, which for Cavalcanti was earlier than it was for most of the others. In the 1930s, in fact, all the documentary people were rather differently placed in relation to each other from the way they are now.

When Cavalcanti came to England to join the GPO film unit in 1934, he was thirty-seven years old and had a whole career behind him. Born in Brazil, he seems to have been a lot brainier and at least a little more argumentative than average from the beginning. He began law studies at the age of fifteen and remembers being the youngest student in the university, but he was 'expelled because of a quarrel with an old professor'. His father sent him to Geneva on condition that he steer clear of both law and politics, and he trained as an architect. At eighteen he was working in an architect's atelier in Paris. From there he switched to interior decoration and then to the art department of the film studios. He did set designs from 1922 for Marcel L'Herbier, Louis Delluc and others, and he became a member of the avant-garde, which he describes as a movement of inward as well as outward dissent and strife:

> We hated ourselves. . . . We couldn't bear any of the others. We had one thing in common and one only – we were in disagreement with our masters' art, the art of the people we were working for. I thought L'Herbier didn't face films to try to make them speak their

own language. He tried to make films speak literature, and all our masters used films as kind of novels or plays. They weren't concerned in finding a language for films. We all had that in common: we thought there was a language and that it must be searched for, it must be found.

In retrospect Cavalcanti sees something constructive not just in the search but in the whole atmosphere of mutual criticism:

I don't know if that hatred among ourselves was not a good thing. I think it was and we had a trump card in our hands. We were friendly with all the great artists of our time in Paris – all the painters, sculptors, writers. They liked us and they helped us. Now if you compare what they call the *nouvelle vague* with that, the *nouvelle vague* is totally different . . . They don't detest each other at all. They love each other. They praise each other. They push each other. All that should improve on us, on the generation before, but it doesn't because they know nobody among the painters, the people in the other arts. They are completely self-centred in films, film magazines, etc. That is the true difference. When I came to England I was surprised by how much film people there were sort of tied together.

Cavalcanti came to England after several years in which, due to the arrival of synchronised sound, no avant-garde work had been possible. He had even had a period of exile from the studios 'because the French like the Americans thought the silent film directors couldn't do sound pictures', but he came back to make French and Portuguese versions of American films for Paramount. These were followed by a series of French comedies of his own which he claims were 'terrifically successful commercially' but 'very primitive' in their use of sound. 'I had learned sound the hard way,' he says, 'the know-how to record dialogue, but I thought dialogue was one small part of sound and not the sound film.' The moment Grierson's unit got its own recording equipment, he broke a contract to come over to England.

Grierson was happy. 'My boys don't know anything about sound', he said, inviting him by all means to amuse himself for a while at the unit's newly acquired studio in Blackheath. Grierson's boys knew about Cavalcanti, of course. He was one of the names that had

impressed them at Film Society screenings. Grierson was lucky or, perhaps more accurately, knew how to use his luck. First Flaherty, now
Cavalcanti. Apart from any other considerations, the reputation of the
fledgeling school of British documentary was obviously much
enhanced by its ability to attract international names like these.

Cavalcanti settled in contentedly: 'I was so happy I stayed seven
years there, and I think the result was very good. But the atmosphere
in Blackheath was wonderful, you know.' With the exception of Grierson,
who worked mainly from the unit's offices at Soho Square, Cavalcanti
found himself 'the only sort of middle aged person there'. Budding
directors like Harry Watt and Basil Wright and Humphrey Jennings,
then still in their twenties, naturally looked up to him as a film-maker
of stature as well as someone with all the technical knowledge they still
lacked.

> I was enormously grateful to him and always shall be, apart from
> his friendship which I managed to obtain, for all the things he did
> on films I was working on like *Song of Ceylon* and *Night Mail*. His
> ideas about the use of sound were so liberating that they would
> liberate in you about a thousand other ideas,

says Basil Wright. He remembers having both Grierson and Cavalcanti
in the same set-up as 'absolutely magical . . . worth a million pounds
to any young man to be there'. Harry Watt goes further. 'I believe fundamentally that the arrival of Cavalcanti in the GPO film unit was the
turning point of British documentary', he says. 'If I've had any success
in films I put it down to my training from Cavalcanti, and I think a lot
of other people should say the same thing.' Grierson's relationship with
Cavalcanti was always a little different. 'He only came to the studios to
upset my work', Cavalcanti claims now. 'He used to shift everybody all
the time, which upset me a lot . . . Indeed everybody knew this well in
Blackheath.' People knew it and, like Cavalcanti himself perhaps, chose
mostly to make a joke of it?

'It must have been very difficult for Grierson when we technicians
more and more turned to Cavalcanti with our problems,' wrote Watt in
his recent autobiography, 'but he (Grierson) was honest and shrewd
enough to realise how much more polished and professional our films
were becoming under Cav.' In fairness it must be added that Harry
Watt was never quite on Grierson's wavelength as far as work was con-

cerned. For some people, Grierson was still the dominant influence. For instance, despite his warm appreciation of Cavalcanti, it is Grierson's artistic contribution to *Song of Ceylon* that Basil Wright has almost total recall of, and indeed describes in every detail with undiminished gratitude to this day.

In any case, arriving as he did at such a crucial moment in the GPO Film Unit's story, Cavalcanti's influence as a teacher and advisor really goes without saying. More than that, however, the story of Grierson's movement is one from which Cavalcanti, at least in spirit, had never been entirely absent. Himself a pioneer in the making of avant-garde films virtually indistinguishable from what Grierson labelled 'documentary', his example was there from the beginning, and indeed the influence on British documentarists of Cavalcanti's *Rien que les heures* (1926), which was shown in London earlier than the famous Film Society programme introducing *Drifters* along with *Battleship Potemkin*, is put on record by the movement's own historian Paul Rotha.

Rien que les heures, the first film to attempt to show the ordinary daily life of a city, is well worth a fresh look with the eye of today. A great deal about it helps to illuminate Cavalcanti's career as a whole: the dramatic approach, the social consciousness in contrasting the lives of rich and poor (not in fact the prerogative of the Grierson school), the surrealism (for as Cavalcanti points out, the French avant-garde 'included all the surrealist tendencies of that time'). Its reputation suffered an initial neglect because its thunder was stolen by Ruttmann's *Berlin*, completed later but shown first in Britain and America. In subsequent years, like so much to which the British documentary movement laid special claim, it acquired that aura of potential boredom which comes of being taken too seriously. According to Rotha, for instance, 'Cavalcanti may have failed, at the time, to bring a full social realisation' to his aim which, again according to Rotha, was to show 'Man against the Street, against the turmoil of the City'. The conscious aim seems to have been a little different.

'*Rien que les heures* was an accident,' says Cavalcanti:

> because my first film (*Le Train sans yeux*) was shot in the studios in Germany and the producers didn't pay the bills and the film was held up by the studios, who wouldn't release the negative for copies because they hadn't been paid. So I got a few friends together, and we said, 'We must do a film at all costs, because we

are going to miss this winter. My film is not coming out. People will think the worst.' We made a script, and it was the cheapest film you could imagine. It cost at the time 3,000 old francs, which is nothing at all. We had no studio. We shot every thing in the streets, and of course we cut it very quickly and it came out as it was. The idea was that films were always about faraway places, about the sunsets over the Pacific, etc., and nobody had an idea that life in the town in which you lived was interesting. That was made clear in *Rien que les heures* . . . and it immediately came to look like a social document. It is a clumsy social document, but it is a social document about the lack of work, about the lives in miserable places. It had a lot of trouble with the censors, you know.

Rien que les heures is an odd mixture of images of a Paris not fre-quented by tourists. A kind of theme suggests itself in the recurrent shots of a lame and wretched woman dragging herself at a snail's pace along alleys and byways, but these shots seem to be presented quite without comment. They are bizarre, incongruous, even comical – especially in juxtaposition with the light Parisian songs that Cavalcanti himself selected to accompany a recent screening at the National Film Theatre. Perhaps it is because these shots, in their sad hopelessness, come so near to provoking laughter that they remain so strongly in the memory. Cavalcanti has been accused of a certain lack of warmth in this film, and a certain lack of feeling in general. I think it is not fully understood that his vision is surrealist rather than realist, and always therefore had the virtue of avoiding sentimentality. Apart from that, it was to be another eight years before British documentary attempted any comparable social document, in the sense of showing conditions during the Depression.

One of Cavalcanti's earliest experiments at the GPO was a fantasy called *Pett and Pott* which cannot be counted among his best work. According to Basil Wright the idea of recording the sound-track first and putting on the picture afterwards was Grierson's as well as Cavalcanti's; it was a way of getting the unit accustomed to using its newly acquired sound-recording equipment. The idea of making it a grotesque comedy Wright thinks must have been Cavalcanti's, because it stemmed from the kind of films he had been making earlier in France. But Cavalcanti was more successful in the light fantastic vein with avant-garde films like, for instance, the charming *La P'tite Lillie* (1927) which, he says, was shot in the studios in three days when a patch of grey weather prevented exterior filming on *Yvette*, the big production based on a Maupassant story which he was directing at the time:

> I bought the short ends of the big film. It (*La P'tite Lillie*) cost 7,500 francs altogether. We didn't pay the cameraman (Jimmy Rogers) or artists or anybody. When we were looking for a story, Catherine (Hessling) sang the song, and I said 'That's it!' The film lasted seven months at Les Ursulines.
>
> Two features were changed because people used to come and complain 'We want to keep *La P'tite Lillie* in the programme but we are bored to see the big film twice.' It went into all the cinemas, was sold abroad, was made into a sound film with Milhaud's music, and I never saw a penny. The distributors took it all.

Well, *Pett and Pott* wasn't at all like that, although it had the benefit of most of the available talent at the GPO Film Unit. Basil Wright and Stuart Legg were assistant directors; John Taylor photographed it; Humphrey Jennings designed the sets. Perhaps it just went to prove that, like oil and water, frivolity and British documentary don't mix. Certainly Paul Rotha has strayed far from the point when he describes it in *Documentary Diary* as showing 'Cavalcanti's influence at its most mischievous'. This attitude, however, is not unique. John Taylor, for instance, remembers *Pett and Pott* as 'the beginning of the division . . . I mean, looking back on it, it was a great mistake to have Cavalcanti really, because he didn't understand what documentary was supposed to be doing.'

Was Cavalcanti in some way undermining Grierson's work? What exactly was the difference of opinion between them? 'The only fundamental difference was that I maintained that "documentary" was a silly denomination', says Cavalcanti:

> I thought films are the same, either fictional or otherwise, and I thought that films ought to go into cinemas. Grierson little by little started creating the theory that they should be put in a different, what he called non-theatrical circuit, and I thought it was as silly as calling those films documentary. I say, if films are good,

they should and could be shown anywhere. There is no reason why they should be destined only for the parsons and for the church halls, etc.

I had a very serious conversation in the early, rosy days with Grierson about this label 'documentary' because I insisted that it should be called, funnily enough (it's only coincidence but it made a fortune in Italy), 'neo-realism'. The Grierson argument – and I remember it exceedingly well – was just to laugh and say, 'You are really a very innocent character. I have to deal with the government, and the word documentary impresses them as something serious, as something . . .' I said, 'Yes, as something dusty and something annoying.' But that was his argument, that documentary was a kind of name that pleased the government.

Of course this is much more than an argument about labels. Cavalcanti is attacking the whole basis on which Grierson decreed that documentary should develop. Cavalcanti's whole approach to life is so very different from Grierson's that it is possible he never realised the increasing gravity of his offence.

In 1937 Grierson left the GPO Film Unit and set up Film Centre in order to extend documentary into a wider field. Sir Stephen Tallents, who, as secretary of the Empire Marketing Board and public relations officer at the GPO, had always given him such invaluable support, had left the GPO in 1935 to become controller of public relations in the BBC overseas services and was now an active member of the Imperial Relations Trust set up in 1937 by the government. It was this Trust which first sent Grierson as film consultant to Canada, New Zealand and Australia.

After Grierson's departure the GPO Film Unit continued as creatively as ever under Cavalcanti. Humphrey Jennings made *Spare Time* and Harry Watt made *North Sea* – the former being attacked by the Grierson school when it came out, and the latter receiving slightly grudging praise. It was said that Cavalcanti lacked Grierson's ability to deal with the higher civil servants at the Post Office, and certainly there is evidence that Cavalcanti was no political operator. He could inspire creative people whom he approached on a personal basis, but he never really sought power and was never able to make the most of it when he had it. Both Grierson and Cavalcanti were dedicated to their work, but Cavalcanti was the more vulnerable in being, by comparison, politically naive.

When war broke out in 1939, Grierson had gone to Canada to set up the National Film Board – an exceedingly impressive operation that in itself demonstrates the difference between his kind of ambition and that of the unaggressive Cavalcantis of this world. There seemed to be a situation of considerable confusion at the newly created Ministry of Information, which took over the GPO Film Unit. According to Harry Watt, there was a longish spell when nothing at all happened because no instructions came through:'Then Cavalcanti took it upon himself to send us out. This is where Cavalcanti was great. He said, "History is being made. We can't sit here."' All the members of the unit, which included Watt and Jennings, went out and shot everything that looked interesting, and a film was quickly put together. Called *The First Days*, it was quite a promising start to the unit's wartime activities – particularly in the area that would be cultivated by Humphrey Jenrungs.

Before Cavalcanti left the GPO Film Unit, which became the Crown Film Unit when it was taken over by Ian Dalrymple in 1940, Harry Watt made *Squadron 992* and *Dover Front Line*, Jennings made *Spring Offensive*, Jack Holmes had begun *Merchant Seamen* and ideas for *London Can Take It* and *Target for Tonight* were being discussed. In fact, the unit was fairly well set on the course that it would follow throughout the war.

Why did Cavalcanti leave the GPO Film Unit and go to Ealing Studios? According to both Cavalcanti and Ian Dalrymple, it was basically because Cavalcanti could not be officially in charge there as a Brazilian.'They wanted me to get naturalised,' says Cavalcanti, 'and I didn't want to get naturalised . . . I don't believe I could be English just by changing my passport, and as I couldn't become French . . .' And then he adds that there were people appointed to the films division of the Ministry of Information whom he did not like:

I was unhappy . . . So I was looking for a job, and Mick (Balcon) had lost lots of his technical people because they had been mobilised . . . and my contract with Ealing was very pleasant because I had one film as associate producer and one film as director. So that suited me fine, and I felt that I was much better remaining a Brazilian at Mick's place.

'We were all a bit at sixes and sevens at the outbreak of war because there were signs that the government had in mind throwing the film industry overboard and not bothering about it very much', says Michael Balcon:

It was a curious position, because they had founded the Ministry of Information . . . and indeed there was a films division there, but there wasn't very much direction as far as the then Post Office Film Unit was concerned. That was quite in the early days. I think there was an element of dissatisfaction amongst these men who felt that they were capable of making a greater contribution. Many of them, and Cavalcanti in particular, were terribly worried by the sort of bureaucratic control that was even stronger in wartime than in peacetime, and there were signs that the unit was going to break up. Happily it was restored later on, because Dalrymple was made the head of the unit and he whipped it into shape and it did magnificent work during the war. But at this particular time they wanted a breakaway, and there were opportunities at Ealing and Cavalcanti was the first to come over. We told him that if we were allowed to go on – there was some doubt at the outbreak of war – we'd be very happy to have him because, apart from anything else, apart from his great talents as a film-maker, any sort of personnel that could be retained without difficulty was something to be grateful for.

For the second time in England, Cavalcanti found himself in an atmosphere in which he was almost completely at home. His memories of Ealing are full of affection. 'Mick was the best producer I ever had', he says:

He was very understanding. He had been in films for years, and he knew the public and he had a sense of box office that was quite deep, because sometimes he said, when he saw the rushes, 'I don't like this. That must be remade.' If you kept on trying to ask 'Why, Mick?' or 'Can't you tell me what's wrong?' very often he didn't know, but he sensed it was wrong. He had an uncanny sort of instinctive sense of films.

'He fitted into our pattern very well because you see, I was at the crossroads myself', says Balcon:

By the time the war broke out, I'd been at it for twenty years and so had Cavalcanti, but Cavalcanti had devoted his life to what we now call the documentary field. I had spent the whole of my time in the normal commercial field where I suppose, the motives that guided us were (a) to found what we thought to be a native industry without being dominated by America, and (b) of course to make films which were as good in marketing terms as the American films which then dominated the whole world. I don't think we had our minds very much upon finer issues which developed later, as to the importance of the films and what they meant in social terms. We were engaged in a commercial operation.

I felt of course – most of us felt quite definitely at the outbreak of war – that the type of film we'd been making in the past would not do, either in war conditions or in the future, and that is why I was eager to get Cav into the studio. I felt sure, to use these ugly words, some cross-fertilisation of our respective experiences, something different, would emerge – and indeed it did. I suppose, to an extent, because he had certain influences on the Ealing output . . . It's not being egocentric to say that I was in charge of the whole output there and my word went, but it was a very democratic control that I exercised and the whole thing was run on a group basis, and of all the group there – and there were some very talented people – I would say that Cavalcanti was the most important and the most talented of the people available to talk to and work with.

What sort of influence did Cavalcanti have on Ealing films? Balcon pointed out that most of Ealing's young talents like Charles Frend, Penrose Tennyson, Charles Crichton, Robert Hamer got their first chance to direct there:

Now, however talented they were – because take a man like Hamer, he was a minor poet, a brilliant mathematician and could have had a career anywhere – they were still short of experience in dealing with visual images on the screen. And this is what Cavalcanti could do for them. He was a vastly experienced man as to how to transfer images to the screen – a curious man, you know, in some respects, until he got going. By virtue of the fact that he didn't know English very well, he could sometimes be completely inarticulate, especially when he got excited. But some-how when he was on the floor, near the camera, talking to these people, just some little things he could do would make all the difference . . . Men like Charles Frend, good as they were, made better films with Cavalcanti by their side . . . Apart from anything else, he was a man of infinite taste. He knew about settings. He knew about music. He knew about European literature. He was a highly civilised man. They all were, but he was a particularly out-standing figure . . . All those things helped to make good films . . .

This is why, and I may be wrong, I always thought that Cavalcanti was better producer material than he was director material. Now that doesn't in any way denigrate him because, in the days that we were working, I thought the talents were equally important and probably the production talent rather more important. But every-body doesn't think that way, and most producers always want to be directors. Cavalcanti wanted to be a director, and of course he directed some films of some importance, but I still think his great work was, and still could be if he were going on today, in produc-tion and the influences he brings to bear on other people. I think that must inevitably be so with films in the English language because, even if he speaks many languages, there must be some difficulties in directing English actors for anybody who hasn't complete mastery of the language. From the visual side he'd always be all right. Whether he was equally good in the direction of actors is a matter for discussion.

One thing I want to emphasise is that he is a great film man. If I point out what appear to be certain slight weaknesses or imper-fections, it is because it would be wrong if I didn't. It wouldn't be fair to a really very important man . . . I know no better sequence for direction than the last incident in *Dead of Night*. If you look at it and examine it, it's still largely a terrifically visual sequence. This is Cavalcanti at his best. Another film that was well directed by Cavalcanti was *Went the Day Well?*. Oddly enough, it's never been recognised as an important British film. I think it was.

Based on a story by Graham Greene, who seems not to have liked the film ('We added so many episodes', says Cavalcanti, 'that perhaps he couldn't recognise it'), *Went the Day Well?* (1942) is an imaginary account of what happened during the German occupation of the

English village of Bramley End over the Whitsun weekend of 1942. The Germans, disguised in British uniforms but just occasionally giving themselves away by, for instance, bashing a troublesome small boy about the head, writing their sevens in the continental way, or bringing the odd bar of 'Schokolade Wien' from home with them, have their path smoothed by British quisling Leslie Banks. All the adult villagers are rounded up in the church; the children confined in an upstairs room of Marie Lohr's manor. Nice people who try to resist are ruthlessly put down, until the tide turns in favour of the villagers. It is devastating to see the cold-blooded revenge they now wreak on the men they had initially entertained as guests in the vicarage, the manor house and elsewhere according to their station. Sweet young English girls are seizing the guns from German corpses, vying with each other to shoot down as many of the beastly Hun as possible. It's not like killing real people. It's a sort of sport. The main emphasis that Cavalcanti himself puts on the film, which he regards as his best film at Ealing, is its deeply pacifist nature: 'People of the kindest character, such as the people in that small English village, as soon as war touches them, become absolutely monsters.' It says something for the British film industry and government that such a film was able to emerge at such a time, and the fact that there were some reactions against it is hardly surprising.

Went the Day Well? pulls together most of the threads that run through Cavalcanti's work: the documentary authenticity, the drama, the surrealism. A remarkable thing about him is that, despite being a Brazilian with a European background, or perhaps because of it, he could put his finger precisely on the essential Britishness of the British and make it a special point of interest. The documentary movement may have gained more than anyone was aware of from this ability of his to see and draw out what was there already. Michael Balcon describes what his arrival meant to Ealing:

> I don't think that up to that point the films I was concerned with, with certain exceptions, had a special trade mark of their own. We know the Jessie Matthews comedies were this; the Hulbert and Courtneidge comedies were that; but the outputs as a whole didn't have any particular stamp to them. He certainly helped me, probably more than anybody else, to create an image. The whole of the Ealing output had a certain stamp on it. Whether I would

have done it on my own I don't know. But most certainly I acknowledge, and always have acknowledged, that of all the help I got his is the help that was the most important.

That surrealism is part of Cavalcanti's view of life has been evident from the outset, but the British are not naturally given to understanding surrealism or the various extensions or applications of it. As far as Cavalcanti is concerned, we are likely to be much more impressed by the surrealist shock tactics of *Dead of Night* than by the grim humour of certain scenes in *Went the Day Well?* where realism has simply been carried a stage further into surrealism. This kind of effect can be achieved only by first ensuring plausibility and then demonstrating the implausibility of the plausible. The only British director who has become master of it is Lindsay Anderson, and it is interesting to realise that in this way Anderson's documentary roots are much closer to Cavalcanti (himself an ardent admirer of the work of Humphrey Jennings) than to Grierson.

Although the other features Cavalcanti directed at Ealing – *Champagne Charlie* and *Nicholas Nickleby* – are less noteworthy, he was also involved in a programme of short films which Michael Balcon describes as having been 'right up Cavalcanti's street'. Some of these he directed – propaganda films like *Yellow Caesar*, instructional films like *Watertight* which (oddly?) are not included in the main histories of British documentary. Cavalcanti is still very enthusiastic about the distribution that these documentaries got in the cinemas, because each of them went out with a big picture. Balcon finds less significance in this:

They were propaganda films during wartime, and there were fewer films available in wartime than there were in most normal times . . . As you know, short films have always been a difficult market, because only West End houses ran these supporting short feature programmes. Most of the houses in the provinces have always gone for double feature programmes. In wartime it was different . . . Also I might tell you that although they liked us to make them and we could get them into the West End, I can't pretend that even in wartime the rest of the country were falling over themselves to book these films. They had to be forced wherever we could in support of features.

The documentary story never really changes. It only seems to now and then.

At the beginning of the war Cavalcanti also completed an anthology film called *Film and Reality*, which was commissioned by the British Film Institute. A sensible and occasionally exciting collection of excerpts from realist films, including newsreels, produced up to that time, it provoked some extremely angry reactions from British documentarists. According to Paul Rotha, still apparently bitter about it when writing his *Documentary Diary* of 1973, it:

> did less than justice to the social aims of the British documentary group, whose work as shown, when at all, was inadequate and false. In spite of protests by the Associated Realist Film Producers, especially in a strong letter to *The Times*, the film was not withdrawn although some film libraries abroad would not distribute it. It is, I am told, still in use in some places today.

Rotha goes on to report an argument that took place in the *New Statesman* in June 1942, as a result of film critic William Whitebait's remark that Ministry of Information films 'set a very high standard indeed; and the tradition that has produced them owes more to Cavalcanti than to any other man'. To this Rotha replied that 'one man, and one man only, John Grierson, was responsible for the birth and inspiration of the 300-odd British documentary films made between 1929 and 1939, including those of which Cavalcanti was himself director'. Harry Watt then joined in:

> It was Grierson's drive and initiative that obtained the formation and sponsoring of the EMB Film Unit, from which eventually so many offshoots have sprung. But I, as a film worker with both men, would like to say that I am convinced that it was the introduction of Cavalcanti's professional skill and incredible film sense that raised the standard and reputation of British documentary to the pitch where today it has become a considerable influence on the cinema as a whole.

Rotha then claims: 'For my own part, as a result of my letter quoted above, I was told that references to my work were in due course removed from *Film and Reality*.' To this he appends the footnote: 'I am happy to record, however, that Cavalcanti and I have always remained the best of friends.'

Cavalcanti does not deny the friendship. The trouble, he suggests, was because the film was too long and he cut out the only Rotha excerpt along with one or two others.'Rotha was very cross about it. He wanted to be in it.' Cavalcanti also explains:

> With my wrong sense of humour I did a bad turn to Grierson. I put Mendelssohn's 'Fingal's Cave' over *Drifters*, which was putting it back into romantic sort of films, and I don't think that pleased Grierson at all . . . But really you must realise that Grierson at the bottom was quite a demagogue. Yes, his parents being parsons and so on, he had a kind of disposition for preaching. And preaching and that sort of thing delighted him, and he was very good at it too, I thought.

The truth of the matter is that the only thing seriously wrong with Cavalcanti's *Film and Reality* is that it is not the selection that Grierson or Rotha would have made. On the contrary, it gives an encouraging impression of the wide variety of film material shot in a realistic vein long before British documentary was even contemplated. From Marey and the Lumière brothers through early newsreels and interest films, clips from the *Secrets of Nature* and X-ray films used in medical diagnosis, there is no mention of British documentary except to say that Charles Urban, director of *Romance of the Railway* (1907), was grandfather of it. *Song of Ceylon* eventually comes up at the end of a section (mainly devoted to Flaherty) about 'Romantic Documentaries of Faraway Places'. *Drifters, Industrial Britain, Housing Problems* and *Night Mail* occupy part of a section (which opens with *Rien que les heures*) on 'Realistic Documentaries of Life at Home'. Here British documentary is described as a 'movement to use films for civic education'. Here too an extract from a French film made by Jean Benoit-Levy in 1932, showing a potter making a pot, compares very well with one's memory of the similar sequence shot by Flaherty in 1931 for *Industrial Britain* and admired almost to distraction by Grierson. At the end of this section Pare Lorentz's *Plow that Broke the Plains* is described as owing much to the British school. Then Cavalcanti moves on to 'Realism in the Story Film': Stiller, James Cruze, Eisenstein, Zecca, Dieterle, Méliès, Pabst, Renoir, etc., obviously nothing more of British documentary.

I cannot help feeling that Cavalcanti had worked with the documentary movement long enough to realise that Mendelssohn's 'Fingal's Cave' was not the only bad turn he would be accused of having done to Grierson in all this. In fact, he dared to give the impression that his conception of 'realist films' was wider than the idea which Grierson labelled 'documentary'. If it was his 'wrong sense of humour' that made him go so far, I do feel that he has since paid dearly for it.

How is it possible to be fair to everybody in circumstances like these? Pointless to say the arguments don't matter because they do – particularly when the spokesman for a movement famed for its liberal-mindedness can still regret some thirty-five years later that an intelligent and informative film has not been taken out of circulation. I can only say thankfully that I saw the film recently at the British Film Institute, that as long as this applies reassessments are possible, and the chance remains that time will set everything right.

'If there is a British cinema,' says Michael Balcon, 'I would put Cavalcanti's contribution pretty well as high as any ... because in a curious way the work he did doesn't reflect itself in credit titles.' This is the problem. Cavalcanti's reputation is to quite a large extent dependent on the word of those who worked with him, but no injustice is necessarily implied by this. Very often there was no way to indicate by means of credits an influence as varied and subtle as his. Like Grierson's initial feat in getting finance for documentary, the stamp that Cavalcanti subsequently put on it could only be belittled by the sort of abbreviated job descriptions that credit titles amount to. This is perhaps why it still remains unclear whether Cavalcanti really cared about having credits at the time or not. It was always a debatable kind of compliment.

Cavalcanti still speaks warmly of the atmosphere at Ealing: 'There were no petty jealousies, no difficulties at all.' Yet he left Ealing in the late 1940s, basically because it seemed to him that he could earn more as freelance than under the terms of his Ealing contract. He and Michael Balcon disagreed about the fairness of the deal he was getting from Ealing at the time, but both say he left in order to earn more money.

'It was a change of mood', says Balcon:

All the wonderful things, the group things we did, the ideas which made us tick during the war, began to disintegrate. There wasn't the same motive, and it became a harsher and rather more cynical period. People's values began to alter, and their success began to be measured in terms of money, and if Cav were to completely examine himself over these things, he was tempted away the same as all the other people. It was Oscar Wilde who said that a man can resist everything except temptation, and this is what happened . . .

I'm the first to admit that this group work of ours worked for twenty years, but when we gave it up none of us as individuals were as important as we were collectively . . . Everybody went out and had plenty of things to do, but when you come to examine it in terms of results none of us were as good separately as we were together. I think that Cav missed it more than anybody I know, and I'm not talking about the support he got from me or from anybody else. I just talk of it in general terms, the support he got from being with Ealing Studios.

Certainly Cavalcanti's career seems rarely to have been as satisfying or as successful since he left Ealing. Around 1950 he left England altogether, apparently intending to set up home in his native Brazil. When I asked him about this in an earlier interview, in 1971, he said:

Oh, don't talk about it. It was a mistake to go to Brazil, and I lost in fact everything I had. It's quite an unhappy adventure. No, it is a mistake to send a boy of fifteen away from his country, because it's from fifteen to twenty-five you settle your entourage and choose your friends.

In the latest interview he described a very confusing situation in which he was trying to create a film industry which would have a real local spirit in São Paulo, while Italian technicians were plotting to push out the other nationalities, and Americans were accusing him of being a Communist and there were documents reminiscent of the Inquisition deposited in the Brazilian Foreign Office. (I hope I have interpreted his meaning here correctly.) Certainly he said he had a contract for three years, but that at the end of the first year he was thrown out because they didn't understand what he was after. He made two films and was halfway through another. He had six complete scripts ready for the second year, but after he left, production was almost at a standstill for two years.

'Why did you go to Brazil?' I asked him. 'I lost my mother', he said. (His mother was a considerable personality, known to all his friends as a great and good influence on his life.)

> And I had a big project for an independent production. I had the rights of *Sparkenbroke* by Charles Morgan. It was – I still believe it was – the best script I ever made. It's a bad novel, but it's a good film story...I had made all the choice of locations, and I had discovered beautiful places that were quite unknown, and all of a sudden I received from that collaborator of Rank (I was working for him) a letter saying that my script was above the understanding of the public. I had lots of times in my life had it told to me, and of course I was disgusted. It was about four month's work, and very expensive work. To make a long script is a big job. So I had an invitation to go to Brazil to lecture about films to the Museum of Modern Art at São Paulo, and I accepted and went.

Cavalcanti's story is latterly a sad one. There can be no getting away from that, although I feel at a disadvantage in commenting on the later years because there have been a number of films in Brazil, Austria, Romania, Italy (in the 1950s) and more recently a couple of plays (one of them by Dürrenmatt) on French television which I, like most people in Britain, have not seen. The Austrian film, *Herr Puntila und sein Knecht Matti* (1955), was based on the comedy by Bertolt Brecht, and something of the charm that endeared Cavalcanti to the many British film-makers who have been indebted to him emerges very simply from his account of his first meeting with the revered Brecht:

> I had a great, great admiration for him. I thought he was a master – even better than a playwright, he was a great poet. I liked scripting what he did very much, and the first script he refused. The second script (*Herr Puntila*) he sent me (I hadn't met him), I refused. It was the play; he hadn't changed a line. So I said at the start – he had made lawsuits against Fritz Lang, against Pabst, against all my colleagues – so I said, 'I am in the basket. He's going to annoy me no end.' But I had a very intelligent woman producer, who said, 'Look here, this is silly. You and Brecht are made to be friends and to understand each other. You speak the same language. Come with me to Berlin.' And I shall never forget – it was a summer day like this – and I came to his house. The big room had three

windows towards the cemetery. He immediately took me by the arm, as if he knew me all the time. He knew I had refused his script. He knew we were going to try together to make one, and he took me to the window and said, 'Do you know who is buried there?' I said, 'No.' He said, 'Hegel.'

'It's a sad thing to say', Cav added, 'that he is buried just by Hegel now.'

THE EVOLUTION OF CINEMATOGRAPHY
IN FRANCE (1936)

At the International Congress of Independent Cinematography, at Sarrez, my remarks on the growth of cinematography from the dramatic point of view were to indicate the solution of some questions with which my comrades and myself were occupied, questions that were the purpose of the meeting.

The silent cinema is dead. Its decline provoked a crisis so violent that we have neither composure nor recoil. Toward the establishment of an historical view of this silent phase, however, an examination of the material already allows formulation of a certain amount of certitude, and an analysis of the *aesthetique*.

A composite reel made up of a resumé of cinematic work in France since 1893 and selections from French films were projected to illustrate the talk at Sarrez.

The first film I think was a release from the Lumière flat in Lyons in 1894. This film was more self-sufficient than evocative; it was followed by a short period of enthusiasm. It concerned the arrival of people by train, and a boat moving around a dock. It carried sufficient novelty and movement to retain attention. Cinematic art began with *L'Arrosseur Arrose* in 1900. Was the cinema aware of its possibilities? Was it going to interpret human emotion, the comic life itself? Also instead of catching its true voice in the beginning indicated so clearly in this film, the year lost itself in encumbrances with theatrical tradition. Armand Callier has shown us at the Studio des Ursulines several very beautiful examples of theatre-film. How is one to forget *Mimosa la derniere grisette*, with Leonace Perret, and above all, *Werther* with André Brule? The year recalls also *L'Assassination du Duc de Guise*, one of the first of the 'historic reconstruction' class of film that unhappily remains much in vogue among French directors. This did not at all impede development, for the cinema recovered itself, first with Melies who was the author of one of the first fantasy films.

The cue was not found alone in fantasy films, however: Fevillade turned out a little later the first comedies (the series of the Belée, for example) played out of doors, which one has not seen again and which in spite of their twenty years seem scarcely obsolete. The period had not completely passed away when Louis Delluc began to work. He died young, before he had arrived at a fruition of his work. He was a theorist of the first order. Even though they are incomplete, his works for the most part are beautiful specimens and they mark distinctly a new transition.

The cinema reacts definitely against the double influence of the theatre and of letters in the growth of the episodic, the cultural and the comic film. A curious lacuna particularly in French production is the long disappearance of the comic film so abundantly and astonishingly developed in America. Only the films of Max Linder are excepted.

Forthwith in the appearance of masterpieces such as *Judex*, or in America *The Mysteries of New York*, the intrusion of decor in its turn shackled the growth of the cinema from the dramatic point of view. How can we forget apartments grander than the cathedrals and intimate affairs where one saw scores of figures?

By the side of this ostentation which tended to bring to cinema sumptuous spectacles of the bad music hall, dramatic documents took on in their disturbing simplicity all the power of photographic veracity. One will never say too much of what a valuable lesson these actualities have been, one indispensable in the evolution of cinematography. How could one forget the straining vision of an automobile race accident in the United States? You saw the torn form thrown into the air and fall to the ground. In another you saw a ship that starts to flounder careen on the waves; the sailors let her glide and escape the wreck by swimming in the fatal turmoil of the engulfment.

These cruder devices were used for a long time. The technique achieved adequacy for the time; objectives of great works were seen. The panchromatic film was evolved. Then a dimunition of scale cinematography reached a point that would have seemed formerly quite improbable. This has brought forth a precision that seems absolute and consonant to the rhythm of the images. One such reduction of scale was a study of a vivid struggle between a mongoose and a cobra; an extreme dimunition was that of a soap bubble which burst; another of a revolver bullet penetrating a plank, and another of the flight of a dragon-fly – these mysteries gave up their secrets in the excellent photography of these rhythms, movements and solutions.

Today most improvement in the domain of speed hardly seem to astonish us. The achievement that will again appease us will perhaps arise in the growth of greater unification of cinematic elements. How much on the side of semblance of the marvellous should one try to attain in a film? The problem calls for realisation that is profound. To have reverence for life, to guard its wild freedom, to interpret it in an act of true reconstruction – this is something to look forward to in the cinema.

It is not always possible to renew data sufficiently to have actuality, nor to accept the rhythm revealed in the first unification of the picture. One secures an alien rhythm of the flow of images themselves. This is called montage. It is brought out by means of adjusting simple interior rhythms, and powerfully it accents dramatic action. Among the first beautiful examples of concordant rhythms one may name the mounting of the machine in La Rove (Gance) and the summons to battle in *Le Jouer d'echecs* (Bernard).

Reacting in its turn against certain bad usages of montage the travel films, often of great dramatic power, co-operate by their naturalism to re-establish the film in a form that is better balanced. *La Croissière noir* (Poerier), *Le Voyage d'André Gide au Congo* (Allegret) in France, and *Grass, Chang, Moana* and others have had a direct influence on film direction.

In the future the cinema finds in pure photography the material of its unique kind of drama. It exists by itself. It is neither a question of theatre nor of literature. Dramatic structure of the film, it seems to us, has arrived at a degree of purity and perfection that is difficult to surpass when the sound element comes into consideration. We thought the formula already found for cinematography was definitive, but instead of proceeding on a new stage of present growth as one expected, the introduction of sound has produced on the contrary a regressive phenomenon. They do not show us the equal of *Train de la Ciotat* and of *Canot contournant la jettée*, etc. The opera singers and players of the saxaphone whom one likes well enough on discs are works of filmed theatre, and we cannot believe such violations will endure. Rather we are seeking to realise in the new form of cinematography the visual and auditory elements that will make up the developed sound film.

With sound film a new era is upon us, and cinematography should begin to evolve the destiny that the addition of tone now lays upon the silent drama.

THE BRITISH CONTRIBUTION (1952)

The word 'documentary' has a taste of dust and boredom. The Scotsman John Grierson, questioned by me about the birth of our school which, I told him, should really be called neo-realist – before the post-war Italian cinema had come into being – replied that the idea of a 'document', as opposed to a 'film', was of use in dealing with a suspicious Conservative government. Grierson's skill and highly individual methods of diplomacy, based on the simple principle of never accepting no for an answer, achieved a great deal for the documentary in Great Britain.

Grierson's achievements can only now be analysed in perspective. He was basically a promoter. He had little impact as a director or producer, but his flair for finding collaborators, his ease in providing wonderful titles to our worst films, his great capacity as a publicist, and, above all, his curious background, half Presbyterian and half Marxist, made him one of the most influential personalities in the movement. The history of the true British documentary began with the Empire Marketing Board, an organisation designed to develop commercial relations between the different countries of the British commonwealth, and directed with intelligence by Sir Stephen Tallents. It was in this organisation that Grierson launched *Drifters*, his first and, really, only film. However, *Drifters* appears a disappointing work when we review it today, characterised by innumerable montage fusions and undiscriminating camerawork.

In Britain, from 1930 onwards, the screening of prestigious documentaries in cinemas led to profits which made Wardour Street production houses feel restless. The critics were unanimous in praising these films, acclaiming their contribution in the social domain, and their educational value. After a tentative beginning the majority of these films ran in the commercial circuits, as complements to the main programmes. However, in the big commercial feature film productions, the preoccupation with exploring certain basic instincts of the popular masses had become the rule, and nobody was prepared to risk the interest of the cinema-going public over conflicts other than the sexual or the sentimental. It was an aesthetic of ready-made clichés, a style without depth. Against the deserved success of Gloria Swanson, Gary Cooper, Greta Garbo and Mae West, who had the power to create an unarguably sensual atmosphere which succeeded through its simplicity, were invented'ersatz'models: the Joan Crawfords and Marlene Dietrichs, to name but a few, who created caricatures, representative of this sexual obsession which the production houses blamed on the public. However, despite the prejudices of the distributors and exhibitors, some audiences did insist on seeing films which dramatised problems other than those connected with sex.

In the documentary movement, Grierson surrounded himself with those elements which suited his ends. He had the option to choose graduates from the two great British universities, Cambridge and Oxford. By tradition, Oxford would have supplied him with students who were not particularly interested in the solution of practical problems. Cambridge was the opposite, however; it was the country's most prestigious centre of democratic education, and it was here that Grierson went to search for most of his collaborators.

Grierson also brought in Flaherty, whom I only met personally ten years after having seen *Moana*, and Flaherty, like myself, remained connected from then on with the British documentary movement. When I arrived in England, Flaherty had completed a few projects with Grierson's team; he had filmed scenes for *Aero-Engine*, and, from these scenes, Gaumont-British had edited *Industrial Britain*, one of the first British documentaries of the new era. Michael Balcon, today Sir Michael, had financed Flaherty's *Man of Aran* and, when I joined the GPO Film Unit, Flaherty had just left for the Aran islands with his brother David and a small crew, of which John Taylor was one.

On Aran Flaherty saw giant metal pots where the islanders made oil from shark fat. But by then this was already a dead industry. Looking for ways to dramatise the miserable lives of the fishermen of Aran, Flaherty decided to reconstruct shark fishing. A ship was sent to the Bay of Biscay to tow back a shark. The shark arrived, more dead than alive, in the cold waters of the Irish sea. The scenes were filmed, but even a great director could not revive such a sick and exhausted shark, and the episode was certainly not the happiest of the film.

Gaumont-British decided, however, that a shark that had travelled so extensively could not end its destiny so prosaically. Specialists stuffed and boxed the animal, and the shark was sent to Wardour Street. Unfortunately the display windows at Gaumont were not large enough to contain the shark, and it became necessary to cut a large-sized chunk off to shorten the animal. Every time I passed by this window display I reflected that Flaherty had something in common with that fish: too big for a Wardour Street window display, but belonging to the film industry which understood him so poorly.

Flaherty brought the fishermen from Aran who had acted in the film with him back to London. I was introduced to him on a night when he was surrounded by Pat Mullan, Tiger King and others. Pat Mullan later wrote a book about the filming. His daughter, Barbara, became a great actress of the British theatre and cinema, and went on to marry John Taylor. An old fisherman told stories of Irish legend. Meggie, a thin and ugly middle-aged woman, sang traditional ballads from Aran, in a high-pitched voice. Afterwards, some danced the simple steps from the island, and the little fisherman, who had looked so pathetic in the film, slept at Flaherty's feet. Nevertheless, *Man of Aran* disappointed us, because of the weakness of the sound-track, which was little more than a form of musical accompaniment.

Flaherty's psychology was very simple. Before anything it was that of a handsome man, of a happy man, of an honest man. He made films because he felt he had a need to. At that time, for example, he gave much thought to a project about the history of coal mining. It was the story of a boy, who worked underground, and his friend, a blind horse. The boy was the same that appears in all Flaherty's films: Flaherty had only daughters, and always wished for a son. The film about the coal mines was never made because the producers retreated when faced with the social problems that it represented, and Flaherty was not prepared to compromise over this.

Elephant Boy came later. Alex Korda, a Hungarian producer who had settled in England, misunderstood Flaherty, just as Hollywood had. Zoltan Korda, Alex's brother, interfered with *Elephant Boy*, and Flaherty was furious. He had already reluctantly accepted the collaboration of F. W. Murnau in *Tabou* and, with restrictions, that of W. Van Dyke in *White Shadows*, but Zoltan Korda was too much! The film was completed in Denham, with mechanical elephants, and Sabu, the little boy in the film, went to Hollywood, where he became prosperous and overweight. When we see him today we understand that Sabu is the only human being who has had his ghost invoked by Flaherty, long before his own death. In Samoa, where Flaherty filmed *Moana*, almost all of the idyllic natives who appeared in the film suffered from venereal disease. But

Flaherty knew nothing of this, absorbed as he was in creating a world of innocence and beauty. It was only later that his brother David had the courage to tell him the truth about this.

While Flaherty, as a film-maker, continued the struggle on his own for the survival of the documentary as he understood it, in England, together with the GPO Film Unit, Grierson constantly manoeuvred so that, despite the fact that the Unit depended on the government for funding, the government did not interfere too much in the affairs of the Film Unit. This was a considerable achievement for Grierson, making him an exceptional promoter, and his dynamic commitment would be repeated later in Canada, with the creation of the National Film Board of Canada.

The role of producer is a relatively recent development in the history of cinema. Today that role is divided between financial accounting and artistic development, but during that period Grierson made no such a distinction. I had, earlier, struggled with directorial problems which were difficult to resolve without the help of a producer. After having taken part in the development of the French avant-garde, and having experienced a number of problems as a result, I found myself prepared to observe this new documentary group, from which an entire school of British cinema would later be born. The economic infrastructure of the avant-garde was very basic. The directors found a patron, or some generous friends, and, to some extent, organised their own production. When the film was finished it was handed over to people who called themselves distributors. They would accept everything that was given to them . . . but the little capital that we had collected with such difficulty would disappear, and then they would argue, as with Flaherty, that our films were not commercial enough (despite this, however, my *La P'tite Lillie*, which cost only 7,500 francs, was shown as the main attraction for six months at the Ursulines Cinema, one of the most expensive cinemas in Paris). This is an old story, which we know well here in Brazil: profits, which are divided between the exhibitor and distributor, rarely reach the producers. If a film makes a small profit, all the better, but if the exhibitors do not then want to project it, all the worse. In effect, the distributors would not risk anything and, consequently, the French cinema grew up within this atmosphere of uncertainty, only becoming what it is today when the government decided to organise and defend it.

When the sound film arrived in France the major producers, who did not really trust the film directors of the avant-garde, imposed such conditions that many of the avant-garde directors had no choice but to return to earlier ways of developing films; that is, each one started, once again, to improvise with their own low-budget productions. It was in this way that Renoir, Painlevé, Chenal, Carné and some others carried on, albeit precariously. But they were the fortunate few, and many others were sacrificed in the process, with the coming of sound. We should not forget to mention, once again, Jean Vigo, in this respect, who would have been the best of them all, but who died a victim of all of this.

This uncertain situation was bound to produce the disastrous results which made the beginning of the sound film in France a despicable period in the history of French cinema, even more so than was the case with the United States. Meanwhile, in Great Britain, Grierson, backed by Sir Stephen Tallents, simply ignored the sound film. Sustained by Marxist ideas, he accepted the moral leadership of the documentary movement, which had been created by him on competely virgin territory. The sad story of the errors of the avant-garde could not be repeated here. A steadfast group took it upon themselves to make documentaries, about fishing, crafts, methods of communication and social problems – in short, about subjects taken from the reality of the moment.

The documentary movement grew quickly. However, the time taken up by publicity, to which great importance was given, and the absorbing task of linking with government circles, stopped Grierson from being able to closely supervise his team, and from resolving technical problems at the GPO Film Unit. Inspired by Flaherty, who was at the time the instructor of the group, newcomers such as Wright, Elton, Legg and Taylor were able to perfect their techniques. When Flaherty left the group to begin filming *Man of Aran*, towards the end of 1934, I explained to Grierson the impasse within which I found myself. I described with bitterness the stupid and tiresome mechanism of the French commercial cinema, and the ephemeral nature of the 'vaudevilles' that I was making with great commercial success in Paris – an entanglement of false situations, in which the characters would go from table to bed, and vice versa.

I did not then know that, from this period at Paramount, and from this series of French 'vaudevilles', I would aquire a level of technical experience which would serve me well in my future career. I had, at that time, reached a point where, after the introduction of the sound film, I had given up all hope of filming a subject that I liked, using sound in a way that I felt it ought to be used. It was then that Grierson turned to me and said – 'Stay with us, enjoy yourself and explain your ideas about sound to the team. We have done nothing of this nature yet.' And then, later, 'A few weeks from now you will receive a proposal from Wardour Street for a commercial film, and we will lose you . . .

However, as soon as I began work I understood that Grierson was the man capable of satisfying the lack I had sorely felt in France, and I no longer thought of Wardour Street. The experimentation with sound was one of the greatest successes of this rich school of documentary, although sound was not the only thing I explored. Together with this enthusiastic, hard-working and disciplined team of film-makers, I studied narrative construction, camerawork and montage and, little by little, I began to understand how important Grierson was to the documentary movement. Luckily, Wardour Street had already forgotten about me, and I remained working happily at the Film Unit 's tiny studios at Blackheath.

Here in Brazil, I am accused of never having been a director of fiction films, and of limiting my career in Europe to documentary. However, in reality, documentaries account for only a small proportion of the films I have made. Although I was the instigator of a certain form of novel-like documentary, with *Rien que les Heures*, in 1925, I have spent the greater part of my career directing commercial films, of which I have more than twenty to my credit. Anyone who knows cinema will know that this is a significant quantity, because, outside Brazil, only directors whose films have achieved profit are able to continue their careers to this extent. Nevertheless, far from considering myself lessened, I am, in fact, proud of my documentary work, even though that work may be considered to be of minor importance by those in my country who harbour bad intentions against me.

Shortly before my arrival in London, the Empire Marketing Board had suspended its activities, and the EMB Film Unit had been absorbed into the General Post Office, which prided itself on being one of the largest industrial organisations and government departments in the United Kingdom. The publicity for the GPO was directed by a board headed by Sir Stephen Tallents and which also contained, besides Grierson, Jack Beddington, who afterwards took on responsibility for publicity at Shell. The GPO Film Unit put their services at the disposal of the country's social education needs, and it was thanks to this spirit that British documentary (together with Soviet documentary) eventually became the most effective in allied propaganda during the Second World War, and, afterwards, the cradle of post-war British cinema.

Shortly after its foundation some film-makers left the GPO Film Unit, but they did not escape the influence of Grierson. Grierson and I remained at the GPO, and outsiders such as Paul Rotha and Jack Holmes came to join our group. Musicians such as Walter Leigh and Maurice Jaubert, both destined to die during the war, also arrived, and they were followed by other musicians, such as Benjamin Britten, Ernest Mayer and Darius Milhaud, and poets such as W. H. Auden and Montagu Slater.

It was a curious situation, however, that, in Great Britain, where millions of pounds were spent on the cinema, the British film did not really exist. All those concerned with this problem, critics, film-makers and artists, had, moreover, only one hope, the GPO Film Unit. The documentary movement was the first to show the British Isles, and the rest of the world, the landscape, people and work of this country.

To quote Graham Greene:

the impression I want to give is that here, in these small documentary production companies, there are still directors who live normally, gathering imaginative material from the streets, from the neighbours, who are not buried, with hundreds of pounds per week, in great silent, carpeted, offices so much the fashion in commercial cinema, fighting to remember how people live when they still do live, when there was a gas stove, coffee with bread and the landlord's rent. And as the memory carries on diminishing while they scribble their shorthand notes, they sit back with a tired sigh, beginning once again the old story of eternal love. . . .

Some unique themes were tackled by the British documentary in between the two wars, of which it is worth remembering the following:

1. A storm was descending; a fishing boat is in danger. What are the chances of saving it? – *North Sea*
2. A postal train travels the length of Britain, from London to Glasgow in one night: – *Night Mail*

3. One day in the BBC studios – the feverish activity of the trans-
   mitters. The reactions of the listeners. The role of the radio in
   the present day: – *The Voice of Britain*
4. Life in Ceylon, the industrial revolution which goes round the
   island without reaching the piety of the indigenous. The dances
   and the Ceylon temples in all their splendour: – *Song of Ceylon*
5. Internationalism: – *We Live in Two Worlds*
   The coal mines and the coal miners: – *Coal Face.*

All of these films dramatised the real and forced the public to become
interested in important national issues. All were developed with integrity and, despite restricted budgets, all achieved a degree of technical
perfection. All of them, without a doubt, were more dramatic and more
cinematographic than films about the adultery of Mrs X, the jealousy of
Mr Y, or the inconsistency of Miss Z.

In the GPO we worked in conditions which were similar to those of
craftsmen in the Middle Ages. The work was collective, and each person's films were discussed by everyone else. If the film of a companion
required some assistance, it was offered. However, each team retained
their own profile, within a spirit of healthy competition. Sir Stephen
Tallents, John Grierson, Basil Wright and their collaborators will always
be remembered for the way in which they carried forward the neo-
realist movement in Great Britain. As for myself, I feel proud to have
been able to have made my own technical contribution, so soon after
Flaherty, to this great work.

In Brazil, now that hopes for the reorganisation of commercial
cinema are surfacing, the documentary could still offer the Brazilian
people a model and ideas which may prove indispensable. Documentary could, again, begin the task of civic education, and interest the
people in national social and economic questions. Hygiene, agriculture
and many other topics await productive exploration. These questions
are, ultimately, more absorbing than adultery, the police romance,
cheap folklore, easy sentimentalism or false poetry. It will only be from
the base of documentary that our cinema will fulfil its role in the life of
Brazil. To limit film to theatre and romance is to betray the largest of all
the means of expression that we possess today for, without the cinema,
a great nation cannot really exist today.

If I was asked to summarise in a few lines the codes of conduct
which the documentary makers in Brazil should follow, I would repeat

those which, based on my own experience in this field, I expressed to young Danish directors, in 1948:

1. Do not work with general subjects: you can write an article about the post, but you should make a film about a letter.
2. Do not distance yourself from the principles by which three fundamental elements exist: the social, the poetic and the technical.
3. Do not neglect your argument, nor count on chance while filming: when your argument is ready, your film is done; only, when beginning to film, you begin it once again.
4. Do not trust in commentary to tell your story: the images and the sound should tell it; commentary is irritating, and humorous commentary even more so.
5. Do not forget that, when you are filming, each take is part of a sequence and each sequence is part of the whole: the most beautiful take, taken out of place, is worse than the most banal.
6. Do not invent camera angles when they are not necessary: gratuitous angles are distracting, and destroy emotion.
7. Do not overuse rapid 'montage': an accelerated rhythm can be just as monotonous as the more pompous wide shot.
8. Do not make excessive use of music: if you do, the audience will no longer hear it.
9. Do not overcharge your film with synchronised sound effects: sound is never better than when used suggestively. Sounds which complement constitute the best sound tracks.
10. Do not order too many special effects, nor make them complicated: fusions, 'fade-ins' and 'outs' form a part of the punctuation of your film. They are your semi-colons, and your full stops.
11. Do not film too many 'close-ups': save them for the climax. In a balanced film they will come naturally; when there are too many, they tend to suffocate each other, and lose their significance.
12. Do not hesitate to deal with human elements and human relationships: human beings can be as beautiful as other animals, as beautiful as machines, or a landscape.
13. Do not be confused in your argument: a truthful subject

should be told with clarity and simplicity. However, clarity and simplicity do not necessarily exclude dramatisation.

14. Do not miss the opportunity to experiment: the prestige of the documentary was only reached through experiments. Without experiments, the documentary loses its value. Without experiments, the documentary ceases to exist.

Chapter 5

HUMPHREY JENNINGS (1907–50)

COMMENTARY

Jennings was a poet and painter as well as a film-maker. He was strongly influenced by romanticism, idealism and surrealism, and was a member of the organising committee of the 1936 Surrealist Exhibition

Figure 5.1 Portrait of Humphrey Jennings.
Source: BFI. Copyright could not be traced, but the publishers will be happy to make amendments in future editions of this book.

in London. In 1937 he also founded, along with Charles Madge and Tom Harrisson, the organisation Mass Observation, which attempted to explore and record popular cultural phenomena. In his films, Jennings is concerned to explore the revelation of the symbolic in the everyday, through the use of an impressionistic style dependent on juxtapositions and association. Jennings believed that, within the collective consciousness of a people, a distinctive 'legacy of feeling' could be discerned, which could be captured symbolically through art. The task of the documentary film-maker is to record these manifestations through symbols. For Jennings, then, the documentary film-maker is both an observer, capturing what emerges from within the legacy of feeling within the nation, and a creative artist, embodying what is observed within an image containing a multiplicity of meanings.

Jennings's style is most apparent in *Listen to Britain* (1942). Here, there is a move away from dependence on linear narrative, and an emphasis on associative editing. Sound and image are built up through a series of oppositions which express the underlying unity beneath apparant contradiction. *Listen to Britain* is an expression of the connectedness of experience; it projects a fluid and ambiguous space, within which meanings evoke a sense of national identity.

Jennings was strongly influenced by the notion that English national identity had been transformed by the industrial revolution, and that the organic unity of English society had been disrupted by laissez-faire capitalism. In many respects, films such as *Listen to Britain* are an intense reflection on this belief in the underlying unity of the nation. Some critics have argued that Jennings's films, effective though they are, could only have been made during the war, when there was such a focus on the issue of national identity. After the war, in films such as *Diary for Timothy*, the contradictions and oppositions which are synthesised in *Listen to Britain* often remain unresolved. In the post-war period, notions of the connectedness of experience became less appropriate, as political divisions developed within Britain. Jennings's concern with the unity of experience underlying apparent division was, in many respects, close to the theoretical model employed by Grierson in *Drifters*. Although their enterprises were similar, however, influenced by similar idealist sources, Jennings's use of symbolic opposition is far more pronounced than Grierson's.

In 'The English' (1948), Jennings defines contemporary England as a metropolitan, rather than rural nation. He talks of football as one of the

English's 'supreme achievements in the transmission of culture', and applauds the work of popular writers such as Agatha Christie and Edgar Wallace. Jennings's nationalism comes through strongly at the end of the review, when he calls for the re-emergence of a vigorous English nationalism to halt the decline of the empire. In 'Surrealism' (1936), Jennings equates classicism with a 'classical-military-capitalist-ecclesiastical racket', and criticises attempts to define surrealism in terms of romanticism. He argues that surrealism is a form of art which rejects preconceived beliefs, and which explores the unknown through coincidence. He calls for English art to 'awaken from the sleep of selectivity', and to produce a spontaneous art, open to the manifold meanings which emerge in the act of artistic creation.

In the reconstructed 'Introduction to *Pandaemonium*' (c. 1948), Jennings's impressionistic account of the effects of the industrial revolution on the English, he presents an 'imaginative history' of the period. The moments from the past in the book are presented as images which 'contain in little a whole world'. They do not represent truth, but experience, illuminating moments, and acting as 'symbols for the whole inexpressible uncapturable process'. In the Introduction Jennings argues that, under capitalism, the artist has lost the central role which he or she played in pre-industrial societies. He calls for the return of the artist into an active engagement with the cultural life of the people, and talks of the need for the 'factory man' to regain his 'means of vision', so that art can satisfy 'the emotional side of our nature'. His definition of the 'means of vision' stands as an encapsulation of the symbolic style employed in *Listen to Britain*: 'Means of Vision – matter (sense impressions) transformed and reborn by imagination: *turned into an image*'.

LISTEN TO BRITAIN (1942)

The music of a people at war – the sound of life in Britain by night and by day.

Britain in summer. The waving tops of the trees and corn. The sound of larks from above the corn drowned by the roar of two Spitfires. Land army girls at work and Observer Corps men on duty. The sound of the squadrons flying far overhead is interrupted by the busy clatter of a tractor drawing a reaper. A rich harvest landscape. Strong forces of RAF fighters in the evening sunlight. Now the blackout curtains are drawn in a house from which is heard the voice of Joseph McLeod as he reads the six o'clock news. News from overseas or from men in uniform? Some are on leave, contemplating the sunset – others don steel helmets and prepare for night duty. The strains of a dance band are coming from the Tower Ballroom in Blackpool where members of HM Forces dance at half price to the tune of 'Roll out the barrel – for the gang's all here!' Hundreds of them in uniform enjoying themselves with young ladies evacuated from government departments in London. Outside the fire watchers are ready.

The clanging cage at a pit-head where the men are going on night shift is a sharp contrast. In the clear light of the moon the night traffic on the railways is shunted about – holding up a passenger train on which a bunch of Canadians are engaged in telling stories of the old days back home and singing 'Home on the range'.

The line is cleared and the train puffs on into the night.

A bomber factory. The whine of machinery and the clinks of metal as rows of aircraft are assembled.

The lights in the roof of this great factory are like stars in the night sky.

Outside another machine takes off.

The women on night duty in an ambulance station are listening to the 'Ashgrove' sung by one of their colleagues.

Her voice echoes through the big marble hall, one of the many famous buildings put to new and strange uses.

Big Ben rings round the world as the BBC Overseas Service gets into its nightly activity. The British Grenadiers March plays triumphantly from London to the countries all round the globe. Dials and valves quiver with the voices in dozens of languages. A woman announcer in the Pacific service gives greetings to all serving in the armed forces and in the Merchant Navy.

The most natural sound in Britain so early in the day is the sound of the birds, but not long after come the people to the factories.

Coleman Smith wakens up the others with his morning PT song and a new day is in full swing.

A housewife watches her child dancing with others in the school playground below and thinks of the man in a foreign land.

Bren-gun carriers come crashing through the village street – shaking the plaster and timbers of 'Ye Olde Tea Shoppe'.

A bugle call – calling all workers – the BBC programme of *Music*

While You Work every morning in the factories [deleted: Gillettes] – the girls sing 'Yes, my darling daughter' [deleted: and machinery seems the brighter for it].

Uniforms on a station platform. Canteens for rescue squads in a street. Painter on a ladder covering a factory with camouflage. 'And when the storm clouds all roll Over'.

Inside Flanagan and Allen are singing 'Round the back of the arches' to a thousand workers at their lunch.

Menu – Scotch broth, Fried cod and chips, Grilled sausages, Greens, Boiled potatoes, Lemon pudding, Jam sauce, Damsons and custard.

Another lunchtime concert is in progress in the National Gallery. Here office workers and shop assistants listen to the RAF Orchestra playing Mozart's Piano Concerto in G, with Myra Hess at the piano. The ceiling and windows above are cracked by bombs like most buildings in London and the Galleries have been cleared of their treasures, yet in one of them there is an exhibition: War Artist's Paintings. A sailor on leave looks at one of Dunkirk. The place is thronged with lunch-hour Londoners – mostly civil defence workers – the Queen is there listening with the others to Dame Myra Hess.

Outside in Trafalgar Square where Nelson stands, the traffic of London moves on. The factories are making tanks for this country to fight with.

The noise of the factory drowns the Mozart and out of the din comes the thumping of the drums of the marines [*sic*] 'A life on the ocean wave'. The thump of the drums is taken up by the thud of the steam hammers, forging arms from red-hot steel. Listen to Britain. The fire in the heart of our people, the music in their voices, swells into the air, out of the factories, over the fields of grain, and up over the land.

Humphrey Jennings to Cicely Jennings, 3 December 1941

South Cottage,
Chorley Wood, Herts

My darling There have already been two false starts to this letter – which has been hopelessly delayed by the rush-finishing of a picture (*Listen to Britain*) and a second lot of flu. Finishing a pic and flu always seem to coincide.

In the meantime we are working harder than ever. Very lucky to get

Sunday – the country as a whole is doing a sixty-hour week – plus fire watching. *Listen to Britain* is the music film I mentioned I think. Two reels – no commentary – highspots Flanagan and Allen and Myra Hess playing Mozart. Saw George (Reavey, the surrealist writer) and Gwyneth (his wife) the other night back from Spain. Kathleen is down from her Cumberland exile – working in London. Bill Empson married – to a ravishing Africaans girl. I hear (André) Breton is in New York. We are beginning to get large quantities of canned American food over here – especially Spam and that sort of thing. Pretty good – but in any case I must say other complaints about the war-organisation apart – the food situation has been remarkably well handled – we really feed magnificently considering. As for the Russians our enthusiasm is nobody's business. But then you see – we have been misled for 25 years and in a sense enthusiasm now is our revenge on the newspaper peers – since they have now *got* to be enthusiastic to keep going at all. Then there were two excellent things from a propaganda point of view that happened together. One – the USSR resisted as her admirers said she would – and two – even so she had to retire as anybody else would have had to – which in a sense proved the Russians were human beings. A ridiculous thing to have to prove if you like and a wretched way of proving it but never mind – very necessary here. Since the *human* side of the USSR has always been forgotten by its supporters who have done nothing but talk economics. Anyway there is a hell of a warm feeling around now... (Added in handwriting:) Since the above bombs have been dropping on Pearl Harbour and [phrases deleted] we are waiting to see what happens next. Here everybody is really too busy to be surprised – at least so it appears. For me I just feel it's another ancient crime of ours – Manchuria I mean – coming home as Abyssinia and Czechoslovakia and the rest have done . . . Good to be on the same side as China anyway. Have started reading Gorki and also the short stories of Turgenev. Reading and painting and music extra-popular everywhere here. People really fighting for coloured reproductions of Breughel and Renoir for Christmas.

THE ENGLISH (1948)

An Indian, reviewing, on the Third Programme, British rule in India, recently said: 'The most remarkable thing about the character of the

English is their zeal for writing essays about the English character.' He did not stop there.'This', he said:

> launches me straightaway into the melancholy conjecture that self-admiration is the primary English failing. . . . The British have made it clear in their frequent moments of frankness that they want hypocrisy to be enthroned as their characteristic error. . . . I must insist on putting first things first. The root and beginning, I suggest, is self-admiration, and hypocrisy is only its most distinguished product.

So be it. But then, no other nation has so much in itself to admire. This is not saying a great deal. *Homo sapiens* is not doing so tremendously well just now, either in India or elsewhere, that any of his branches can be superior about any of the others. As for the English, it is what they are going to do which will require to excite admiration. There is only one occasion when admiration for past deeds may be given full rein, and that is in an epitaph. It is a dangerous tendency for the living. Narcissus was very beautiful and quite rightly spent a very long time admiring himself; but he died of it. However good our characters are, they all can stand a great deal of improvement.

It is probable that all books about national character should be written by foreigners. A man, or a nation, cannot truly appreciate his own character any more than he can correctly hear his own voice. The reproduction of one's own voice, either by a gramophone record or by a broadcast, is well known to be one of life's most startling experiences.

Character is even more intimate than voice, and must be reflected, preferably by a frontier, to be known. There is a frontier in this island, or at the very least an ex-frontier: that which runs between England and Scotland. Descriptions of the Scots by English investigators have often differed most remarkably from the Scots' conception of themselves. So a Scot, reading a book by the English on the English, compares it with his own mental picture of that great race. The two do not at all coincide; but here, as elsewhere, the onlooker may be seeing most of the game.

Looking at the English from outside, one or two obvious facts stand out which the English themselves ignore completely. Their ruthlessness, for example. The English in America exterminated one race, the Red

Indians, almost completely, and imported another race, the Negroes, as slaves, on whom they inflicted unspeakable brutalities. The English in Australia carried extermination even further than in America. They accomplished a good deal of it by the simple use of arsenic, though there were other ways, more horrible and straightforward, which the Australians themselves have chronicled. This characteristic has not passed away. Some of the English achievements in the late war, notably the burning of Hamburg, make the blood run cold.

There is also the English habit of buccaneering, of dropping honest work and taking to simple, bluff, hearty plunder. A buccaneer was originally a man in the West Indies who boucaned, that is, who cured meat by drying it in the sun. But the English knew a trick worth two of that. They took to piracy. Very few people nowadays associate buccaneers with honest toil; indeed, its termination has passed into an acknowledged suffix of disreputableness.

There are other characteristics of the English well known to their neighbours, but altogether unmentioned by themselves. Their propensity for endless aggressive war, for example. The Hundred Years' War looks quite different from the French side of the Channel. Let those who think it simply a piece of medieval romanticism ask the Scots – or the Welsh – about their experiences. It would be inadvisable to ask the Irish.

But these are very necessary traits nowadays; very desirable; not at all to be apologised for. There is nothing more dangerous than the current cant phrase, 'We must gather together all the peace-loving nations.' Unless the peace-loving nations can induce one or two war-loving nations to join the club it is simply an invitation to be plundered. The larger the assembly of sheep the more it appeals to the wolves.

Now, for some strange reason, the Englishman likes to think of himself as a sheep; and so great is his artistry, so thoroughly does he see himself in any part which he has assumed, that he frequently deceives not only himself, but others. This mild, beneficent, benevolent, trustful creature, easily imposed upon, unmindful of injury, is a pose. But, like all the best poses, it takes in its author as well. The English are not hypocritical. They are sincere. In that lies their deadly danger to others.

The English are in fact a violent, savage race; passionately artistic, enormously addicted to pattern, with a faculty beyond all other people of ignoring their neighbours, their surroundings, or in the last resort, themselves. They have a power of poetry which is the despair of all the rest of the world. They produce from time to time personalities transcending ordinary human limitations. Then they drive other nations to a frenzy by patronising these archangels who have come among them, and by indicating that any ordinary Englishman could do better if he liked to take the trouble. As exemplified in Ben Jonson's insufferable appreciation of Shakespeare.

An exasperated opponent said of Gladstone that he did not mind the Grand Old Man having aces up his sleeve; what he resented was the assumption that God put them there. This exemplifies another habit of the English: a belief that the story is meant to end happily – that is to say, with an English victory; moral or material. Bernard Shaw draws attention to it in *Saint Joan*. The attitude has not weakened in the passage of time. Nobody can make out whether the English believe they will overcome their enemies because they have looked up the answer at the end of the book, or whether it comes out that way by accident. No doubt it was one of the problems that embittered Hitler's last hours in his bunker. It remains a question-mark still, to the new challengers.

There are other things the English have done besides riding their luck and making poetry, but they are not so important. Poetry certainly appears in *The Character of England*. There is a scholarly essay on this subject by James Sutherland. But there is no chapter on the Englishman's luck. That is what we should like to know about. Can they do it again?

Because they are hard pressed just now. The English have been a Great Power for quite a long time, and the adjustments necessary if they are to remain in that class are profound. They will require to people continents from their loins, as they did after the discovery of America; but at the same time they will have to recreate the Anglo-French state of the Angevins, and add to it the conquests of Charlemagne. This is an extensive programme. It is certainly worthwhile for them to take stock. What sort of people are they, the oldest of the Old Powers, the youngest – indeed the unborn – of the Newest Powers, starting to challenge Fate again?

The formidable volume before us sets out in 575 pages to answer this question. Yet it balks completely at the threshold of the problem. What relation to Old England is Newest England, the England of the streets? In the index you will find under the heading 'city life' two pages only – pages 4 and 5 – where this, the essence of modern England, is sandwiched between a few words on the Pleistocene age and a description of the 'dry Boreal period . . . when pine forests grew over much of the country and the North Sea was still advancing for its final isolation'. There is, it is true, a chapter on town life. But that is not the same thing at all.

The furious industrial epoch, of which England was the pioneer, and of which she is still much the most extreme example, cannot be so put aside. There is no country so urbanised as England. There is no country with so small a percentage of its population engaged upon the land. There is no country with such an energy of horsepower heaped and crammed into so small a space. In spite of the fact that a grocer's calendar will carry the picture of a cottage in the snow, or that the frontispiece of the *Listener* may show a village spire, England, modern England, is a series of city streets. The streets of London are paralleled by the streets of the Midlands, by the streets of Yorkshire and Lancashire. Nine out of every ten Englishmen anywhere are born in the towns and bred in the streets. Yet out of those streets came the men who could outlast the Arabs in the desert, who could outfight the Japanese in the forests, who flew above the birds and dived below the whales.

It is true that Lord Kennet has written a chapter on town life, just as Miss Sackville-West has written a chapter on country life. But read these two chapters, side by side, and you will see that country life is described from the inside, and town life from the outside. This is not surprising. Miss Sackville-West lives in the country, loves the country, and only with reluctance comes to town, for as short a period as she can possibly arrange. Nobody ever said the converse about Lord Kennet. As for the intense appreciation of city life, such as that possessed, for example, by Dr Johnson, or by Damon Runyon, it would be to him simply incomprehensible. Even his title is drawn from the loneliest and loveliest of little English rivers, famous for the most solitary of sports; and his delight is in watching birds – which, unlike horses, or pigs, or even rats, all of which have their devotees, are positively repelled by cities.

The English carry into almost every department of modern life their great unwillingness to admit facts, their power of pretending that things are not so. Only in their unconscious literature do they reveal themselves. The chapter on English city life, that is to say, on the life of nine-tenths of the English who make up the present nation, ought in logic to have been written by someone who could and would write, sing, whistle, dance and watch for his or her own personal pleasure 'The Lambeth Walk'.

The chapter on recreation and games comes nearer to the mark, because no Englishman could possibly write an uninteresting chapter on this subject. Mr I. J. Pitman comes to the core of the matter when he directs our attention to the part which team work plays in the attraction which games have for the Englishman:

> An eight going perfectly on the tideway, English figure-skating perfectly called and executed with precision and timing, the reverse pass with which a stand-off half sends his centre three-quarter racing for a clearly certain try, carry a satisfaction in corporate human relationships which can be felt but not described.

This is the English love of pattern, of order, referred to above, one of their fundamental qualities. It is responsible for their delight in ships, the supreme example of a patterned life, for their fame abroad as troupe dancers ('les Girls'), for the spectacle of Trooping the Colour. The most extreme example is that of bell-ringing. Give a continental campanologist a spire full of great bells, and he will begin to play a tune on them. Only the English will undertake an endless series of ringing-the-changes; pulling sally after sally, for hour after hour, with no other purpose than to pursue some intricate rhythm in company, through peal after peal, clanging over a countryside, to the grave admiration of the whole parish.

This absorption in pattern is one aspect of the general power of absorption, of concentration, which the Englishman so specially enjoys. It is possible that this has enabled him to pass into a civilisation of the streets without becoming a part of it. So the English travel in trains; not a company, but a collection of individuals; first turning each carriage into a row of cottages – the word 'compartment' is a word of praise – and then sitting in each corner with the same blank denial of any other presence that the lovers show in the parks. The English live in cities, but they are not citified; they very seldom produce, for example, that characteristic symptom of a city, the mob. They are urbane without being urban; creating their own environment within their own being, they can dwell in the midst of twenty miles of paving stones and pretend, with the aid of a back green or even of a flower-pot, that they are in a hamlet on the Downs. Or so it seems to the outsider. Perhaps the English have something completely different in their heads.

Because they are also very inscrutable. Don Salvador de Madariaga has said that the wisdom of the English is so far above that of other races as to be of no use to them. This is horribly true. They cannot communicate their fine flowers – cricket, for instance – to other nations. They are unaware that among their supreme achievements in the transmission of culture – something not forced upon foreigners, but sought out by them – is association football. They cannot communicate – perhaps it is incommunicable – their angelic mastery of lyric poetry. They do not know that the art form which they have perfected and launched upon the modern world is not what the common man regards as the pretentious nonsense of their avant-garde poets, or the gibber-ish, to him intentionally unintelligible, of Joyce and the followers of Joyce, but Sherlock Holmes and all that has flowed from him.

In the detective story the English lose their self-consciousness; they move easily and naturally in the world which they normally inhabit. The world recognises this and takes them to its heart. Sherlock Holmes in lodgings in Baker Street, Sherlock Holmes going to classical concerts on Saturday afternoons, Sherlock Holmes discussing with his brother, the great civil servant, the affairs of the Diogenes Club, Sherlock Holme displaying, as naturally as a courting blackcock, the whole naive, inti-mate, enraging – and strengthening – snobbery of the English - here is a description of contemporary manners in the vein of the everyday passage of Chaucer or of Shakespeare. Edgar Wallace, the English Dumas, pouring out an endless succession of ephemeridae, Jack London in America knocking off thrillers with the power and enjoy-ment of a blacksmith fettling for the great grey dray-horse his bright and battering sandal: these are the authors whose works are studied and appreciated abroad along with Milton, Byron and the romances of Oscar Wilde. These current authors are not mentioned, let alone analysed, in this volume.

The English are deserting Kipling, but the French are discovering him; the Russians, weary of Dostoevsky and Tolstoy, want to be able to write like Miss Dorothy Sayers or Miss Agatha Christie. None of this the English know. They certainly will not learn it from the pages before us. They will find a great number of very charming and well-informed essays. They will find Miss Rebecca West on the Englishman abroad (it is always worth while reading anything that Miss West writes). They will find a chapter on England and the sea, and another on England at war. But they will not find that the authors have laid hold, singly or collectively, of the inner genius of this extraordinary people. In particular, the essays do not emphasise their singular originality of thought. The chapter on the sea, for instance, omits mention of the fact that the English invented, in Elizabethan times, the fore-and-aft rig, an invention almost as revolutionary as that of the internal combustion engine. The chapter on war omits mention of either the longbow or the tank, and though it mentions the Spitfires, leaves out radar, on which the whole strategy of air defence and the short-range fighter pivoted. It does not mention the inland voyage of Marlborough, via the Rhine, to the Danube, or Wavell's switch backwards and forwards of his Indian Division, from the Mediterranean to the Central African mountains and – only just in time – back to the Mediterranean again. The feat of holding a quarter of the world together for so many long years 'with twelve battleships', as Hitler querulously remarked, and a corporal's guard, merits greater consideration. The boldness, the presumptuous quality of English thought is seen as well in their conduct of war as in any of their other exploits.

This quality was outstandingly demonstrated in the last war. But no doubt the authors are right to lay little stress on this portion of English history. For one thing it is too near to have any real knowledge of the facts or any proper perspective upon them. For another, the English were at bay and staking everything they had. If they won, all would be well. If they lost, nothing would greatly matter. Yet for all that, the decision to fight in the Levant at all, in 1940, is a decision so arrogant that it is not easy to see where history will rank it. Some of Hitler's decisions will seem inexplicable to history; but that was because they failed. The decision to fight in the Levant succeeded. Otherwise history would have found it just as inapplicable to any reasoned appreciation of the facts.

The chapter on the universities by Sir Maurice Powicke mentions the strange division between Oxford and Cambridge and 'the eight other English universities whose history begins with the foundation of the Owen's College at Manchester in 1851'. (!) 'Foreigners', he says, 'find our universities very English. There is nothing like them in the world. This perhaps is the only generalisation about them to which nobody would demur.' It is very true. If one could understand the English universities, one would understand at least half of England. But here also the mystery is withheld from us.

Perhaps the most revealing of all the essays, because the least assuming, is that of Lady Violet Bonham-Carter, on the subject of children and education. Anyone reading it will learn a great deal of the English view of children and a great deal more besides. An essayist who can discern and describe that characteristic English contribution to social life 'the Nannie', and who has the courage to assert, of one of the unrecognised peaks of English literature, the nonsense rhymes, that for sheer poetry 'The Dong with the Luminous Nose' can hold its own with 'Kubla Khan', is not only an author; she is the very thing of which she writes; she is no less than the English character itself.

All these considerations, all these essays, have a very practical and immediate bearing on our present times. The most important political and economic fact of the day is the break-up of the British Empire. The question is whether, and, if so, in what shape, it will reform. It has already broken up twice. Once when the Anglo-French state, so necessary, so impossible, so nearly achieved, collapsed under the stroke of Saint Joan. After that, the English state abandoned the Channel and reformed upon the ocean. Then the Atlantic commonwealth, also so necessary, split under the impact of General Washington. Very few societies have done this trick twice. None, except perhaps the Greek, with Athens, Alexandria and Byzantium to its credit, has done it a third time. The English have to do it a third time; or perish.

Or perish. There is no middle way. The structure is too tall, too boldly conceived to be dismantled arch by arch and beam after beam. It must stand, or crash. We are watching one small corner cracking – in Palestine; we recognise with horror how great a series of stresses will be opened by the buckling of even a single girder.

The English at present are sleeping, as a sailor sleeps after a storm, cast up on a beach, in the sun. But in their dreams they know very well that they will have to rise and go forth. There are traces of this in their current light writing, in their action, even in their thought. Miss Rebecca West, an outside observer, suddenly breaks into it – *à propos de bottes* – at the end of her essay. 'We were to know again', she says, 'the conflict of continental faith and local genius: there came back into life something of a Tudor strength and richness: the hammer was striking on the anvil again.'

These quick, tremendous, inventive, bold people are to be tested once more. They will have to move suddenly from the period of Racine to the period of Villon. One of the great epics of the world is to be played out before us, and played out now.

SURREALISM (1936)

How can one open this book, so expensive, so *well* produced, so con-
formistly printed, with so many and such mixed illustrations, so assorted
a set of articles, containing so *protesting* a number of English statements
and so stiffly pathetic a presentation of French ones, and compare it
even for a moment with the passion, terror and excitement, dictated by
absolute integrity and produced with all the poetry of bare necessity,
which emanated from *La Révolution surréaliste* and *Le Surréalisme au
service de la révolution*, without facing a great wave of nostalgia, and
bringing up a nauseating memory of the mixed atmosphere of cultural
hysteria and amateur-theatricality which combined to make the
Surrealist Exhibition of June so peculiar a 'success'?

Mr Sykes Davies assures us that there is no need to worry ourselves
with such comparisons. The course of historical development will
justify blind faith. Mr Read simply resolves all difficulties by the disso-
lution of the 'universal truths of classicism'. That is to say, they find
writing articles on surrealism an excuse for another affirmation of their
favourite theses: Mr Davies's article becomes a lecture on Coleridge,
and Mr Read's a defence of romanticism.

A romanticism, however, which can only pity Michelangelo (p. 45) even
if not patronisingly, which still imagines Pope to have been just a classical wit (p. 78) and lumps Hardy with Dickens in opposition to the Black
Novel (p. 56), can hardly be said to have a dialectic grip on the human
situation. Mr Read does not venture to commit himself about Homer.

Now a special attachment to certain sides of surrealism may be
defendable, but the elevation of definite 'universal truths of romanticism'
(pp. 27–8) in place of the 'universal truths' of classicism is not only a
short-sighted horror, but immediately corroborates really grave doubts
already existent about the *use* of surrealism in this country. We all agree
with Mr Read that the eternally fabricated 'eternal truths of classicism'
constantly appear as the symbols and tools of a classical-military-cap-
italist ecclesiastical racket. But then we remember a recent query in a
film-paper: 'Is it possible that the business of national education is
passing, by default, from the offices of Whitehall to the public relations
departments of the great corporations?'

Is it possible that in place of a classical-military-capitalist-ecclesiastical racket there has come into being a romantic-cultural-*soi-disant*-
co-operative-new-uplift racket ready and delighted to use the 'universal

truths of romanticism – co-eval with the evolving consciousness of mankind' as symbols and tools for its own ends? Our 'advanced' poster designers and 'emancipated' businessmen – what a gift surrealism is to them when it is presented in the auras of 'necessity', 'culture' and 'truth' with which Read and Sykes Davies invest it.

To the real poet the front of the Bank of England may be as excellent a site for the appearance of poetry as the depths of the sea. Note the careful distinction made by Breton in his article (pp. 112–13): 'Human psychism in its most universal aspect has found in the Gothic castle and its accessories a point of fixation so precise that it becomes essential to discover what would be the equivalent for our own period'. He continues to say that surrealism has replaced the 'coincidence' with the 'apparition', and that we must 'allow ourselves to be guided towards the unknown by this newest promise'. Now that is talking; and to settle surrealism down as romanticism only is to deny this promise. It is to cling to the apparition with its special 'haunt'. It is to look for ghosts only on battlements, and on battlements only for ghosts. Coincidences have the infinite freedom of appearing anywhere, anytime, to anyone: in broad daylight to those whom we most despise in places we have most loathed: not even to us at all: probably least to petty seekers after mystery and poetry on deserted sea-shores and in misty junk-shops.

'Imagination' says Eluard (p. 173) 'lacks the imitative instinct.' Its mysteries are not mysterious. 'It is the spring and torrent which we do not re-ascend' (ibid.). Creation is *not* the re-presentation of 'the truth', however much it may at times look like it. But at those times (the 'Greek' drawings of Picasso are instances) the eruptions of doubt and the magic of treachery are precisely at their greatest. It is the next generation that *believes* in the results. So it is that the enduring statements of Picasso, early Chirico, Duchamp, Klee, Magritte, and of certain Dalis, are due to their unquestioning acceptance of *all* the conditions of the moment: forgetting all 'beliefs' preceding the picture, which would deny the promise of the unknown. But so deadly agile is man's mind that it is possible, even easy to form a series of 'truths' and 'loyalties' which produce imitations of the creative powers of non-selectivity; forgetting that surrealism is only a means and believing in the 'universal truth' of it; or again, still relying on aestheticism (as admitted by Read, p. 63) to the rules of which surrealism has now been added. 'To the poet everything is the object of sensations and consequently of sentiments. Everything becomes food for his imagination' (Eluard, p. 174). But for the English to awaken from the sleep of selectivity, what a task. And to be *already* a 'painter', a 'writer', an 'artist', a 'surrealist', what a handicap.

INTRODUCTION TO *PANDAEMONIUM* (*c*.1948)

In this book I present the imaginative history of the industrial revolution. Neither the political history, nor the mechanical history, nor the social history nor the economic history, but the imaginative history. I say 'present', not describe or analyse, because the imagination is a function of man whose traces are more delicate to handle than the facts and events and ideas of which history is usually constructed. This function I believe is found active in the areas of the arts, of poetry and of religion – but is not necessarily confined to them or present in all their manifestations. I prefer not to try to define its limits at the moment but to leave the reader to agree or not with the evidence which I shall place before him. I present it by means of what I call images.

These are quotations from writings of the period in question, passages describing certain moments, events, clashes, ideas occurring between 1660 and 1886 which either in the writing or in the nature of the matter itself or both have revolutionary and symbolic and illuminatory quality. I mean that they contain in little a whole world – they are the knots in a great net of tangled time and space – the moments at which the situation of humanity is clear – even if only for the flash time of the photographer or the lightning. And just as the usual history does not consist of isolated events, occurrences – so this 'imaginative history' does not consist of isolated images, but each is in a particular place in an unrolling film.

And these images – what do they deal with? I do not claim that they represent truth – they are too varied, even contradictory, for that. But they represent human experience. They are the record of mental events. Events of the heart. They are facts (the historian's kind of facts) which have been passed through the feelings and the mind of an individual and have forced him to write. And what he wrote is a picture – a coloured picture of them. His personality has coloured them and selected and altered and pruned and enlarged and minimised and exaggerated. Admitted. But he himself is part, was part of the period, even part of the event itself – he was an actor, a spectator in it. So his distortions are not so much distortions as one might suppose. Moreover they altered him. The event had its effect on him. Undistorted him, opened his eyes.

What have these extracts in common? They have no political or economic or social homogeneity. They are all *moments* in the history of the industrial revolution, at which clashes and conflicts suddenly show themselves with extra clearness, and which through that clearness can stand as symbols for the whole inexpressible uncapturable process. They are what later poets have called 'illuminations', 'moments of vision' – some obviously clearer than others – some intentional, others unintentional – but all in some degree with this window-opening quality – it is this which differentiates these pieces of writing from purely economic or political, or social analyses. Theirs is a different method of tackling, of presenting the same material, the same conflicts, the method of poetry. These extracts are to be considered as documents which illuminate – in one way or another – the conflicts of the industrial revolution in Britain. In what ways? What conflicts?

1. Class conflicts – in their simplest form Luddite riots, Peterloo
2. The conflict of animism and materialism
3. The conflict of the expropriated individual with his environment
4. Conflicts of ideas
5. Conflicts of systems –
    religious systems
    political systems
    moral systems

But do not expect to find each of the extracts dealing with one of these conflicts only. That is precisely what they do not do. They are *not* texts to illustrate histories of economics, etc. In treating separately the trade union, the political-historical, the social, the economic sides of the industrial revolution, the writers have themselves simply perpetuated the law of division of labour. But this should not blind us to the fact that life – of which their analyses are analyses – is a synthesis and that the interactions between its parts are infinitely more complex than any analytical machine can follow. This is not in any way to invalidate the analytical method – or to suggest that the poet, for example, is more capable of presenting the whole: of course he is not. But what he can present is the sense of complexity – the type of pattern and so the type of interactions of which it consists. The analytical historian's business is to disentangle shred by shred like plucking the strand out of a rope. The result is the length of the rope but only one strand's thickness, and although the strand may still be twisted from its position among the other strands it is presented nevertheless alone. The poet might be compared to a man who cuts a short section of *the whole* rope. The only thing is he must cut it where it will not fall to pieces.

The history of poetry is itself a history of mechanisation and specialisation. At the time of Homer, Hesiod, Moses, Lao-Tze, poet–sages dealt with *all* problems of life – religious, scientific, social and personal. In the course of history, the actual mental process of poetic production has hardly altered, but the division of labour has produced specialisation here as everywhere. Since that time we have seen the appearance of specialist writers on every subject, who have in the main avoided poetry as much as possible – since their reason for specialisation was in reaction against the universal poetic writer. In the last two hundred years the division of labour and specialisation have gone so far that the poet can only write about the subject of poetry itself (Gray, 'The Progress of Poesy') or definitely poetic subjects (Keats – supreme example) or his own thoughts.

It would take a large work on its own to show, in the great period of English poets 1570–1750, the desperate struggle that poets had to keep poetry head into the wind: to keep it facing life. But by 1750 the struggle – like that of the peasants – was over. *In other words poetry has been expropriated.*

Poetry was created in primitive and feudal societies – patriarchal societies – and in these societies the subjects with which the poet dealt were not *then* political subjects; they were vital everyday facts and necessities – *religion* – the cosmos and the fate of the human soul . . . *kingship* – the character of the man in power and the fate of the people under him. As agriculture was the principal means of subsistence of these societies, the language and metaphors of poetry (what is called 'flowery' language) are full of agricultural memories.

But in a process (conflict) which culminated between 1660 and 1880 the peasants were destroyed and the land capitalised – the power of money capital substituted for the power of the crown and the religion. The poet, as an individual, reacted to this major crisis of his career in many differing ways, but it must be admitted not very successfully. We cannot say that any poet understood this process – much less applied it to his own view of the world or in any way modified his writings through it.

But the written language itself – the poets' raw material – did not stand about unused – unwritten. I mean that the conflict between animism and materialism – between poetry and science – the conflicts between agriculture and industrialisation – the fundamental class conflicts – did not go unrecorded. *Poetry survived* – although it would be untrue to say that a synthesis was evolved from any of the above conflicts. In what ways may we say it survived?

In the work of certain well-known poets – Milton, Blake, Shelley; plus novelists – Disraeli, Dickens: who from time to time, but only rarely, found a point in their work where it *met*, so to speak, the current economic and political and social revolutions on equal ground and where they were capable of recording the conflict: adaptation of the classic line of poetry to industrial revolution.

In the work of scientists and philosophers (natural philosophers as they were called) where very occasionally they are looking beyond the immediate scientific issues and recording the conflict of their own new systems with others such as religion – Newton, Berkeley, Darwin. In the work of social critics as we may call them – Cobbett, Swift, Carlyle, Ruskin, Arnold – who made it their business of life to comment on the conflicts they saw in front of them and whose commentaries are often passionate, and lively. Also social documents as by Defoe, Head, Hawthorne.

In the autobiographies, memoirs, letters, diaries and so on of scientists, artists and especially in the nineteenth century of working men and social workers – Samuel Bamford, Hugh Miller, Charles Kingsley, Caroline Fox – which not only record some of the conflicts but also show the growing consciousness of those conflicts among the people most nearly involved in them: principally the newly formed working class.

In other documents in which the authors were in the main unconscious of the effect and value of what they were recording – memoirs of capitalists (Nasmyth, Bessemer) – newspaper accounts – would-be comic writers.

The means of vision and the means of production

The means of vision – matter (sense impressions) transformed and reborn by imagination: *turned into an image.*

The means of production – matter is transformed and reborn by *labour.*

At a certain period in human development the means of vision and the means of production were intimately connected – or were felt to be by the people concerned – I refer to the magical systems under which it was not possible to plough the ground without a prayer – to eat without a blessing, to hunt an animal without a magic formula. To build without a sense of glory. In the two hundred years 1660–1860 the means of production were violently and fundamentally altered – altered by the accumulation of capital, the freedom of trade, the invention of machines, the philosophy of materialism, the discoveries of science.

In what sense have the means of vision kept pace with these alterations? I am referring not to the arts as a commodity for Bond Street, or as a piece of snobbery in Mayfair, or as a means of propaganda in Bloomsbury, or as a method of escapism in Hampstead . . . but to the means of vision by which 'the emotional side of our nature' (Darwin's phrase) is kept alive and satisfied and fed – our nature as human beings in the anthracite drifts of south Wales, in the cotton belt of Lancashire, in the forges of Motherwell – how the emotional side of their nature has been used, altered, tempered, appealed to in these two hundred years.

Man as we see him today lives by production and by vision. It is doubtful if he can live by one alone. He has occasionally, however, tried. Dr Ure speaks of a factory as ideally 'a vast automaton, composed of various mechanical and intellectual organs, acting in an uninterrupted concern for the production of a common object, all of them being subordinated to a self-regulated moving force'.

At the other extreme we have the Tibetan living naked in the caves of the Himalayas, eating only nettles and devoting himself to contemplation, and turning green in consequence. But in fact the factory man is living on the vision of others and the Buddhist yogi on the production of others. In some societies (civilisations) the two have been mixed, in others clearly distinguishable. The relationship of production to vision and vision to production has been mankind's greatest problem.

Unless we are prepared to claim special attributes for the poet – the attribute of vision – and unless we are prepared to admit the work of the artist (that is to say the function of 'imagination') as an essential part of the modern world there is no real reason for our continuing to bother with any of the arts any more, or with any imaginary activity. No reasons except money, snobbery, propaganda or escapism. In this book, however, it is assumed that the poet's vision does exist, that the imagination is a part of life, that the exercise of the imagination is an indispensable function of man like work, eating, sleeping, loving. I do not propose to ask the obvious next question 'What then is the place of imagination in the world of today?' I prefer to inquire what may have *been* the place of imagination in the making of the modern world.

Chapter 6

BASIL WRIGHT (1907–87)

COMMENTARY

Basil Wright was one of Grierson's closest associates. He was one of Grierson's first recruits, and remained close to Grierson throughout his career. His 1935 film *Song of Ceylon* showed that he was capable of making impressive films. However, he made few films of consequence after that. In 'Documentary Today' (1947), Wright draws on Grierson's model of the need, in a complex society, for instruments of mass communication to explain society to the people. He often draws on the same language used by Grierson, sometimes stating Grierson's positions in terms even stronger than Grierson himself would. For example, he argues that documentary film-makers should be 'in the forefront of policy' and 'several steps ahead of the politicians'. Similarly, he puts even more strongly the view expressed in Grierson's writings of the 1940s that 'documentary is not this or that type of film, but simply *a method of approach to public information*'. It is, however, difficult to square such a statement with a film such as *Song of Ceylon*.

Wright gave a number of interviews throughout his career, and these often tend to be more informative than his written work. Consequently, I have included an interview which I conducted with him in 1983, and which provides interesting insight into the various intellectual influences on the documentary movement during the 1930s.

DOCUMENTARY TODAY (1947)

What is a documentary film? A swift canvass around the country would provide a curious collection of answers to the question. A documentary

Figure 6.1 Portrait of Basil Wright.
*Source: BFI. Copyright could not be traced, but the publishers will be happy to
make amendments in future editions of this book.*

would be variously defined as a short film before the feature, as a
travelogue, as a description of how things are made, as an instructional
film, as an aid to teaching, as an artistic interpretation of reality and,
by some theoreticians in the documentary field, as a film made by
themselves. In point of fact, confusion of public thought as to what
documentary film is doesn't matter much. It is the creators of documentaries who must essentially be quite clear about what it is they are
trying to do.

The first thing to note is that there is, in the end, little need to define a documentary film. Those two words now cover such a multitude of activities and approaches that the real underlying purpose becomes daily less clear. The great expansion of the documentary movement in Britain during World War II took place because a number of public needs had to be met under conditions of critical urgency. The expansion was *ad hoc*, and it was successful because the foundations of documentary had been firmly laid during the thirties.

Today there are infinite possibilities of further expansion, because this uneasy period of so-called peace has revealed greater and more profound public needs which imaginative, efficient services of information can materially help to satisfy. These needs basically reflect world problems, and a purely parochial approach is no longer possible. It was perhaps not unnatural that during the war documentary workers in this country worked within a somewhat circumscribed horizon. The circumstances of the battle fell that way; and if the parochial slant was often too pronounced, it was in part redressed by the international approach of Canadian film-workers whose position in global war took them (once the road was indicated) in that direction. But today in all countries, and particularly Britain, some revaluation is necessary.

Returning to definitions – if it is agreed that a definition of the documentary film is no longer really necessary, it becomes quite plain that documentary is not this or that type of film, but simply *a method of approach to public information*. The documentary method must be based on a functional conception of needs and problems. However short-term much of the product may be, the approach to all work must essentially be long-term, if only because world problems and needs are in themselves capable only of long-term solution. The short-term products can only succeed if they are the links in a long-term chain. There is therefore urgent need for deeper and more serious thinking, and deeper and more serious planning.

The documentary method embraces all known media of information, particularly films, film-strips, slides, radio, television, stills and illustrations of all sorts, the press (daily, weekly and periodical in general), diagrams, wall-newspapers, pamphlets, books, lectures and exhibitions. It is within a field as wide as, certainly no narrower than, this that documentary groups in all countries must operate. At this time the original conceptions on which documentary theory was based are clearer than ever, since the need of ordinary people for information and explanation is greater than ever. If the world of the first quarter of this century was so complex and so rapid in movement that ordinary citizens could not keep pace with it, and therefore could not assess or make adequate judgements – thus jeopardising any proper practice of democratic government – how much more complex is the world of the second quarter? The jigsaw of modern civilisation is now finally in pieces. How to see where all the pieces fit, and how to put them together? And still the educationists are behind in the race for those new conceptions of world understandings and responsibilities which should arise in the local classrooms or the local study groups. Just as in the thirties the documentalists acted as pacemakers (or, if you prefer, gadflies) in the educational field, so today they must work unceasingly for the co-ordination of all informational and educational media to agreed ends. The ends themselves they will find – not too easily – by deep and serious study of economic and sociological problems, by discussion and consultation on a world rather than a local basis, and by an intensification of imaginative techniques. In this their job will be all the easier the more they realise themselves by contribution to the needs of functional international ideas and organisations.

Here we return to the film medium. It will continue to be the pace-maker of information. It was no chance that the cinema was chosen as the developing ground for the documentary method. The moving picture – vivid, convincing, lending itself especially to imaginative expression – forms a natural dynamo supplying power and current to other media. Today, for instance, we may note the dramatic impact of television, which overnight will bring to radio the imaginative factors of the film medium. What documentary has done for movies provides television with a springboard of no mean value. Note, too, the increasing production of books and pamphlets described both by publishers and critics as 'documentary'.

The visual is so important, and, as Jean Benoit-Levy has stressed so rightly in his recent book, visuals *in motion* are so pre-eminently con-vincing, that the film, with its powers of imaginative analysis and synthesis, its attributes both of excitement and cohesion, is the natural nucleus of the visual unit. Visual units, by the way, are not (as some seem to think) the prerogative of the Ministry of Education. They are an essential approach to all problems of public information and education.

A documentary worker, faced with a problem, must assess the respective values of the various media, and apportion his efforts accordingly. Sometimes he may reject the film medium altogether, and hand the problem to other colleagues. More often he will, after study, decide on what film, or groups of films, are required – that is, what angles of approach and statement over what period and to what audience groups. He will combine with workers in other media at the earliest possible stage, so that the fullest planning may be achieved when the situation is still fluid enough to allow of alteration in detail and the discovery of new growing-points.

Thus in documentary it is not only the making of film which is (inevitably) a group activity. The whole process is a group activity of all the related visual media. Truism though this may be, it still needs stressing, because only group effort can satisfactorily solve group problems. We are dealing with groups, not individuals – however unpalatable that may sometimes appear to old gentlemen like myself who were brought up in the deeper traditions of Gladstonian liberalism. The individual is interesting because he is part of a group. His relation to the group – his aspirations, achievements, participation or lack of it; his function as a unit with free will working in consideration of a group unit with a group will – all this makes the individual more moving, thrilling, real and valuable than any conception of him in a sanctified vacuum as a solitary, golden creature of nature.

Imaginatively, therefore, and with primary respect for the individual in the group, we must break down our audience (potentially everyone on earth) into categories. These categories fall under two main headings – *mood* and *interest*. Both of these are, of course, aspects of audience attitude. The former, however, represents a general thesis, the investigation of which early in the thirties led directly to the development of the non-theatrical showing of films. Most non-theatrical shows are for people who normally go to public cinemas to see entertainment films, but in the case of the non-theatrical film they are in a different mood – a mood of enquiry, or discussion – rather than in a mood of relaxation. It might indeed be said that theatrical audiences tend to be passive, non-theatrical audiences active; but, like all generalisations, this one should be accepted with caution. In both cases the calibre of the films shown is a prime factor. If the films are stimulating, the effect in both cases will be active; and vice versa.

This brings us automatically to the second factor, that of *interest*. Another word for this, in *common use*, is box office, but its implications are a bit narrow for a field which embraces free shows of all sorts, including the use of films in classrooms. The point here is that a film, for whatever mood and purpose it is designed, must capture and hold the interest of the audience. This is obvious enough in the case of a film in the movie houses – but there are too many film-makers who do not realise sufficiently clearly that it is equally important elsewhere. A film, say, on penicillin, designed for audiences in public cinemas, must at the least match up to known criteria of box office. But a film on penicillin for, say, doctors or medical students must also, in the terms of reference concerned, provide an equal level of 'box office' for its more specialised audience. It would no doubt bore or exasperate a cinema audience, but it must on no account, however academically correct it may be, have the same effect on the doctors or students. Obvious enough – but still forgotten too often, largely because in making technical films the element of imagination is too often jettisoned. It needs as much imagination to devise a method of explaining a surgical or biological process as for anything else. It has been one of documentary's distinctive contributions that it has brought a vivid and lively-looking eye to bear on the problems of technical exposition.

The planning of films and related media is comparatively simple as regards meeting audience mood. But as far as audience interest is concerned the job is more complicated. There are five main groups of audience types: (1) The audience of the public cinema. (2) The general non-theatrical audience (e.g. in village or town halls, factory canteens, public libraries, etc.). (3) The *selected* non-theatrical audience – that is, groups within the community with common interests; for instance, housewives or trade unionists or farmers. (4) The *specialised* non-theatrical audience – that is, groups concerned with common expertise; for instance, biologists, surgeons, construction engineers, stamp-collectors, veterinary surgeons, miners, etc. These groups can be summed up under the heading of 'shop'. It will be noted that the margin betweeen the selected and specialised audiences is somewhat blurred, but the distinction is none the less important. Selected audiences can be shown a wide range of films in any given programme; a women's institute show may include films on international affairs in addition to those on cooking, housekeeping, care of children, or what have you. On the other hand, most specialised audiences need shows of a wholly technical nature. The fact is that audience mood is the yardstick by which the selected or specialist show may be judged; so that a group of specialists of varying interests as regards expertise may meet as a scientific film society to see a selected show, or a show partly selected and partly specialised. (5) The final category is the educational audience, children and students in particular. Here the problems of visual aids crop up in full measure, but in an article of this scope there is no space to deal with them. It must be sufficient here to note the vital importance of this field, and the especial need for close and continuous liaison between the teachers, LEAs, Ministry of Education and the makers of the visual aids, particularly films.

Granted that films are the centre from which the other visual media radiate, it is obvious that the basic problem for documentary today is summed up in one word – screenspace. By screenspace we mean that the maximum number of people in all groups must see the maximum number of cogent films in the minimum time, and that this conception must be continuous and long-term, with plan overlapping on plan. Films and their related media need, in general, much more careful planning than they at present get. Too often today one sees not only single films, but whole series of films, put into production without a sufficiently clear conception of the audience groups they are to serve. It is not enough for the purpose of the job to be assessed and under-stood. The interest and mood of the various community groups must be examined, the number and type of films must be carefully plotted, and the plan drawn up must be rigorously kept to; it is no use starting a film for, say, non-theatrical selected audiences only, to find it eventually goes to the theatres, for this only means that through lack of pre-thought one audience group at least will go unsatisfied.

But behind all the necessary planning and production and distribu-tion machinery must be the basic analysis and understanding of needs and purposes. It is the task of the documentary worker to be in the forefront of policy, which means he must always try to be several steps ahead of the politicians and indeed of the administrators. More partic-ularly must he be expert in the international field, for it is to this field that his major contribution is to be made.

Gone is the old heresy of internationalism *per se* – the vacuum in which the League of Nations perished. We cannot contribute to inter-national needs by setting up central production units, multilingual in personnel, making films to loyalties which do not yet exist and have not yet been clearly specified. The international job must for some time yet, if not always, be the function of specific national groups. These groups will do two things. They will on the one hand produce material for local purposes; and as local needs like food, housing, health and work are also world needs, much of this material will also be of international validity. On the other hand, they must also concentrate – much more than at present – on material which is designed as a contribution by their groups (or nation) to discussion, and the action arising from discussion, in all countries and among all people. Again, such films will be of local as well as of world significance.

What, therefore, is of paramount importance is the closest mutual relationships between producing groups in all countries. It is here that the functional basis of information as regards UNO, Unesco; FAO, UNRRA and other international bodies essentially lies. Co-ordination of effort by documentary groups in the various countries was inevitably curtailed during the war (despite joint efforts on a military basis), and it is of the utmost urgency that this situation be reversed as quickly as possible. There should be annual conferences, held in different countries, of documentary workers, as well as constant and continuous exchange of personnel.

By such means we can make certain of direct contribution on an international level, and can avoid the selfish and useless outpouring of unilateral propaganda. For in all fields of information today national and international needs (which mean, simply, common humanity) can only be met if they are regarded as equivalent and identical. This is the basis of the documentary method, and in its further development this country, rich in its past experience, has a great contribution to make.

INTERVIEW WITH IAN AITKEN (1987)

I.A. The EMB was established in order to promote trade in the British Empire. I get the impression that Stephen Tallents was a firm believer in the empire, and more concerned with this than with questions of film.

B.W. That is probably true. In terms of film, Tallents had no idea about the visual world, or about how a visual medium could be used for educational purposes. He was strongly influenced by Grierson's ideas on public relations, which Grierson derived from his experience of the yellow press in America.

I.A. Was Grierson concerned about the empire, or more concerned with using film to improve social and political relations in Britain?

B.W. Grierson was not very interested in the empire as such, not as much as Tallents was. He wanted to make documentaries about educational and sociological questions in Britain.

I.A. Were you an empire enthusiast? Were you interested in the EMB? Or did you just want to make films?

B.W. I couldn't give a fuck about the EMB. I wanted to make films, and to begin with I was mainly interested in film aesthetics. I had read classics and economics at Cambridge, and had made some student films between 1926 and 1929. However, I did not know what I really wanted to do with film until I saw the first screening of *Drifters* at the Film Society in 1929. Then I knew what I wanted to do. Grierson had seen my student film and wrote to me asking to meet him at the 1917 Club in Gerrard's Street.

I.A. What sort of club was that, and why did you meet there?

B.W. It was a club where people met who were interested in developments in Russia. Grierson was a highly energetic individual, though without strong convictions about Russia. He preferred to observe situations, and to absorb ideas. I think, however, that he was also a member of this club because it had a large ping-pong table. Grierson, like Ivor Montagu, was a very good and enthusiastic ping-pong player. After that meeting I knew that I wanted to make films; films of high artistic quality, but with an educational and sociological purpose too.

I.A. You say that you studied economics at Cambridge. Did that influence you in any way?

B.W. I think probably it did in a vague way, in that I realised how important the means of production were and how important it would be to control the means of production if good documentary films were to be made. Ivor Montagu felt the same: that a separate organisation would have to be established in order to make films worth showing. I think I also understood a little of how the film industry operated in terms of economics.

I.A. You became involved with the documentary movement after seeing *Drifters*. What impressed you most about the film? Was it the Russian-style editing, or the representation of working-class life?

B.W. Well, you must remember that *Drifters* was a great success, because here was an English film competing with the best Russian films. It created a new interest in film aesthetics in England, and I think the film stands the test of time. At that time the Film Society was becoming very influential, and you never knew what you would find there at their Sunday afternoon showings. It was a sort of dreamworld, and we were all on the crest of a wave about what could be done with film. It was a period of great possibilities in relation to film aesthetics and the sociological uses of film. Eisenstein gave some lectures at the time, and these had a considerable impact. I was most impressed by the Russian montage in *Drifters* and by the romantic and dramatic storm sequences.

I.A. You were more interested in the Russian montage than the representation of working-class life?

B.W. Probably. It was the montage which really inspired me with the possibilities of cinema.

I.A. Arthur Elton, Paul Rotha and Edgar Anstey were all in the audience at the first screening of *Drifters*. Did you know any of them then?

B.W. Well, Arthur Elton was at Cambridge with me, and I knew him there. I did not know Edgar Anstey then, he joined the EMB later on. Rotha, I did not know then. Rotha was a lone wolf who could not work with anybody. Although he was a very fine film-maker, he could not get on with anybody, and his relations with Grierson could be best described as a permanent state of unarmed combat.

I.A. When the EMB Film Unit began it had a strange relationship with the commercial company New Era. I wondered whether there were any conflicts or tensions in this relationship.

B.W. I was employed by New Era on a commercial employment contract to make film for the Film Unit. This arrangement enabled us to have some control over our production, rather than let New Era make the films entirely themselves. Grierson did not want to be dominated by a commercial company, and he was anxious to protect Tallents from film industry tycoons.

I.A. How did you relate to the people from New Era whom you had to work with?

B.W. We regarded them as rather boring, though we knew that we needed their technical expertise. Some of them changed for the better through coming into contact with us. Davidson for example, his character changed for the better, and he came to sympathise with our aims and ideals. One of the worst was the managing director, Gordon Craig. He was only interested in getting the best bargain he could from the Treasury.

I.A. Were you aware that Craig had tried to make Tallents abandon the production of *Drifters*?

B.W. That doesn't surprise me at all. Craig was only interested in money.

I.A. During the whole period of the EMB Film Unit attempts were being made by the Treasury to restrict the development of the Unit, and possibly close it down. Were you aware of that, and were you conscious of restrictions on what kinds of films you could make?

B.W. We were all aware that the Treasury was constantly trying to have us closed down, and I felt – and so did the others – that the EMB was the wrong place for us to be. It did not make sense to be there anyway. We also knew that the political right wing were particularly hostile to us, and regarded us as leftists.

I.A. Were you conscious of hostility from the film industry?

B.W. Not really. Some may have been, but many in the industry were sympathetic, and I don't recall feeling particularly strongly about hostile treatment by the film industry. The main trouble was from politicians and civil servants.

I.A. Were any of you involved in the making of the Walter Creighton film, *One Family*?

B.W. That film was a disaster, and was written off after its first night. I believe that it was only shown twice. I was not involved in its production, and I assume that New Era were largely responsible for production, as well as exhibition.

I.A. What films were you and Grierson most impressed with at that time?

B.W. *Turksib* was one of Grierson's favourite films, and we bowed down low before Dovzhenko. His *Earth* was the most outstanding film of the period in its simple representation of peasant life and use of montage.

I.A. I believe that you and Grierson helped Turin on the English subtitles of *Turksib*. Could you say something about that?

B.W. We helped him prepare the English subtitles, that's all. *Turksib* made a great impression on us because of its depiction of the building of the trans-Siberian railway. Turin had arrived in Britain in conjunction with a first showing of his film at the Film Society.

I.A. In *Song of Ceylon* there seems to be a considerable shift between the main body of the film and the last section, which dealt with the marketing of produce. The bulk of the film is very poetic and lyrical, dealing with history, religion and tradition, but the last section deals with modern trade. Were you obliged to include this final section? Would you rather have done without it? Were you influenced by a similar kind of sequence in *Drifters*?

B.W. *Song of Ceylon* was overwhelmingly my best film, and one of the best films to come out of the documentary movement.

I.A. Was it the best film from the documentary movement?

B.W. That is not for me to say, but it was definitely my best film. John Taylor and I spent a month in Ceylon researching, reading everything we could. During that time I became very impressed by the Buddhist religion, by its depth and contemplative nature. I tried to put that feeling into *Song of Ceylon*. As for the last sequence, I think that was my EMB training – about connecting up the past to the future. The film is in four movements, that was my idea, and the sequence concerning the voices of trade was also my idea. One reason why it might seem so different from the rest of the film today is that we were experimenting with a new sound system then. The film was an experiment with sound.

I.A. I understand that Grierson insisted that some changes be made to the final sequences of *Song of Ceylon* when he first saw it. What sort of changes were made?

B.W. When Grierson saw the film he said it was a marvellous film, but that I had destroyed it towards the end. We had a big row about this, I thought the film was fine and did not require any changes, but Grierson insisted. So I went home and drank a bottle of whisky, then got in my car and drove to Blackheath where I worked through the night until I had made the changes that Grierson had suggested.

I.A. What changes?

B.W. Grierson had suggested that the film lacked dramatic development, suspense and climax. So I made alterations to the scenes of native dancing, in order to build from anti-climax to climax in a scene showing a man praying before the Buddha, and the dance. Grierson had said that I had two climaxes and no anti-climax.

I.A. So the alterations which Grierson suggested were entirely concerned with improving the dramatic aspect of some sequences, improving aesthetic aspects, rather than alterations to the information content of the film?

B.W. That is correct. Grierson was also very helpful as a protector. The Ceylon Tea Board were expecting four short travelogues, and Grierson spent three and a half hours convincing them to allow the film to be finished. *Song of Ceylon* was an unusual film for its time, and the Tea Board did not know what to make of it.

I.A. Do you recall Grierson ever referring to philosophers such as Hegel, Kant, Bradley or Russell?

B.W. We had a great deal of respect for Bertrand Russell, and of course Grierson always talked a great deal about Kant, particularly Kant's aesthetic. I also recall him mentioning the names of Dewey, James and Bradley, and Hegel. I remember him often mentioning these names, and they may have influenced his ideas about film-making.

I.A. Grierson went to India in the 1970s and was very taken by the country and by Hinduism and Buddhism. Do you think that he may have been influenced, throughout his life, by religion and metaphysical systems?

B.W. When Grierson went to India he developed a kind of love affair with Mrs Gandhi. The two of them became very close friends, and it was tragic that Grierson had to cancel his last meeting with her in order to return home through illness. This was the lung cancer which eventually killed him. You know, no one has ever asked me these kinds of questions about Grierson before, and they do strike a chord in my memory. Grierson always had an interest in oriental philosophy, and that interest may have been greater than I have previously suspected. I may also have underestimated the extent of his liking of *Song of Ceylon*.

I.A. Later in his life, when Grierson was asked to name the films directed and produced by him which he was happiest with, he named the more poetic films, such as *Drifters, Song of Ceylon* and *Granton Trawler* as opposed to the didactic documentaries which one would normally associate him with, such as *Housing Problems*. Do you think that his concern with art and aesthetics has been underestimated?

B.W. You may be correct, but I don't quite understand the dictinction you are making between aesthetic and didactic films. A film must be made well in order to tell a story or express a messsage, and I think that the aesthetic and educational parts of the documentaries are integrated. Some of the documentary films were more aesthetic than others, but I don't accept the distinction you are trying to make.

I.A. But the standard image of Grierson and documentary is of didactic information films?

B.W. Although Grierson was always interested in questions of art and aesthetics, dating back to his American period, and he advised us to study painting, poetry and theatre.

I.A. How familiar were you and Grierson with the avant-garde film movement of the time, and what were your favourite avant-garde films?

B.W. We were familiar with the avant-garde movement. Film seemed to offer a wonderful freedom of expression, and I was particularly impressed by the surrealist films of Salvador Dalí and Buñuel. Dalí was a straightforward honest anarchist, whilst Buñuel showed how film could have a political function. I fe1t that the period was one of great change and possibility, following the total disruption caused by the First World War. Society was in transition, and film offered a way of participating in a new way in social change. We were looking for new uses for the film, and for a new type of cinema.

I.A. So you felt that there was a connection between questions about film as art, and questions about film as an instrument of social change?

B.W. Yes. The two were connected in my mind. The possibilities of film as a medium of expression were connected to the new situations and social changes thrown up in the post-war period.

I.A. Do you know whether Grierson had read anything by Bela Balazs at that time?

B.W. Yes he had, and he knew Balazs quite well. I think he was impressed and influenced by Balazs. I myself met Balazs in the twenties and thirties, and I would say that he was buggered up by the need to toe the Stalinist line. He had to do and say what he was told in other words. But Grierson was certainly familiar with his writings. We were familiar with a number of those theorists, the whole thing was an intellectual movement – a movement in which people were trying to contact each other.

I.A. Very few documentaries were made on historical subjects, or had a clear historical approach. Why was that?

B.W. Partly because we wanted to record what was happening around us, rather than record what had happened in the past. As I said, we felt that the period we were working in was one of great change, and we wanted to record those changes. Grierson also felt that history was happening here and now, and that the here and now had the seeds of history in it, so that we were recording history in the making. It was also easy to make a bad historical film because it involved research and generalisation, whereas a film about the present only had to describe an existing situation. So, because we were learners we avoided historical subjects to some extent. On the whole though I don't think we ever thought much about this problem.

I.A. Documentary consists of using actuality footage. Did this affect your approach to historical subjects?

B.W. It may have, but I think that the main thing was the technical difficulty and expense involved in making a film about a historical subject.

I.A. When you worked on *The Country Comes to Town*, your first film for the EMB, you spent some time on location with Robert Flaherty. What influence did that experience have on you, and what impressed you most about Flaherty's style of work?

B.W. Flaherty had a tremendous ability for'seeing' through the camera. He was able to look at a landscape and capture all the key elements of that landscape, then translate that into the film image. The most important thing which I learned from him then was the importance of knowing how to 'look' through the camera. This included learning how to compose within the camera frame, and in terms of montage, how to connect images togetber. So you could say he was an important influence upon the development of my visual sense.

I.A. When I spoke to Alberto Cavalcanti in Paris, in 1983, he said that the alleged rift between him and Grierson had been exaggerated. Do you think that was the case, or were you aware of any antagonism between them?

B.W. Grierson and Cavalcanti complemented each other, I would say. Both were great men in their own right. Grierson was an organiser and administrator, as well as a theorist; whilst Cavalcanti was a gifted producer who was able to help us with great technical knowledge. I was very fond of Cavalcanti, and we were very close friends during our period together. They were very different people, with different ideas about how documentary should develop, and it should be remembered that Grierson could often be argumentative and stubborn. However, I don't think that there was any serious rift between Grierson and Cavalcanti, though there was a difference of opinion about how documentary should develop.

I.A. What sort of difference of opinion?

B.W. Cavalcanti believed that the documentary should become more integrated into the feature film, so that the distinction between the two became less clear cut. But I don't think that Grierson really understood feature films, and so he argued that the two should remain quite separate.

WORKS CITED

—◦◦—

JOHN GRIERSON

'English Cinema Production and the Naturalistic Tradition', 'The Character of an Ultimate Synthesis' and 'Untitled Lecture on Documentary', all previously unpublished papers held at the Grierson Archive, University of Stirling.

'*Drifters*' (*The Clarion*, October 1929), reprinted in H. Forsyth Hardy (ed.), *Grierson on Documentary* (London and Boston, Faber and Faber, 1979).

'First Principles of Documentary' (*Cinema Quarterly*, Winter 1932), reprinted in Forsyth Hardy op. cit.

'Education and the New Order' (Canadian Association for Adult Education, 1941), reprinted in Forsyth Hardy op. cit.

'The Documentary Idea 1942' (*Documentary Newsletter*, 1942), reprinted in Forsyth Hardy op. cit.

'Preface' to Paul Rotha's *Documentary Film* (London, Faber and Faber, 1952).

'Art and Revolution', previously unpublished paper held at the John Grierson Archive.

'Answers to a Cambridge Questionnaire' (*Granta*, 1967).

'*I Remember, I Remember*' (1970), developed from a draft script held at the Grierson Archive.

PAUL ROTHA

'Afterthought', in idem, *Documentary Diary* (London and New York, Hill and Wang, 1973).

'Films and the Labour Party' (Address delivered at a Special Labour Party Conference on Film Propaganda, Edinburgh, 3 October 1936). Reprinted in Paul Marris (ed.), *Paul Rotha* (BFI Dossier no. 16, 1982).

253

ALBERTO CAVALCANTI

'Cavalcanti in England' by Elizabeth Sussex in *Sight and Sound*, 44:4 (Autumn 1975).
'The Evolution of Cinematography in France', *Experimental Cinema*, 1:2 (June 1930).
'The British Case', from *Film e Realidade* (originally published in 1952) (São Paulo, editoria artenova, 1976).

HUMPHREY JENNINGS

'Introduction', in idem, *Pandaemonium: The Coming of the Machine as seen by Contemporary Observers*, ed. Charles Madge and Mary-Lou Jennings (London, André Deutsch, 1985).
'The English', 'Surrealism' and 'Listen to Britain', in Kevin Jackson (ed.), *The Humphrey Jennings Film Reader* (Manchester, Carcanet Press, 1995).

BASIL WRIGHT

'Documentary Today', in *The Penguin Film Review*, 2 (January 1947).
'Interview with Ian Aitken', 1987.

SELECT BIBLIOGRAPHY

Aitken, Ian, 'Grierson, Idealism and the Inter-War Period', *Historical Journal of Film, Radio and Television*, 9:3 (1989).

—— *Film and Reform: John Grierson and the British Documentary Film Movement* (London, Routledge, 1990)

—— 'The British Documentary Film Movement', in Robert Murphy (ed.), *The British Cinema Book* (London, BFI, 1997).

—— 'Representations of Work in the Films of the Documentary Film Movement', in John Hassard and Ruth Holliday (eds), *Organization-Representation* (London, Sage, 1998).

Barnouw, Erik, *Documentary: A History of the Non-Fiction Film* (London, Oxford University Press, 1974).

Barsam, Richard, *Non-fiction Film: A Critical History* (London, Allen & Unwin, 1974).

Bernays, E. L., *Crystalizing Public Opinion* (New York, Boni & Liverweight, 1923).

Beveridge, James, *John Grierson: Film Master* (London, Macmillan, 1979); 2nd edn 1986.

Bond, Ralph, 'Cinema in the Thirties', in John Clark et al. (eds), *Culture and Crisis in Britain in the Thirties* (London, Lawrence & Wishart, 1979).

Bradley, F. H., *Essays on Truth and Reality* (London, Clarendon Press, 1914).

Branson, Noreen and Margot Heinemann, *Britain in the 1930s* (London, Panther, 1973).

British Film Institute, *The Film in National Life* (London, BFI, 1943).

Cavalcanti, Alberto, 'The Evolution of Cinematography in France', *Experimental Cinema*, 1:2 (June 1930).

Cavalcanti, Alberto, *Film e Realidade* (São Paulo, editoria artenova, 1976).

Clark, John et al. (eds), *Culture and Crisis in Britain in the Thirties* (London, Lawrence & Wishart, 1979).

Cockburn, Claud, *The Devil's Decade* (London, Sidgwick & Jackson, 1973).

Ellis, Jack C., 'The Young Grierson in America 1924–1927', *Cinema Journal*, 8:17

(Fall, 1968).

—— 'Grierson at University', *Cinema Journal*, 12:41 (Spring, 1973).

—— *John Grierson: A Guide to References and Resources* (Boston, Boston University Press, 1986).

Evans, Gary, *John Grierson and the National Film Board: The Politics of War-time Propaganda* (Toronto, Buffalo and London, University of Toronto Press, 1984).

—— *In the National Interest: A Chronicle of the National Film Board of Canada from 1949 to 1989* (Toronto, Buffalo and London, University of Toronto Press, 1991).

Forsyth Hardy, H. (ed.), *Grierson on Documentary* (London, Faber & Faber, 1946); later editions 1966, 1979.

—— *John Grierson: A Documentary Biography* (London, Faber & Faber, 1979).

—— (ed.), *Grierson on the Movies* (London, Faber & Faber, 1981).

Gallacher, William, *Revolt on the Clyde* (London, Lawrence & Wishart, 1936).

Glover, Janet, *The Story of Scotland* (London, Faber & Faber, 1960).

Gloversmith, Frank (ed.), *Class, Culture and Social Change* (London, Harvester Press, 1980).

Higson, Andrew (ed.), *Dissolving Views: Key Writings on British Cinema* (London, Cassell, 1996).

Hillier, J. and A. Lovell, *Studies in Documentary* (London, Secker & Warburg, 1972).

Hogenkamp, Bert, 'Making Films with a Purpose: Film-Making and the Working Class', in John Clark et al. (eds), *Culture and Crisis in Britain in the Thirties* (London, Lawrence & Wishart, 1979).

Hood, Stuart, 'A Cool Look at the Legend', in E. Orbanz (ed.), *Journey to a Legend and Back: The British Realistic Film* (Berlin, Edition Volker Spiess, 1977).

—— 'John Grierson and the British Documentary Film Movement', in Vincent Porter and James Curran (eds), *British Cinema History* (London, Weidenfeld & Nicolson, 1983).

Jackson, Kevin (ed.), *The Humphrey Jennings Film Reader* (Manchester, Carcanet Press, 1995).

Jacobs, Lewis (ed.), *The Documentary Tradition* (New York, Hopkinson & Blake, 1971).

Jennings, Humphrey, *Pandaemonium: The Coming of the Machine as Seen by Contemporary Observers*, ed. and intro. Charles Madge and Mary-Lou Jennings (London, André Deutsch, 1985).

Jennings, Mary-Lou (ed.), *Humphrey Jennings: Film-maker/Painter/Poet* (London, BFI and Riverside Studios, 1982).

John Grierson Project, *John Grierson and the NFB* (Montreal, ECW Press, 1984).

Johnston, Claire, 'Independence and the Thirties', conference contribution in D. Macpherson (ed.), *British Cinema: Traditions of Independence* (London, BFI, 1980).

—— *Undercut*, 9 (Summer 1983).

Kuhn, Annette, 'British Documentary in the 1930s and Independence: Recontextualising a Film Movement', in D. Macpherson (ed.), *British Cinema: Traditions of Independence* (London, BFI, 1980).

Laing, Stuart, 'Presenting Things as they Are', in F. Gloversmith (ed.), *Class, Culture and Social Change* (London, Harvester Press, 1980).

Lippmann, Walter, *Public Opinion* (New York and London, Allen & Unwin, 1922).

Low, Rachel, *History of the British Film* (London, Allen & Unwin), Vol. 5, *Documentary and Educational Films of the 1930s* (1979), Vol. 6, *Films of Comment and Persuasion in the 1930s* (1979).

Margolies, David, 'Left Review and Left Literary Theory', in F. Gloversmith (ed.), *Class, Culture and Social Change* (London, Harvester Press, 1980).

Marris, Paul (ed.), *Paul Rotha* (London BFI Dossier no. 16, 1982).

Marwick, Arthur, 'Middle Opinion in the Thirties', *English Historical Review*, 79 (1964).

—— *The Deluge: British Society and the First World War* (London, Bodley Head, 1965).

—— *Britain in the Century of Total War: War, Peace and Social Change 1900–1967* (London, Bodley Head, 1968).

Middlemas, R. K., *The Clydesiders* (London, Hutchinson, 1965).

Montagu, Ivor, *Film World* (London, Penguin, 1964).

Mowat, C. L., *Britain Between the Wars, 1918–1940* (London, Methuen, 1955).

Nelson, Joyce, *The Colonized Eye: Rethinking the Grierson Legend* (Toronto, Between the Lines, 1988).

Nichols, Bill, 'Documentary Theory and Practice', *Screen*, 17:4 (Winter 1976–7).

Orbanz, Eva (ed.), *Journey to a Legend and Back: The British Realistic Film* (Berlin, Edition Volker Spiess, 1977).

Political and Economic Planning, *The British Film Industry* (London, PEP, 1952).

Priestley, J. B., *English Journey* (London, Heinemann, 1934).

Pronay, Nicholas, 'John Grierson and the Documentary – 60 Years On', *Historical Journal of Film, Radio and Television*, 9:3 (1989).

Rotha, Paul, *The Film Till Now: A Survey of World Cinema* (London, Cape, 1930).

—— *Documentary Film* (London, Faber & Faber, 1936); later editions 1939, 1952, 1966.

—— *Rotha on the Film* (London, Faber & Faber, 1958).

—— *Documentary Diary* (London and New York, Hill & Wang, 1973).

Samuel, Raphael, 'The Middle Class Between the Wars', *New Socialist* (January, February and March 1983).

Stevenson, John, *British Society 1914–1945* (London, Penguin, 1984).

Stevenson, John and Chris Cook, *The Slump* (London, Cape, 1977).

Sussex, Elizabeth, *The Rise and Fall of British Documentary* (Berkeley, Los Angeles and London, University of California Press, 1975).

Swann, Paul, 'John Grierson and the GPO Film Unit 1933–1939', *Historical Journal of Film, Radio and Television*, 3:1 (1983).

—— 'The Selling of the Empire: The EMB Film Unit', *Studies in Visual Communication*, 9:3 (1983).

—— *The British Documentary Film Movement 1926–1946* (Cambridge and New York, Cambridge University Press, 1989).

Symons, Julian, *The Thirties* (London, Faber & Faber, 1960).

Tallents, Stephen, *The Projection of England* (London, Faber & Faber, 1932).

—— 'The Birth of British Documentary', *Journal of the University Film Association*, 20:1 (1968).

Taylor, A. J. P., *English History 1914–1945* (London and Oxford, Clarendon Press, 1965).

Taylor, P. M., *The Projection of Britain* (Cambridge, Cambridge University Press, 1981).

Taylor, P. M. and M. Sanders, *British Propaganda During World War One* (London, Macmillan, 1982).

Tudor, Andrew, *Theories of Film* (London, Secker & Warburg, 1974).

Valentinetti, Claudio and Lorenzo Pellizzari, *Alberto Cavalcanti* (São Paulo, Instituto Lina Bo e P. M. Bardi, 1988).

Watt, Harry, *Don't Look at the Camera* (London, Elek, 1974).

Widdowson, Peter, 'Between the Acts? English Fiction in the 1930s', in John Clark et al. (eds), *Culture and Crisis in Britain in the Thirties* (London, Lawrence & Wishart, 1979).

Williams, Raymond, *Culture and Society 1780–1950* (London, Chatto & Windus, 1958).

Winston, Brian, *Claiming the Real: The Griersonian Documentary and its Legitimations* (London, BFI, 1995).

Wollheim, Richard, *Bradley* (London, Harmondsworth, 1959).

Wright, Basil, *Use of the Film* (London, Bodley Head, 1948).

—— *The Long View* (London, Secker & Warburg, 1974).

INDEX